KUNTU DRAMA

KUNTU DRAMA

Plays of the African Continuum

Collected and with an Introduction by
PAUL CARTER HARRISON

Preface by Oliver Jackson

Grove Press, Inc.
New York

Illustration on page 11 designed by Nelson Stevens.

ISBN: 0-394-17806-8
Grove Press ISBN: 0-8021-0027-9

Library of Congress Catalog Card Number: 73-6638

First Evergreen Edition

Manufactured in the United States of America

Distributed by Random House, Inc., New York

DEDICATION

These works are dedicated to Kenny Harrison (All-American three-years-in-a-row) in memory of our father. Also to the elder members of the Carter clan: Thelma (mother), Buddy, Beatrice, and Gladyce.

PREFACE

by Oliver Jackson

I. THE AFRICAN CONTINUUM

Kuntu drama is a reflection and an objectification of the concepts of the African continuum. Those concepts and beliefs common to African peoples the world over are the basis of the unbroken continuity of the African continuum. Foremost among these concepts is the belief in the fundamental spiritual nature of the universe, as well as the attendant belief that man is essentially spirit, and as such basically irreducible.

The African continuum is therefore those fundamental concepts that the black man has created in the universe that reflect his own image. The strong ancestral base (Africa, the potent ancestor) is the force for statehood, independence, freedom, and all else that truly reflects the African spirit wherever it is located. It is particularly evident, this African continuum, in the music of Africans, and in the use of words, images, and sounds.

The African continuum is a modal concept* in that it views the cosmos as a totally integrated environment in which all spiritual

---

* "Mode" is defined as a reality—an active force that determines all states of existence within its active perimeter. There are many realities or modes. An example is the dream state, in which there are two or more realities: the physicality of the dreamer (his bed, the room, the city in which he lives, the time of his sleep) and the dream, which may have a different place, time, and sequence of actions.

forces interact. In the African continuum, the concept of death, terrible as it is to the living, is basically the living spirit giving way to spirit without body. There is no "finish," "end," or "death" to the spirit: its immortality is as constant as the cosmos. This concept is aptly reflected in the Akan proverb, "If God could die, I would die."

The moral sanctity of all life derives from the idea that all is spiritual and that the Supreme Power embodies the totality of the cosmos in one spiritual unity. Therefore, regardless of how it appears, the African continuum is essentially harmonious. Men, in building their societies, endeavor to reproduce this "divine or cosmic harmony." This is the basis of all ethical and moral behavior in community life. The human microcosm must reaffirm the harmonious modality of the cosmic macrocosm.

The spiritual continuum never breaks down, even when violated on the human plane to the extent of causing unharmonious consequences in the world of man. It is the nature of the cosmos to seek harmony, but the cosmic harmony of the universe is not fully comprehensible to men in its totality.

People of the African continuum see power as the basis of all endeavor. It is through the use of this power, or "life-force," individually and collectively, that people of the African continuum seek to establish and maintain their proper relationship to other men, to the force referred to as Nature, and to the cosmos itself. Individually, man's uniqueness cannot and does not have significance in isolation of family, clan, or society. (Uniqueness, here, is defined as existence through recognition and re-affirmation by individual societal groups.) Individuality, then, is not a definitive characteristic of spiritual man and has no cosmic force of significance; therefore, society is its proper and only meaningful context. Collectively, man is perceived as a societal animal and is obligated by his cosmic role to maintain cosmic harmony in his societal living. Specifically, man has in this view fundamental duties to other men.

These fundamental duties are put into effect through the supreme source of power in man—his intelligence. His intelligence is comprised, basically, of the individual power of experience, but becomes much more effective when generated as the collective strength or intelligence of the community or race. This intelligence is brought into focus through the use of psychic conjuring that employs concentration, objects, word gestures that are potent in the achievement of desired action, through what has been incorrectly labeled "magic." The most powerful and far-reaching manifestation of intelligence is the collective religious ceremony, in which collective power summons and brings forth the forces of the ancestors, the forces of their sons, and the forces of God.

It is this bringing forth the power or force of God that is the supreme test of a man's spiritual power and the power of the collective community which is comprised, for the greater part, of the ancestors. God is brought forth to empower the community with the spiritual power to manipulate its total existence into harmony with the other forces of the universe. In the continuum, numerous sacred ceremonies focus that power, including the theatrical ritualization—Kuntu drama.

II. KUNTU DRAMA

Kuntu drama is drama that has, as its ultimate purpose, to reveal and invoke the reality of the particular mode that it has ritualized. This theater style depends on power and power invocation. It is magical in that it attempts to produce modification in behavior through the combined use of word power, dance power, and music power. It is sacred theater in the sense that it seeks to fulfill a spiritual revelation.

The play is the ritualized context of reality. The ritual confirms the mode: it is a living incantation that focuses power to invoke and release beneficent power to the audience.

In this theater there is no separation between audience and actors. The mode is the event; its success as a reality depends on its power to persuade to action its audience. Kuntu drama recognizes no separation—distance perhaps—but no separation. The mode is one. It may have many aspects—the audience being a very forceful one.

However, the mode's total reality is true to itself and to its degree of power. Power is the activating force of the particular reality and the reality, in turn, determines the characteristic of the power. In Kuntu drama, power is understood, invoked, and revealed in contextual relationships. It is necessary to relate to the proper power relationships in order that the mode becomes definitive and revelatory. Certainly, the degree of power depends upon dialogue, presentation, tensions, etc., for these elements of the ritual are its bones; but the bones are only the vehicles of modality. The content is the principal thing.

As stated, the drama's purpose is to be a beneficent moral force in its society (i.e., audience, people). Like man, it derives its purpose from a cosmic source: that is, it is defined by man's role in the cosmos. It owes its existence to need for social and cosmic order. It is ritual—not drama—and everything within the play should be a description of the contextual power that the ritual intends to invoke. However, it may be dramatic and employ all the known devices of a drama.

Everything within the play, then, should be the vehicle of the power described; therefore, the description—the vehicle of power—is ideally one thing. For example, the attitude, speech, dress, song, and music of a performer will describe and project the aspect of the force or power needed or eventually revealed within the mode. The performer, or participant, must be the force or an aspect of the force proper to his role in the ritual or power context.

In the ritual, participants[1] act as spiritual forces who are designated by intent. (Intent, here, is the creative force that determines the form and content of all aspects of the ritual. The aesthetics of the ritual are the tools of intent. Intent is spiritual in nature and is a will to power in a given context.) These spiritual forces are focused by the use of attitude, dress, speech, movement, etc.

The participants are not defined by sociological or psychological premises, although they may have a sociological setting or psychology. The participants are the fundamental determinants in the ritual

[1] "Characters." "Actors" imply the performance, of which they are a part, they are not of the real world.

or mode. They possess the power to manipulate the other determinants, i.e. things, time and place, and ultimately the mode.

. . . Things are, generally, those inanimate objects used in a play to set the mode, i.e., sets, props, music, and song. Things have latent force that the participants activate.

. . . Place and Time in ritual involves, first, the event and the particular environment in which the event occurs. The arena of the event has to be possessed by the ritual each time the ritual is given.[2] The arena is an inertial force that has a modality of its own. The event must dominate the arena's mode continually. For example, if the ritual designates a known time and place, i.e., Chicago in the 1930s, the ritual may use all of the representative effects unique to that particular time and place. The representative effects will not necessarily bring forth that life force unique to Chicago in the thirties. The actualization of this life force depends upon the skills of the participants.

. . . The mode has been aptly described in the text. However, as a determinant, the mode is the ritual, the event, the power evoked within the event—it is the particular reality, in all its dynamic intensity and forms.

The determinants must, through their use—description, attitudes—convey and focus the aspect of the power to be revealed, invoked. Nothing is really representation; everything used or selected is in the focused contextual power—its reality, its actions, its truth. Therefore, the ritual environment is powerful, dynamic, harmonious; it focuses, not merely represents. Kuntu drama is testimonial.

---

[2] As implied, the role of the participant is fundamental to the invocation of the definitive power.

(*Oliver Jackson* is an artist and scholar of African thought at the State University of California at Sacramento.)

CONTENTS

KUNTU DRAMA

INTRODUCTION
Black Theater in Search of a Source

Perhaps the most promising aspect of the black theater is its continued visibility over the past ten years: what is most visible, however, is the kitchen sink and living room couch, those familiar frayed household objects that tend to serve no other purpose than to indentify the ear-marks of oppression. Such naturalistic detailing of social neglect tends to focus black life as a monolithic, strident cry. Though "cry" may be an accurate description of the pain manifest in our suffering, it often seems suspended, as if locked in an ice-box; and the pathos generated by such a fabrication of reality fails to move us beyond an absurd indulgence in self-pity. Yet, it is such fabrication of reality, the so-called black experience at its most sensate level, that receives immediate approbation in the white market. The *experience* is invariably articulated in forms that eschew any uniqueness in content: black anguish becomes committed to the human laws of so-called universal truths. It would seem that the aesthetic ambivalance of such works is designed to achieve commercial success in the American mainstream without any regard for a specific source of ethnic reference other than content. These authors accept the traditions of social realism which unavoidably preempt the cultural priorities of Afro-Americans that might perpetuate the black theater as a permanent and unique institutional experience in the lives of black people.

While it should be clear that every culture owns a specific experiential syntax which can be identified by their responses to familiar cultural artifacts, there has been a tendency for black Americans to allow their particular perceptions of form and content to be subordinated by the demands of white American standards of excellence. In songs and dance, a given rhythm and tonal expressions signals special illumination of a cluster of social references for a specific group, while owning littlc meaning for the alien group. As late as 1973, we find the revival of Lorraine Hansberry's *A Raisin in the Sun* resurrected on the Broadway stage in a musical form without idiomatic reference in the music. *Raisin* becomes a facile, uninspired event in which the gifts of the talented black performers are subordinated to the priorities of traditional American music. The descriptive folk idiom of Gershwin and the quasi-syncopation of Bernstein are ineptly used to focus the black family's problems in a "soap-opera" mode calculated to arrest the attention of white audiences. Despite the power and grace of the gifted black performers, their vitality was not able to raise the reality of the experience beyond the frozen conditions of an undistinguished folk operetta.

In the mid-sixties, Imamu Amiri Baraka broke through the ice that chilled the vision of Lorraine Hansberry and James Baldwin in the fifties, with his *Dutchman,* and received authentication by the American cultural mainstream. Since then, lesser and equally skilled black playwrights have emerged on the theater-circuit to receive almost indiscriminate, similar applause for their spleenic gut-thrusts into the belly of the white whale, if for no other reason than the forceful expurgation of America's historical guilt. During the height of social havoc in the mid-sixties, careful detailing of black problems brought relief to the buckra who was concerned about the rude behavior of his orphans; however poignant may have been these distress signals, very little illumination was provided for the black community who was all too familiar with the content of oppression.

As the commercial stage doors opened to receive images of black life, there was a rush of image-products served up by authors who seemed motivated by an overzealous need to re-define the black experience; however, they inadvertently created carbon copies of ghetto life which merely sensitized whites and froze the black experience into limited frames of reference such as black poverty, black power, and black is beautiful. Ed Bullins had referred to his work as being "the theater of reality," in which case the revolutionary priority is "not of style and technique but of theme character."[1] Certainly, it cannot be said that the thematic references above created the limitations of dramatic focus since, categorically, they are indeed aspects of black life: the references become troublesome, however, when allowed to be focused through sociological imperatives that codify, thus freeze, our relationships to the known aspects of oppression. Rather than heightening the inscrutable, black life is often treated like a slice/hunk out of a stale pie to be reviewed up close by white producers whose principal concern, beyond immediate exoneration of guilt, is how to translate so much potent anguish into potent bucks.

Authentication, then, seems to come to the author who diligently details black life in a manner receptive to white curiosity, rather than to the author who attends the native ethos of the African/American community. Authors from the Caribbean or Africa are often allowed legitimacy because they clearly represent a unique social frame and whet the palates of the tastemakers who own an unassuagable curiosity for the exotic in so-called native cultures. But the Afro-American is discouraged from the landscape of his culture. He is not rewarded for seizing upon its myths, its rhythms, and its cosmic sensibilities so as to designate a mode of theater which reflects the African continuum, one that has permanency and provides cultural/educational consequences for the future of black life.

But who are the arbiters that sanction the credibility of a particular staged event? It must be quite painful for the black community, if not otherwise incredulous, to discover that a reviewer of the *New York Times* reviewing a black play—equipped with the rule-of-thumb made formidable by sociology—presumes to know more about what motivates black life than the author. Small wonder that so few black playwrights have ever received legitimacy from the black community, including Ed Bullins, whose works were often performed at the New Lafayette Theater in Harlem.

---

[1] William Couch, Jr., from *Introduction to New Black Playwrights* (Avon Books, New York, pp. xxii).

While there is an urgent concern for the presentation of images which reflect the positive goals and aspirations of black people, the most salient feature of our lives is oppression, and thusly, survival within such a deadly context. The mode[2] of oppression is so real for most authors that it invariably leads him/her head-on into a realism that, more often than not, focuses the most negative properties of oppression. One would be hard-pressed to indict the sincerity of compassion found in Lonnie Elder, III's *Ceremonies In Dark Old Men,* which examines the conditions of oppression that emasculate black maleness in the most literal, sociogrammatic terms; or even take serious opposition to J. E. Franklin's banal description of a young sista's growing pains in a "typical" black family in *Black Girl;* and despite the fact that we are passing through these fragile times when criticism of an artless reproduction of black life seems tantamount to self-hate, G. E. Gaines' raw, noxious photo-copy detailing of street ethics in *A Hard Head Makes A Soft Behind* offers little wisdom to the black audience who is left to ponder the simple-minded truism that "it bees that way sometime!" Authentication of works represented by the latter, simply for the purpose of immediate gratification, merely serves to arrest the development of a possibly useful talent; it allows the black experience to receive accolades for a theatrical representation owning a premature vision, one which might have been larger in scope and intention if criticized within the scale of its limited achievement. If musicians can woodshed, why can't authors? Woodshedding may result in the highly esteemed growth shown in G. E. Gaines' *What If It Turned Up Heads* which explores, in a very accomplished fashion, the absurd nature of oppression afflicted on black humanity.

Ideally, the black playwright/dramatist should have the opportunity to investigate the viability of his ethnic impulses in a black non-commercial environment, such as a black university could nurture, so that his aesthetic judgments may be exercised with a potency freed of economic concessions: a place away from the marketplace which fails to recognize that when we address ourselves to the sensibilities of our particular humanity, no less than the disciplines of the Kabuki, we have accomplished a universality which can be ap-

---

[2] Mode is used here to suggest Kuntu, or context that gives shape to image.

prehended by all people once the works have matured. At the moment, works owing their style and vision to African sensibility are not often solicited for commercial production since they tend to be emotionally/humanly outside of the marketing formula. Yet, it is such works that must be given a chance to demonstrate their force, and hopefully, receive legitimization from the black community.

Many of our authors seem to have accepted the common Euro-American notion that "the play is the thing," and having no fixed source of aesthetic priorities, end up explaining their lives, reporting rather than grappling with the rhythms of oppression that create a certain spontaneity of effect, the same dynamics that are common to story-telling sessions in beauty-parlors, barber shops, and saloons, places where a certain musicality is generated that causes the story to soar while uncovering hidden meaning—signifyin'—bringing to bear all the folk wisdom of antiquity and, in the process, creating a heightened experience that is at once exhilarating and cathartic.

Rather than the play, the *event* is the thing, the total impact of environmental rhythms which massage our sensitivities and rouse the spirit. The souls of black folks cannot be dredged with carefully chosen words alone. If the soul is to be quickened, the event must own the sensate power and vitality of experience witnessed in the store-front church where the sins of natural life are assigned mythic relationships and focused through a cosmic source of light, utilizing those powerful Kuntu forces—Song, Dance, and Drum—to capture the rhythms of that life, committing the community to a form of total engagement of body/spirit, thereby testifying to our continuation as an African people on this continent, in this unnatural mode of primal chaos.

Clearly, such a presentation in the theaters downtown, the marketplace where most black plays seem to end up, does not own the commercial aesthetics of studied mediocrity cranked out by a Neil Simon for Broadway. Still, it cannot be denied that more black people get to the Abyssinian Baptist Church on a single Sunday than to all the theaters presenting black plays in an entire week. The event is larger than the word/play: here one witnesses the fundamental spiritual inclination of African people. Essential to the arousal of the spirit is an orchestration of words, sounds, and images into a potent reality, a fluid mode that evokes testimony from the participants who have struggled through the undivined state of their humanity all week, trusting the wisdom of the preacher who ultimately, once the spirit has been awakened, restores a sense of harmony to the community, reaffirming its natural divine-ness.

The *event,* then, becomes the context of reality, a force-field of phenomena which is ritualized. In order for such an event to be illuminating, we need authors who can see beyond the descriptive, sociogrammatic character of oppression; directors who have prepared themselves with the knowledge of corresponding African and African/American mythologies, and who are able to discern the motivating responses of black people to certain rhythms; and actors who are not afraid to throw off the shackles of stiff-necked thespianism so that they may move securely within the rhythms of the mode with natural grace and potency. And most certainly, such a theater requires black producers who are courageous enough to disengage themselves from the white-collar commercialism that locks him/her into the traditional American definition of "play" at a time when we need a liberated stance to advance the prerogatives of African/American culture. Just as the sacred ceremony of the church focuses on the power of God, the secular theatrical event invites the potency of supreme spirits such as Charlie Parker, Sojourner Truth, or the Signifying Monkey to shed light on the miasma of oppressed life: it is a love supreme! While Barbara Teer's National Black Theater, which resides in Harlem, approximates the means toward an invocation, Gil Moses' production of Imamu Amiri Baraka's *Slave Ship*[3] is indicative of the ends.

Yet, invariably, due to commercial pressures, black theater finds itself capitulating to the references of humanity designated by the American ideal. It would almost seem that white Americans learn more from the theatrical experience than blacks. Howard Sackler's Pulitzer Prize scripting of a black hero, Jack Johnson, in *The Great White Hope*[4] must surely give credence to the fact that facile description of a black experience makes that experience readily avail-

---

[3] Produced by the Chelsea Theater in January 1970, under the modally conceived direction of Gil Moses.

[4] The success of this work must be largely credited to the vitality of James Earl Jones, who created the role.

able to even white authors who may earn greater remuneration and/or acclaim for their efforts than blacks. True definition of the experience requires an apprehension of the attendant forces/rhythms of black life, an acquisition of peculiarly ethnic motivations that are often outside of white commercial manipulation. Ossie Davis' musical, *Purlie,* was clearly designed for legitimacy on Broadway, despite any tentative entertainment value it may have had for some blacks; and the Broadway production of Melvin Van Peeble's *Ain't Supposed to Die a Natural Death,*[5] was an attempt to kill two birds with one razor: engender in blacks a sense of pride in the most unfortunate aspects of our lives, while introducing to whites palatable cameos of the abrasions found in ghetto life without bitterness.

Undoubtedly, Richard Wesley's arresting rhetorical drama *Black Terror,*[6] provided an intriguing political forum for both black and white intellectuals downtown. However limited may have been considerations of style and techniques, or even accommodations to commercialism, the lesson being taught might have summoned a more profound ritual if it had been served in the black community where the possibility for active participation in the arguments might have moved us toward taking distinct sides of the issues, fostering greater illumination of the problems of political choice, rather than becoming a frozen exhibition of confused black allegiances, an intellectual exercise inhibited by the gaze of Shakespeare's ghost. The poetess Jayne Cortez once observed "Happiness is black people being together away from profane eyes." However, it would seem that the black theater, having few places in or out of Harlem where the most viable ethnic sensibilities may be exercised without being compromised, faces the reality of becoming "a hostage . . . a recent killing!"[7]

Where, then, are the models? The plays/events of Kuntu drama afford us a handle on the tradition. Included are writers of Pan-African origin: Jean Toomer, Aimé Césaire, Imamu Amiri Baraka,

---

[5] Original production at Sacramento State University, and conceived by Harrison as an organic, virulent mode of oppression that threatened our humanity and had to be broken.

[6] Produced at the New York Shakespeare Company Theater in 1971.

[7] A line from Imamu Amiri Baraka's *A Recent Killing.*

Adrienne Kennedy, Lennox Brown, Clay Goss, and myself. Each of these works, as well as examples from other Pan-African writers such as Sonia Sanchez, N. R. Davison, and Derek Wolcott, demonstrate, in varying degrees, a race memory that reflects certain aspects of traditional African ceremony while dealing with the specificity of experience their cultures dictate: they all share in common a peculiarly native resonance.

Admittedly, even in the contemporary play-form of home-based Africans such as Wole Soyinka and Efua Sutherland, there are some western influences: the written word often appears as with a certain lyricism, a sort of European transmutation of the oral traditions. Despite such influences, these works, even when conceived in a literary/poetic mode such as crafted by Jean Toomer, tend to eschew the dramaturgy of western tradition, with its expositional plots, middle-scene conflicts, and final-act resolutions: rather, those works are characteristically *modal*[8] in conception, much like black music, treating time/space, spirit/corpus, and social/moral in a single force-field of reality, as if the event were located in a matrix of notes grafted on a B-flat scale. Within the matrix, changes are played: an orchestration of light and shadow, character transformations, object/mask animism, and Song, Dance, and Drum. The image/drama unfolds in a matrix/mode that is fluid: rather than fixity or static representation, the mode is manipulated/massaged in a manner which allows the dramatic elements/forces to move transitionally into new relationships so as to produce a testimonial quality potent enough to excavate the surface of reality, a sort of heightening the apperception of black experience, somewhere between the eye and the pie of life. Imamu Amiri Baraka asks that the theater "isolate the ritual and historical cycles of reality": these works achieve that end.

Thus, the Kuntu[9] of these plays are determined by modal relationships of forces, and are not limited to the scientific laws of

---

[8] Modal used here to suggest a fluid matrix, an orchestration of many stage elements in a manner similar to ensemble configurations in dance, or mode permutations in music.

[9] Kuntu signifies mode of image, or rather the cluster of elements that make up the context in which an image is formed. It may be used synonymously with the term "mode."

cause and effect, nor the motivations of modern psychology which atomize the personality in order to arrive at the core of dramatic conflict. The core of reality is total, the forces of experience are manipulated into a synthesis with the entire environment—including audience/participators. And just as the remnants of traditional ceremony can be witnessed in Caribbean carnivals or the black Baptist Church, focus is augmented in the theatrical mode through those Kuntu forces—Song, Dance, and Drum—to reinforce the vigor of the desired revelation.

Since the theatrical experience borders on being a spiritualized secular event, it might be useful to examine a sacred institutional frame that exhibits a high degree of theatricality while owing its rituals to African traditions: the black church.

AFRICAN/AMERICAN RITUAL MODE

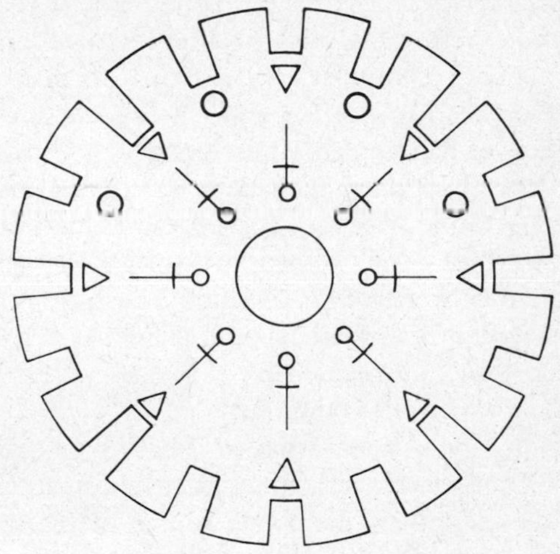

ENVIRONMENT: EDIFICE/HOUSE

Preacher: Spiritual Leader

Sacred Images: Spiritual Force

Congregation: Community

Chorus/Musicians: Sacred Community

Elders: Spiritual Models

First, there is the edifice, a house; but we are reminded by ancient Dogon wisdom that the house receives its magnificence/magic from the people that enter it:

In Molu the houses have storeys.
But it is the men who are fine,
Not the storeyed houses!

The chorus is composed of singers and musicians and represents the sacred component of the community, having more direct access to the spirits. The altar displays objects of worship—idols, icons, fetishes, symbols—that own a potency for animism; and inasmuch as they are sacred representations of ancestral spirit[10]—in this case, European ancestors—they may be ritualized in a manner that produces an epiphany. The preacher is a spiritualist who, quite like the traditional medicine man, mediates between spirit and corpus, light and shadow, manipulating all the forces in the mode with proper word-force (Nommo) so that the spirit will be revealed. And then there is the congregation/community, the participators in the ritual whose response to the preacher's call is a necessary ingredient in the incantative process of focusing the directives of the spirit. Sitting at the front of the congregation are the elders, the custodians of the tradition who, owing to the wisdom afforded them due to their spiritual proximity with the spirit, authenticate—or deauthenticate when necessary—the procedures of the ceremony, passing judgment on the potency of the preacher's skill in activating the forces within the mode into the kinds of relationships, historically/spiritually, that will be illuminating for the community.

The preacher, having been assigned the task of orchestrating all aspects of the mode into harmonious relationships, uses a script, a story-book—the Bible—as the object source of his story-telling to bridge myth with reality; the spirit must come through strongly in an oppressed condition if the social and moral directives of the story are to be accepted by the congregation/community. As any good

[10] While the idols may own European features and do not resemble the African ancestors, they are simply useful tools; implements of the Christian mode of ceremonial worship, and used to invite the essence of the ancestral spirit.

stage director, the preacher must utilize the proper devices—phonically, physically, and visually—to produce images that will urge the emotions of the community to coalesce around the goals of the ceremony: once the entire mode has become unified, the total experience becomes a testament of the truth—and the truth don't move!—a revelation of reality.

While there is no intention here to suggest that *all* black plays *must* duplicate the ceremonial process of the black church, most black works, even those that are clearly naturalistic in form, reflect some aspect of the model/tradition. Lorraine Hansberry's *A Raisin in the Sun* indicates an acquisition of the invocative power of the church when the mother scolds the son for recklessly losing the money she had bestowed upon him from her dead husband's insurance policy: here we find the mother invoking the proper rhythm and repetition in her word-force to call up the spirit image of the father to subdue her outrage:

MAMA I seen . . . him . . . night after night . . . come in . . . and look at that rug . . . and then look at me . . . the red showing in his eyes . . . the veins moving in his head . . . I seen him grow thin and old before he was forty . . . working . . . working . . . working . . . and working and working like somebody's old horse . . . killing himself . . . and you —you give it all away in a day . . . Oh God . . . look down here . . . and show me the strength . . . strength . . . strength!

And in Langston Hughes' pithy, ironic playlet, *Soul Gone Home,* we find a mother conversing with her dead son after he had been conjured up with the appropriate word-force, Nommo:

MOTHER Oh Gawd! Oh Lawd! Why did you take my son from me? Oh Gawd, why did you do it? He was all I had! Oh, Lawd, what am I gonna do? (*Looking at dead boy and stroking his head.*) Oh, son! Oh! Ronnie! Oh, my boy, speak to me! Ronnie, say something to me! Son, why don't you talk to your mother? Can't you see she's bowed down in sorrow? Son, speak to me, just a word! Come back from the spirit world and speak to me! Ronnie, come back from the dead and speak to your mother!

Responding to the cadence of African invocation, the boy speaks; and while he dialogues with the mother, he becomes part of her immediate reality, rather than treated as an illusion.

Phillip Hayes Dean also allows the conjuring forces of the church tradition, with its call and response devices, to transform memory/illusion into an immediate sense of reality in his *The Sty of the Blind Pig.* The potency of the rhythms closes the gap of time/space, bringing the event into Alberta's living room where she stands alone to bear witness to the sweet agony of grief experienced at the funeral of her departed lover:

ALBERTA (*standing and swaying to the music, which has started to build*) How long!!

CONGREGATION How long!!

REVEREND GOODLOW How long, oh Lord.

ALBERTA How long, Jesus!

CONGREGATION How long, Lord!!!

REVEREND GOODLOW How long the night!

ALBERTA Yes, Lord! Oh, yes, Lord!

CONGREGATION Mercy, Lord! Lord, have mercy!

REVEREND GOODLOW How long this darkness!

ALBERTA (*falling to the floor*) I wanna shout Jesus! And dance! Amen! (*Lies out on floor.*) Fill me with the Holy Ghost. Let me tremble with the Holy Ghost! (*Her body trembling with the Holy Ghost. On her feet.*) Let me dance the dance of happiness! (*The* CHOIR *still can be heard humming.*) I want to dance the dance of happiness! (*She goes into a wild, frenzied dance.*) Let me speak in tongues, oh Lord. Twist my words into confusion, Jesus. Let the meaning of my words be withheld even from me. Only you, Jesus, and the beautiful Purple Angels understand my utterances. (*Still dancing, she speaks gibberish.*)

And finally, without doubt Jesse Jackson's "Operation Push" is consummate theater: here we observe how the traditional Baptist ceremony is manipulated into a secular, theatrical mode which focuses the politico-social objectives of the organization: it's the best show in town!

It would seem, nonetheless, that there must be a way to translate the experimental power of the sacred ritual into the secular ceremony called theater without necessarily using the literal model of the church. What we seek is power. And there is power in the familiar sound/word designations of an event. The proper manipulation of space/sound will activate the necessary rhythms of the mode that will heighten the force of images. Imamu Amiri Baraka is one of the writers who owns the capacity to send language through the sonorous changes that intensifies images in a manner redolent of the great Bird, Charlie Parker: be it a blues scat, riff, or ballad, its potency emanates from a spiritual place. Further, like all musicians, language is used in the service of illuminating familiar symbolic references germane to our experience.

In Baraka's full length drama, *A Recent Killing,*[11] the protagonist-poet confronts, on stage, a chorus of European bedfellows and an aphrodisiac nymph who occupy his mind. When viewed from the tradition of the western continuum, the chorus is considered illusory, the plot earmarked for an exercise in the surreal. However, as orchestrated—at least on paper—within the reality of the young soldier-poet, they become epiphanies of a certain spirit force: he must deal with them in real terms, not as apparitions, but as forces that intrude on his reality. One such chorus member, Sebastian Flyte, appears from out of the shadows in appropriate Edwardian garb to assert his force on young Len:

FLYTE *The Wasteland!* Uhuhmmm. (*Clearing his throat haughtily.*) "April . . . (*trilling his "r's" very conspicuously*) . . . is the cruelest month, breeding/Lilacs out of the dead land, mixing/Memory and desire, stirring/Dull roots with spring rain."

LEN (*getting up and joining in the recitation, without even glanc-*

---

[11] Performed by New Federal Theater, New York, in 1973.

ing over his shoulder at FLYTE) "Winter kept us warm, covering/Earth in forgetful snow, feeding . . ."

FLYTE (*stopping his recitation*) What on earth do you think you're doing?

LEN (*still not looking at him*) I know that poem.

Len has managed at least a temporary harmonizing of the force/Flyte which contains all the prerogatives of western civility; an imposing and unrelenting force that sets about the action to capture the imagination of the young black poet who admits not understanding the function of poetry. Flyte takes off:

FLYTE Huzzah! (*Mockingly.*) Selah! An honest youth. (*Making believe he is a dainty airplane.*) Broooooooom! (*Coming back to* LEN.) Poetry? Is that what this discourse is about? Poesie, the gentle art. Ah, love, ah, birds, ah gentle things disappearing . . . It is sad business, isn't it? The wretched hoax of sensitivity. (*Fake despair.*) Ahhh . . . ahhhhhh. But I wanted to lecture you and now I've quite forgotten what the wretched thing was to be about.

And later, when Len announces to Flyte the first image that comes into his mind is gold, the color gold, Imamu takes Flyte through lyrical changes that focuses the ghost of western sensibility; a lofty Flyte singing like a flower-child of the mythic fairy-godmother:

FLYTE Well, then, we'll take it as poetry. As the glittery image of life you see. Something to be captured, that is that feeling . . . what gold can make you feel, as color, as something somehow just beyond your reach, but part of you. As color, poems are gold. The act of poetry is gold. And the poet himself. (*Kissing* LEN *behind his ear.*) My golden boy. All gold and energy. What do you feel now?

Obviously like Sad Sack. Baraka has infused into the language of this western mythic creature a word-force emanating from a spiritualist tradition, with its connotative sounds, and repetitions that urge the rhythms to soar, making Flyte a formidable force to contend with.

When *A Recent Killing* was first performed at the New Federal Theater in New York it faced a cool reception from the usual arbiters of the New York theater, one reviewer of the *New York Times* even finding the experience disappointing because of its "uncharacteristic moderation," the absence of the familiar "hysterical fury" that allows a purging of guilt. It is not difficult to see how this full-length drama could be misread, appearing to the traditionalist American viewer as supra-realistic, or abstract realism, even clumsy allegorical melodrama. Misappropriation of the work's intention, however, was largely due to its production which attended the scenes in a linear fashion belonging to the conventions of naturalism. The characters were set into motion from a naturalistic frame of reality: unfortunately, if one chooses to initiate the experience from such a reference, any shift from naturalism would necessarily have to be viewed as illusion. At this point, the play becomes elusive, obscure. However, if the characters had been treated as archetypes—including the chorus—the entire event might have been realized in one field of reality, rather than appearing as separate states of consciousness.

Rather than a linear treatment, the work well afforded a modal conceptualization, one that would have allowed for multiple scenes—at least simultaneous actions—to be played without disturbing the focus of the language. Orchestration of the total mode would have provided, at least, several layers of consciousness, if not otherwise, sheets of energy that would galvanize the images, giving them purpose; an intensity is required here that would shake our spirits when reality reveals itself to young Len, forcing us to experience the revelation along with the poet, thereby creating an impact on our consciousness that would make the drama monumental.

Archetypes, as opposed to phototypes, are often characterized in black plays, as was evidenced in Douglas Turner Ward's *Day of Absence*, or even the comedic/satiric version of Ossie Davis' *Purlie Victorious*. Such characters lend themselves appropriately to Kuntu, and allow for more global metaphors than do personalized characters, however often the archetype may be misapprehended as being merely stereotypic. But then, parenthetically, there are times when archetypical character traits are assigned to stereotypes in order to dignify or heighten our interest in a character's conflict. Such may be observed in the alter-personality conflict of Johnny and Gabe, an obscured vision of the "tragic mulatto" in Charles Gordone's *No Place to Be Somebody.* On the surface, it would appear that the conflict rests with the darker-skinned Johnny's efforts to buck the white system that oppresses him; yet, in a very subtle, and far more profound sense, the inner turbulence of the "tragic mulatto," Gabe, screams out for some cosmic redemption in his fragmented personality:

GABE

Whiter than snow, yes!
Whiter than snow!
Now, wash me, and I shall be
Whiter than snow!

(*He chants.*)

We moved out of that dirty-black slum
Away from those dirty-black people!
Who live in those dirty-black hovels,
Amidst all of that garbage and filth!
Away from those dirty-black people,
Who in every way,
Prove daily
They are what they are!
Just dirty-black people!

Gabe is pursued by a tormenting ambivalence throughout the play which remains unresolved at the end when he kills his alter-personality, his darker-side, Johnny. There is a tragedy here that has far greater implications—dramaturgically and socially—than the demise of an archetypical anti-hero. End parenthesis!

Transformation of character is quite common to the archetype. A single character, such as Booboo in Oliver Pitcher's theater piece, *The One,* can become several characters in transition. The same may be said of Sonia Sanchez' Sista Son/Ji who, as an Old Black Woman, traverses the memory of youthful naïveté toward nationalism, on to warring mother, and back to resignation. And in N. R.

Davison's thoroughly modal event *El Haig Malik,* Malcolm is played by both male and female performers, depending upon the scenic demands of the event. Or, as Adrienne Kennedy indicates in her stage notes to *The Owl Answers:*

> Seated is a plain, pallid Negro woman, wearing a cotton summer dress . . . She is Clara Passmore who is the Virgin Mary who is the Bastard who is the Owl.

At times, even objects may transcend their objectness and own archetypical character values when properly manipulated in the mode, such as the animism of the ax in Miss Kennedy's *A Beast Story,* or the juju-cane in *The Great MacDaddy,* or the fork used in the ritual of Lennox Brown's *Devil Mas'.* Even light has its archetypical cosmic weight when used, as in Baraka's *Great Goodness of Life,* to suggest an antagonistic character. The cosmic insinuation of light is not exclusive to the black theater, for it has always held a strange fascination for the European as a theatrical device or a metaphysical reference to the unencroachable. However, Baraka attributes a substantive role to light which is animated into character.

The ubiquitous presence of a chorus is another aspect of the African continuum found in the black theater. A chorus usually personifies community, both living and dead. It signifies the spiritual imperatives of the community's moral universe which revitalizes the features of black humanity. At times the chorus may be otherworldly, emanating from that place where the ancestors reside, committing itself to the security of a community member who dialogues with his race memory, as did Sweetback[12] in his efforts to elude his pursuers. Once again, dialogue between living and dead members of the community should not be misconstrued as surrealism: what is important to the mode here is simply the materialization of the ancestral spirit so that one is able to identify the precise source of a particular piece of wisdom. A chorus may also be subsumed in one character, as was Johnny's alter-personality, Gabe, in Charles Gordone's *No Place to Be Somebody:* even here, the magical wisdom of character transformation should not be confused with the psychic

---

[12] *Sweet Sweetback's Bad Ass Song,* a film by Melvin Van Peebles.

manifestations of the dream theory. And in *Devil Mas',* we discover Borbon, a black street sweeper, Lalsingh, an East Indian bottle vendor, and Achong, a Chinese grocer, used as manifestations of the community—the same three characters appearing in other works of Brown's—thus serving as a chorus. And when properly orchestrated into a direct relationship with elements of the mode, even the non-material can be used as a chorus, as was the silent, screen projections of black militant leaders who are unrecognized by Court Royal in *Great Goodness of Life.* Or the ever-present choral configuration in Jean Toomer's *Kabnis,* which pursues the protagonist with the chill of race memory as Song blows through the Georgia pine:

White-man's land
Niggers, sing.
Burn, bear black children
Till poor rivers bring
Rest, and sweet glory
In Camp Ground.

As early as 1933, Hall Johnson in his drama, *Run Little Chillin',* pitted the Hope Baptist Church revivalists in conflict with the New Day Pilgrim voodoo ritualists, attempting to grapple with the commercial priorities of Broadway in a manner that would not totally compromise his native sensibilities. Orchestrated with Song, Dance, and Drum, Johnson assigned to one of the Pilgrim rituals mythic relationships commensurate with what Alaine Locke refers to as "native traits":

> The general impression should be of something approaching voodoo—not too directly African, but with a strong African flavor . . . There should be . . . references (in the chants) to Sun, Moon, Water, etc. . . . The whole betokens and partly expresses a religious attitude of joy and freedom toward life, in sharp contrast to the well-known spiritual joy of suffering which characterizes the more orthodox religious services of Negroes.

Here we find that the ritual experience, rather than deferring to a hocus-pocus spectacle, was made sensible by familiar indices to the experience found in African/American life. On the other hand,

Song, Dance, and Drum might be committed to a more rigorous, formal, and dramaturgical structure when geography and experience dictates a different manner of attending a theatrical mode.

Such is the case of many Caribbean writers, most notably Aimé Césaire, where there is a tendency to use the strict dramaturgical forms fashioned by African stage writers. In both cases, there is a penchant for a stylized lyricism; thus an acquiescence to the influence of colonial domination which colors the author's perception and guides the execution of his sensibility.

In Aimé Césaire's *A Season in the Congo,* a solo chorus member in the motherland, the sanza player, forbodingly passes Lumumba who had just been pardoned from jail.

> *Kungo Mpaka Dima*
> (Be watchful, brothers, the Congo is moving)

But Lumumba was a man driven by conspiratorial winds; he was a man of imagination, observes Césaire:

> (Lumumba is) . . . always on top of the present situation, and because of this also a man of faith; thus he is the African, the "muntu" at once the man who shares the vital force (the "ngolo") and the man of words (the "nommo").

Thus, Césaire has Lumumba announce:

> We have danced the dance of life! When I am
> gone, when I
> am spent like the blinding meteor in the night
> sky,
> when the Congo is no more than a season seasoned
> with blood,
> be beautiful, still beautiful . . .

Upon reading the works in this collection it should become apparent that black language owns an idiom which is elegant, syntactically poetic. In almost all cases, let alone the stylized poetic forms characteristic of the Caribbean and African writers, there tends to be a penchant for verse, an exacting of speech rhythms on a fine metered course, one that is direct and testimonially consummate.

Toomer has Kabnis make an assessment of the night:

> Night, soft belly of a pregnant Negress, throbs evenly against the torso of the South. Night throbs a womb-song to the South. Cane and cotton fields, pine forests, cypress swamps, sawmills, and factories are fecund at her touch. Night's womb-song sets them singing. Night winds are the breathing of the unborn child whose calm throbbing in the belly of a Negress sets them somnolently singing. Hear their song.

And Imamu Baraka has the voice of light cryptically exonerating Court Royal from behind a shadow:

> The rite must be finished. This ghost must be lost in cold space. Court Royal, this is your destiny. This act was done by you a million years ago. This is only the memory of it. This is only a rite. You cannot kill a shadow. This is only a rite, to show that you would be guilty but for the cleansing rite . . .

In *Mars,* Clay Goss invokes the changes of scatology:

> Maybe it's because we're married, baby. Maybe it's because we've been married so long . . . you know . . . like the whole routine and shit that it's kinda become a standard . . . like "Moon River" . . . with us. Between us. "Moon River" between us . . . "Moon River" between us. Noise between the scratched-up grooves with Jerry Butler groanin' over and over again "Moon River . . . Moon River."

Song, Dance, and Drum are as important to the modes of contemporary black experience as they always have been in traditional African life. While the experience of the New World may have colored these expressive indices, the resonance of Africa remains apparent. As connotative references, they are invaluable. In the theatrical sense, Song has the power to transcend the static nature of literal word-meaning. Dance codifies and makes sensible the wide range of gestural signification in black life. And Drums makes evident the acoustic syntax of black speech with its varying tonal choices. These references to sound and movement are culturally cultivated. They are concerned with specific meaning in the Afro-American experience. Yet while race memory cannot be denied its progenitive place of value, it is not necessary to regard Africa as the primary source of expressive inclination. To do so would encourage a gross and erroneous self-mockery of ancestral traditions. What is important, however, is the free expression of the sensibility within the new social context. But, in order for the sensibility to own a liberating quality, as in gospel singing, it must be clearly identifiable in the Afro-American theater mode, so as to extricate itself from being an illegitimate, if not otherwise, exotic aspect of a melting-pot culture.

The inherent spirituality of our music has always mystified. It is certainly consonant with the tonalities and rhythms of the African continuum. Music plays a focal role in the lives of black people everywhere; it is said, and correctly so, that all black people have rhythm.

But so do Europeans have rhythm, though of a different drummer. It is not a particularly elegant rhythm; it is contained in the awesome surge of the epic, that agonized pursuit of emotions that erects steel bridges and concrete walls, the episodic cataloguing of human failing and successes protracted over a long duration of excavations of the mind/heart. The epic owns a rhythm which is unquestionably forceful, invoking the spirit of nostalgia in the European until catharsis brings about the rude awakening of reality. It is truly moving. Yet, observing the European epic and the African ritual is like attending the difference between a lullaby and a flatted fifth blues chord. A lullaby almost seems to generically suggest lull-on-by or lull-into-past; wherein the flatted fifth tends to augment the present state of things through the materialization of the spirit, the spirit, the forceful emergence/convergence of shadow into light, an animation of what's happening now.

Adrienne Kennedy's *A Beast Story* is no lullaby; it is an active matrix of forces gradually locking in several pieces of light passing through a prism: at a certain moment it becomes apparent that the spectrum radiates from a single source of power, the Sun. Miss Kennedy's story comes at us in fragments, each new detail augmenting the horrific mode, the intricate polyrhythm of language and movement adding light on the shadow guarding a terrible scar on the mind/heart: the change amounts to a sort of malefic blues ballad.

And why not? If black culture can produce a Charlie Parker, a John Coltrane, or a Thelonius Monk, it should very well take advantage of such models when exercising theatrical modes. These men perform with a power that cannot be easily overwhelmed or corrupted. Even when such force is placed in an artificial/alien mode, say, Charlie Parker and a symphonic string accompaniment, the power remains focused, the African ethos penetrates without being subdued by the alien context. Even if the sound should seem smooth, appearing, on first inspection, to accommodate the subtleties of the alien mode, it would be so smooth that the mode will shift in mysterious ways without realizing that it has become subordinate to the sound; thus a harmonious relationship is realized.

In February 1973, the *New York Times* posed the moot/mut question "Should Black Actors Play Chekhov?"[13] soliciting responses from two black theater artists, playwright Ed Bullins and actress/author Maya Angelou. They both intoned affirmatively to the arrogant query which asks blacks to authenticate the traditions of western culture. While it is not unreasonable for a great people to recognize greatness outside of one's own culture, Bullins seems to have been forced into a posture of being in awe, if not enamored of the master:

> Upon hearing of the production concept before attending a performance, I thought the ideal abominable, but the man's work has survived revolutions, wars, and evolution, so one must remember that Chekhov was read and studied even before one matured enough to read and study himself.

And Maya Angelou signals a regressive attitude of ambivalence among many black theater artists when she notes:

> . . . a black actor would expose subtleties in a white character that a white actor might never see, or might not have the heart to reveal.

---

[13] *New York Times,* February 4, 1973.

It would seem that the black actor is once again burdened with defining white humanity with the depth of perception accrued an oppressed/alienated minority; his energies/vision preempted to the point of even excavating the dead rather than focusing on the subtleties of majesty in the black experience. At best, participation in the Chekhov frame can only offer novelty, while giving a host of great black actors a chance to exercise the power of their skills. But to legitimize the experience as being "imperative" abstruse analysis of aesthetic/cultural priorities, even Miss Angelou cannot resist the call of her mother-wit which urges her sensibilities toward demanding a spirituality in *The Cherry Orchard:*

> The play desperately needs the rippling sensuosity of James Earl Jones and the exhausted langor of Gloria Foster. In fact, to make it come alive really it could use a few impersonations by Sammy Davis, Jr., "Young, Gifted, and Black" sung by Nina Simone and a rousing sermon by the Rev. Jesse Jackson. Ray Charles and the Rayettes ought to be humming in the background.

Black music has clearly made a formidable contribution to the shape/form of many black theater works. Imamu Amiri Baraka's *Slaveship* is certainly characteristic of a modal composition. On paper, it is a mere few pages which serve as charts upon which the attitude of scenes, some dialogue, and types of activities are designated within space/time relationship. The script then provides for the kind of spaces that allow for improvisation within the mode. With deft manipulation/orchestration of the mode, as was the case in Gilbert Moses' production, the desired rhythm is induced to amplify the horrors of the slaveship at its most sensate/spiritual level of experience. The improvisations lock us into a rhythm that focuses our historical outrage, while heightening our unrelieved acuity of oppression.

Just as Archie Shepp's music abetted the vitality of the *Slaveship* mode, his own dramatic piece, *Junebug Graduates Tonight,* is a musical model in structure, complete with band, chorus, and scenic transitions that focus the message of a black youth's disillusionment in the blues changes of sharps or flats, the entire matrix giving expression to the kind of harsh lyricism of an oppressed reality. The *Washington Post* observed:

> The script attempts to make a fluid shift between real persons and abstract personification, between the allegorical and the literal, the factual and the fanciful . . . Similarly, the dialogue slips without transition from realistic banter into symbolic reverie, and from there right into music . . . The exchange between the discursive and the lyrical mode is managed with wonderful skill . . . When the emotions of the play reach the critical temperature, the words automatically give way to song and dance, and in context, this seems to be the most natural thing in the world.[14]

Music designated the mode, and all aspects of production were in harmonious relationship to its invocation.

Archie Shepp's music also made a formidable contribution to the production of Aishah Rahman's *Lady Day: A Musical Tragedy.*[15] In this case, an eighteen-member band/chorus was utilized to activate the forces in the mode that overtook a mythic heroine, Billie Holiday. Stylistically, the production was designed to create an organic cohesiveness between the rhythms of word/song and movement, iconographic images and color textures of black life, hoodoo, and life force, all orchestrated in a manner that allows time/space the fluidity which gives the past the immediacy of the present: such a Kuntu eschewed the awakening of a vapid nostalgia which cannot be useful to the spirit, nor did it seek refuge in sociological explications that would freeze the content of experience into the static condition of melodrama.

Instead, the forces of oppression are focused so as to invite the spirit of Billie to guide us past similar pitfalls. The work intended a spiritual awakening to an earth-bond crisis, employing the syntax of black music—its Nommo force—to bridge the "now" generation to parents, and parents to ancestors. It became an expression of our African continuation, a testament of urgency to survive the crisis of oppression.

---

[14] 1970 production at Howard University, directed by Harrison.

[15] Produced by the Chelsea Theater in New York under the direction of Harrison.

Clay Goss's *Mars*[16] appears almost like a studied composition in black music. The Kuntu is given shape by an instrumental ensemble, a chorus/community that designates the physical space/images through initiating call/response changes, establishing polyrhythms/meters, and at times, transforming into specific musical instrumental tone/characters to take fours with the principal character who, due to the nature of his scat/riff, assumes the personage/quality of a lead vocalist evoking the myriad colors of the blues. Silence—pregnant pause—is also manipulated in the mode: Goss asks that the wife never speak, but insinuate the potency of her thoughts/responses to the male lead through body movements. Further:

> Also the chorus should have body movements that are exaggerated; after all, this is a *monumental* play. And all the characters are monumental.

It had not been until 1964 that one felt secure enough with one's native intuition to assign to a musician the same character values in a play traditionally given to actors. *Tophat*[17] was thus conceived as a dramatic tone-poem with one musician, a female vocalist who had all the lines, and an itinerant *speechless* male who became the "rests" in the total composition. This experiment led to *Tabernacle* in 1967 which employed the new music attitude of Ayler, Shepp, and Coltrane scored by Eric Gravatt to galvanize the action of the play. These techniques were further advanced in the creation of the original production of Melvin Van Peeble's *Ain't Supposed to Die a Natural Death,* where the rhythms committed the community/characters to a mode of continued assaults of oppression without relief until the forces are revealed: at this point of revelation, the mode is broken and the spirit released through the house. *The Great MacDaddy,* then, attempts to formalize the style of work that

[16] First produced at Howard University in January 1972, under the direction of Eric Hughes.

[17] *Tophat:* performed at Buffalo University Summer Theater in 1965, revised for production at Negro Ensemble Company in 1972: both under Harrison's direction.

grapples with the demands of African memory and African-American consciousness.

In the process of pursuing African-American mythic relationships in the continuum of our tradition—particularly urban—the structure of the work is described in a musical Kuntu. Rather than scenes, there is the designation of Primal Rhythms, Beats, Transitional Beats, and Terminal Rhythm. These designations are not simply arbitrary, i.e., designed as a reactive, spurious departure from American theatrical conventions; they are necessary conditions to achieve the clearest focusing of the image in the mode without compromising the vitality and integrity of an African sensibility nurtured in the wasteland.

Lennox Brown, the Trinidadian playwright who currently resides in Toronto, observed that "any race of people should see themselves as part of a stream that runs way back."[18] *Devil Mas',* which is one of a cycle of plays dealing with black Caribbean ghetto life, attends the mythos of the black community. As demonstrated in his *A Ballet Behind The Bridge*[19] and *Prodigal In Black Stone,*[20] the complexities of ghetto life are too great to be locked into psychological categories which merely freeze the problems for closer inspection without any palliative effect. Thus Brown tends to place the characters into mythic relationships which might be liberating to the spirit sense, "you give the human being a link in the continuum, a link to the human past when you approach him mythologically."[21] In *Devil Mas',* the forces/problems of contemporary life are given focus through the dynamics of a community's understanding of its cultural antecedents.

The collection of works in *Kuntu Drama* do not exhaust the number of possible representatives of the sensibility. Aside from the aforementioned Douglas Turner Ward, and Oliver Pitcher, Archie Shepp and Aishah Rahman, one might include Oyamo's *Revelation,* and perhaps even *The Game,* the fifth play of Charles

---

[18] *Trinidad Guardian,* August 25, 1972.
[19] Staged by Negro Ensemble Company, Spring 1972.
[20] Staged by Eugene O'Neill Playwrights Conference, Summer 1972.
[21] *Trinidad Guardian,* August 25, 1972.

Fuller's epic-cycle *In My Many Names and Days.* In the Motherland, almost all of Wole Soyinka's work would be representative; and from the Caribbean, Derek Wolcott's *Ti-Jean and His Brothers* and *The Dream on Monkey Mountain.*

In the production note to *The Dream on Monkey Mountain,* Wolcott advises:

> The producer can amplify it with spectacle as he chooses, or, as in the original production, switch roles and limit his cast to a dozen or so. He will need dancers, actors, and singers, the same precision and vitality that one has read of in the Kabuki.

Kuntu drama, or modally conceived plays/events utilizing our native traditions, however shaped by American experiences, demand the same seriousness of attention and precision of execution that is considered unique in other cultural forms, such as the Berliner Ensemble, flamenco dance, or a Scottish military band. The works of Kuntu drama should be paid the kind of deference given any sociopolitical force that might liberate the black theater from a frozen cultural reference which identifies black life with the priorities of the American dream. Despite economic considerations, there is a future for the black theater when we begin to accept Africa as the antecedent reference to our contemporary American folk styles. It is the source that gives expression to our walk/dance, talk/song, and provide rhythm/silence at the Sunday chicken dinner table, urban/rural: all of it must be attended in a manner which creates the strongest reality of our power to summon the dynamics of black life into harmonious relationships with the mode.

—Paul Carter Harrison
W. E. B. Dubois Department of Afro-American Studies
University of Massachusetts

KABNIS
by Jean Toomer

Jean Toomer was perhaps one of the most innovative writers of the 1920's Negro Renaissance movement. His epic novel, *Cane,* is as important to the annals of black literature as Wright's *Native Son* and Ellison's *Invisible Man.* Stylistically, Toomer achieves the highest form of invention in literature on a par with Pound and Eliot. Among black writers of the time, he owned the sole distinction of having been one of the forerunners of the modern idiom in American letters. *Kabnis* is taken from the last part of *Cane,* which was first published in 1923.

CAST OF CHARACTERS

KABNIS

HALSEY

LAYMAN

HANBY

LEWIS

MR. RAMSAY

CARRIE K.

CORA

STELLA

OLD MAN (FATHER JOHN)

I

RALPH KABNIS, *propped in his bed, tries to read. To read himself to sleep. An oil lamp on a chair near his elbow burns unsteadily. The cabin room is spaced fantastically about it. Whitewashed hearth and chimney, black with sooty saw-teeth. Ceiling, patterned by the fringed globe of the lamp. The walls, unpainted, are seasoned a rosin yellow. And cracks between the boards are black. These cracks are the lips the night winds use for whispering. Night winds in Georgia are vagrant poets, whispering.* KABNIS, *against his will, lets his book slip down and listens to them. The warm whiteness of his bed, the lamplight, do not protect him from the weird chill of their song:*

White-man's land.
Niggers, sing.
Burn, bear black children
Till poor rivers bring
Rest, and sweet glory
In Camp Ground.

KABNIS' *thin hair is streaked on the pillow. His hand strokes the slim silk of his mustache. His thumb, pressed under his chin, seems to be trying to give squareness and projection to it. Brown eyes stare from a lemon face. Moisture gathers beneath his armpits. He slides down beneath the cover, seeking release.*

KABNIS Near me. Now. Whoever you are, my warm glowing sweetheart, do not think that the face that rests beside you is the real Kabnis. Ralph Kabnis is a dream. And dreams are faces with large eyes and weak chins and broad brows that get smashed by the fists of square faces. The body of the world is bullnecked. A dream is a soft face that fits uncertainly upon it . . . God, if I could develop that in words. Give what I know a bullneck and a heaving body, all would go well with me, wouldnt it, sweetheart? If I could feel that I came to the South to face it. If I, the dream (not what is weak and afraid in me) could become the face of the South. How my lips would sing for it, my songs being the lips of its soul. Soul. Soul hell. There aint no such thing. What in hell was that? (*A rat had run across the thin boards of the ceiling.* KABNIS *thrusts his head out from the covers. Through the cracks, a powdery faded red dust sprays down on him. Dust of slave fields, dried, scattered . . . No use to read. Christ, if he only could drink himself to sleep. Something as sure as fate was going to happen. He couldnt stand this thing much longer. A hen perched on a shelf in the adjoining room begins to tread. Her nails scrape the soft wood. Her feathers ruffle.*) Get out of that, you egg-laying bitch. (KABNIS *hurls a slipper against the wall. The hen flies from her perch and cackles as if a skunk were after her.*) Now cut out that racket or I'll wring your neck for you. (*Answering cackles arise in the chicken yard.*) Why in Christ's hell cant you leave me alone? Damn it, I wish your cackle would choke you. Choke every mother's son of them in this God-forsaken hole. Go away. By God I'll wring your neck for you if you dont. Hell of a mess I've got in: even the poultry is hostile. Go way. Go way. By God, I'll . . . (KABNIS *jumps from his bed. His eyes are wild. He makes for the door. Bursts through it. The hen, driving blindly at the windowpane screams. Then flies and flops around trying to elude him.* KABNIS *catches her.*) Got you now, you she-bitch. (*With his fingers about her neck, he thrusts open the outside door and steps out into the serene loveliness of Georgian autumn moonlight. Some distance off, down in the valley, a band of pine-smoke, silvered gauze, drifts steadily. The half-moon is a white child that sleeps upon the tree-tops of the forest. White winds croon its sleep-song:*

rock a-by baby . . .
Black mother sways, holding a white child on her
bosom.

when the bough bends . . .
Her breath hums through pine-cones.
cradle will fall . . .
Teat moon-children at your breasts,
down will come baby . . .
Black mother.

KABNIS *whirls the chicken by its neck, and throws the head away. Picks up the hopping body, warm, sticky, and hides it in a clump of bushes. He wipes blood from his hands onto the coarse scant grass.*

KABNIS Thats done. Old Chromo in the big house there will wonder whats become of her pet hen. Well, it'll teach her a lesson: not to make a hen-coop of my quarters. Quarters. Hell of a fine quarters I've got. Five years ago; look at me now. Earth's child. The earth my mother. God is a profligate red-nosed man about town. Bastardy; me. A bastard son has got a right to curse his maker. God . . . (KABNIS *is about to shake his fists heavenward. He looks up, and the night's beauty strikes him dumb. He falls to his knees. Sharp stones cut through his thin pajamas. The shock sends a shiver over him. He quivers. Tears mist his eyes. He writhes.*) God Almighty, dear God, dear Jesus, do not torture me with beauty. Take it away. Give me an ugly world. Ha, ugly. Stinking like unwashed niggers. Dear Jesus, do not chain me to myself and set these hills and valleys, heaving with folksongs, so close to me that I cannot reach them. There is a radiant beauty in the night that touches and . . . tortures me. Ugh. Hell. Get up, you damn fool. Look around. Whats beautiful there? Hog pens and chicken yards. Dirty red mud. Stinking outhouse. What beauty anyway but ugliness if it hurts you? God, he doesnt exist, but nevertheless He is ugly. Hence, what comes from Him is ugly. Lynchers and businessmen, and that cockroach Hanby, especially. How come that he gets to be principal of a school? Of the school I'm driven to teach in? God's handiwork, doubtless. God and Hanby, they belong together. Two godam moral-spouters. Oh, no, I wont let that emotion come up in me. Stay down. Stay down, I tell you. O Jesus, Thou art beautiful . . . Come, Ralph, pull yourself together. Curses and adoration dont come from what is sane. This loneliness, dumbness, awful intangible oppression is enough to drive a man insane. Miles from nowhere. A speck on a Georgia hillside. Jesus, can you imagine it—an atom of dust in agony on a hillside? Thats a spectacle for you. Come, Ralph, old man, pull yourself together. (KABNIS *has stiffened. He is conscious now of the night wind, and of how it chills him. He rises. He totters as a man would who for the first time uses artificial limbs. As a completely artificial man would. The large frame house, squatting on brick pillars, where the principal of the school, his wife, and the boarding girls sleep, seems a curious shadow of his mind. He tries but cannot convince himself of its reality. His gaze drifts down into the vale, across the swamp, up over the solid dusk bank of pines, and rests, bewildered-like, on the courthouse tower. It is dull silver in the moonlight. White child that sleeps upon the top of pines. His mind clears. He sees himself yanked beneath that tower. He sees white minds, with indolent assumption, juggle justice and a nigger . . . Somewhere, far off in the straight line of his sight, is Augusta. Christ, how cut off from everything he is. And hours, hours north, why not say a lifetime north? Washington sleeps. Its still, peaceful streets, how desirable they are. Its people whom he had always halfway despised. New York? Impossible. It was a fiction. He had dreamed it. An impotent nostalgia grips him. It becomes intolerable. He forces himself to narrow to a cabin silhouetted on a knoll about a mile away. Peace. Negroes within it are content. They farm. They sing. They love. They sleep.* KABNIS *wonders if perhaps they can feel him. If perhaps he gives them bad dreams. Things are so immediate in Georgia.*

Thinking that now he can go to sleep, he re-enters his room. He builds a fire in the open hearth. The room dances to the tongues of flames, and sings to the crackling and spurting of the logs. Wind comes up between the floor boards, through the black cracks of the walls.) Cant sleep. Light a cigarette. If that old bastard comes over here and smells smoke, I'm done for. Hell of a note, cant even smoke. The stillness of it: where they burn and hang men, you cant smoke. Cant take a swig of licker. What do they think this is, anyway, some sort of temperance school? How did I ever land in such a hole? Ugh. One might just as well be in his grave. Still as a grave. Jesus, how still everything is. Does the world know how still it is? People make noise. They are afraid of silence. Of what lives, and God, of what dies in silence. There must be many dead things moving in silence. They come here to touch me. I swear I feel their fingers . . . Come, Ralph, pull yourself together. What in hell was that? Only the rustle of leaves, I guess. You know, Ralph, old man, it wouldnt surprise me at all to see a ghost. People dont think there are such things. They rationalize their fear and call their cowardice science. Fine bunch, they are. Damit, that was a noise. And not the wind either. A chicken maybe. Hell, chickens dont wander around this time of night. What in hell is it? (*A scraping sound, like a piece of wood dragging over the ground, is coming near.*) Ha, ha. The ghosts down this way havent got any chains to rattle, so they drag trees along with them. Thats a good one. But no joke, something is outside this house, as sure as hell. Whatever it is, it can get a good look at me and I cant see it. Jesus Christ! (KABNIS *pours water on the flames and blows his lamp out. He picks up a poker and stealthily approaches the outside door. Swings it open, and lurches into the night. A calf, carrying a yoke of wood, bolts away from him and scampers down the road.*)

KABNIS Well, I'm damned. This godam place is sure getting the best of me. Come, Ralph, old man, pull yourself together. Nights cant last forever. Thank God for that. Its Sunday already. First time in my life I've ever wanted Sunday to come. Hell of a day. And down here there's no such thing as ducking church. Well, I'll see Halsey and Layman and get a good square meal. Thats something. And Halsey's a damn good feller. Cant talk to him, though. Who in Christ's world can I talk to? A hen. God. Myself . . . I'm going bats, no doubt of that. Come now, Ralph, go in and make yourself go to sleep. Come now . . . in the door . . . that's right. Put the poker down. There. All right. Slip under the sheets. Close your eyes. Think nothing . . . a long time . . . nothing, nothing. Dont even think nothing. Blank. Not even blank. Count. No, mustnt count. Nothing . . . blank . . . nothing . . . blank . . . space without stars in it. No, nothing . . . nothing . . .

KABNIS *sleeps. The winds, like soft-voiced vagrant poets sing:*

White-man's land.
Niggers, sing.
Burn, bear black children
Till poor rivers bring
Rest, and sweet glory
In Camp Ground.

II

The parlor of FRED HALSEY'S *home. There is a seediness about it. It seems as though the fittings have given a frugal service to at least seven generations of middle-class shopowners. An open grate burns cheerily in contrast to the gray cold changed autumn weather. An old-fashioned mantelpiece supports a family clock (not running), a figure or two in imitation bronze, and two small group pictures. Directly above it, in a heavy oak frame, the portrait of a bearded man. Black hair, thick and curly, intensifies the pallor of the high forehead. The eyes are daring. The nose, sharp and regular. The poise suggests a tendency to adventure checked by the necessities of absolute command. The portrait is that of an English gentleman who has retained much of his culture, in that money has enabled him to escape being drawn through a land-grubbing pioneer life. His nature and features, modified by marriage and circumstances, have been transmitted to his great-grandson, Fred. To the left of this picture, spaced on the wall, is a smaller portrait of the great-grandmother. That here there is a Negro strain no one would doubt. But it is difficult to say in precisely what feature it lies. On close inspection, her mouth is seen to be wistfully twisted. The expression of her face seems to shift before one's gaze—now ugly, repulsive; now sad, and somehow beautiful in its pain. A tin wood-box rests on the floor below. To the right of the great-grandfather's portrait hangs a family group: the father, mother, two brothers, and one sister of Fred. It includes himself some thirty years ago when his face was an olive white, and his hair luxuriant and dark and wavy. The father is a rich brown. The mother, practically white. Of the children, the girl, quite young, is like Fred; the two brothers, darker. The walls of the room are plastered and painted green. An old upright piano is tucked into the corner near the window. The window looks out on a forlorn, box-like, whitewashed frame church. Negroes are gathering, on foot, driving questionable gray and brown mules, and in an occasional Ford, for afternoon service. Beyond, Georgia hills roll off into the distance, their dreary aspect heightened by the gray spots of unpainted one- and two-room shanties. Clumps of pine trees here and there are the dark points the whole landscape is approaching. The church bell tolls. Above its squat tower, a great spiral of buzzards reaches far into the heavens. An ironic comment upon the path that leads into the Christian land . . . Three rocking chairs are grouped around the grate. Sunday papers scattered on the floor indicate a recent usage. Halsey, a well-built, stocky fellow, hair cropped close, enters the room. His Sunday clothes smell of wood and glue, for it is his habit to putter around his wagon shop even on the Lord's day. He is followed by* PROFESSOR LAYMAN, *tall, heavy, loose-jointed Georgia Negro, by turns teacher and preacher, who has traveled in almost every nook and corner of the state and hence knows more than would be good for anyone other than a silent man.* KABNIS, *trying to force through a gathering heaviness, trails in behind them. They slip into chairs before the fire.*

LAYMAN Sholy fine, Mr. Halsey, sholy fine. This town's right good at feedin folks, better'n most towns in th state, even for preachers, but I ken say this beats um all. Yassur. Now aint that right, Professor Kabnis?

KABNIS Yes sir, this beats them all, all right—best I've had, and thats a fact, though my comparison doesnt carry far, y'know.

LAYMAN Hows that, Professor?

KABNIS Well, this is my first time out—

LAYMAN For a fact. Aint seed you round so much. Whats th trouble? Dont like our folks down this away?

HALSEY Aint that, Layman. He aint like most northern niggers that way. Aint a thing stuck up about him. He likes us, you an me, maybe all—its that red mud over yonder—gets stuck in it and cant get out. (*Laughs.*) An then he loves th fire so, warm as its been. Coldest Yankee I've ever seen. But I'm goin t get him out now in a jiffy, eh, Kabnis?

KABNIS Sure, I should say so, sure. Dont think its because I don't like folks down this way. Just the opposite, in fact. Theres more hospitality and everything. Its diff—that is, theres lots of northern exaggeration about the South. Its not half the terror they picture it. Things are not half bad, as one could easily figure out for himself without ever crossing the Mason and Dixie line: all these people wouldnt stay down here, especially the rich, the ones that could easily leave, if conditions were so mighty bad. And then too, sometime back, my family were southerners y'know. From Georgia, in fact—

LAYMAN Nothing t feel proud about, Professor. Neither your folks nor mine.

HALSEY (*in a mock religious tone*) Amen t that, brother Layman. Amen. (*Turning to* KABNIS, *half playful, yet somehow dead in earnest.*) An Mr. Kabnis, kindly remember youre in th land of cotton—hell of a land. Th white folks get th boll; th niggers get th stalk. An dont you dare touch th boll, or even look at it. They'll swing y sho. (*Laughs.*)

KABNIS But they wouldnt touch a gentleman—fellows, men like us three here—

LAYMAN Nigger's a nigger down this away, Professor. An only two dividins: good an bad. An even they aint permanent categories. They sometimes mixes um up when it comes t lynchin. I've seen um do it.

HALSEY Dont let th fear int y, though, Kabnis. This county's a good un. Aint been a stringin up I can remember. (*Laughs.*)

LAYMAN This is a good town an a good county. But theres some that makes up fer it.

KABNIS Things are better now though since that stir about those peonage cases, arent they?

LAYMAN Ever hear tell of a single shot killin moren one rabbit, Professor?

KABNIS No, of course not, that is, but then—

HALSEY Now I know you werent born yesterday, sprung up so rapid like you aint heard of th brick thrown in th hornets' nest. (*Laughs.*)

KABNIS Hardly, hardly, I know—

HALSEY Course y do. (*To* LAYMAN.) See, northern niggers aint as dumb as they make out t be.

KABNIS (*overlooking the remark*) Just stirs them up to sting.

HALSEY T perfection. An put just like a professor should put it.

KABNIS Thats what actually did happen?

LAYMAN Well, if it aint sos only because th stingers already movin jes as fast as they ken go. An been goin ever since I ken remember, an then some mo. Though I dont usually make mention of it.

HALSEY Damn sight better not. Say, Layman, you come from where theyre always swarmin, dont y?

LAYMAN Yassur. I do that, sho. Dont want t mention it, but its a fact. I've seed th time when there werent no use t even stretch out flat upon th ground. Seen um shoot an cut a man t pieces who had died th night befo. Yassur. An they didnt stop when they found out he was dead—jes went on ahackin at him anyway.

KABNIS What did you do? What did you say to them, Professor?

LAYMAN Thems th things you neither does a thing or talks about if y want t stay around this away, Professor.

HALSEY Listen t what he's tellin y, Kabnis. May come in handy some day.

KABNIS Cant something be done? But of course not. This preacher-ridden race. Pray and shout. Theyre in the preacher's hands. Thats what it is. And the preacher's hands are in the white man's pockets.

HALSEY Present company always excepted.

KABNIS The Professor knows I wasnt referring to him.

LAYMAN Preacher's a preacher anywheres you turn. No use exceptin.

KABNIS Well, of course, if you look at it that way. I didnt mean— But cant something be done?

LAYMAN Sho. Yassur. An done first rate an well. Jes like Sam Raymon done it.

KABNIS Hows that? What did he do?

LAYMAN Th white folks (reckon I oughtnt tell it) had jes knocked two others like you kill a cow—brained um with an ax, when they caught Sam Raymon by a stream. They was about t do fer him when he up and says, "White folks, I gotter die, I knows that. But wont y let me die in my own way?" Some was fer gettin after him, but th boss held um back an says, "Jes so longs th nigger dies—" An Sam fell down ont his knees an prayed, "O Lord, Ise comin to y," an he up and jumps int th stream.

Singing from the church becomes audible. Above it, rising and falling in a plaintive moan, a woman's voice swells to shouting. KABNIS *hears it. His face gives way to an expression of mingled fear, contempt, and pity.* LAYMAN *takes no notice of it.* HALSEY *grins at* KABNIS. *He feels like having a little sport with him.*

HALSEY Lets go t church, eh, Kabnis?

KABNIS (*seeking control*) All right—no sir, not by a damn sight. Once a days enough for me. Christ, but that stuff gets to me. Meaning no reflection on you, Professor.

HALSEY Course not. Say, Kabnis, noticed y this morning. What'd y get up for an go out?

KABNIS Couldnt stand the shouting, and thats a fact. We dont have that sort of thing up North. We do, but, that is, some one should see to it that they are stopped or put out when they get so bad the preacher has to stop his sermon for them.

HALSEY Is that th way youall sit on sisters up North?

KABNIS In the church I used to go to no one ever shouted—

HALSEY Lungs weak?

KABNIS Hardly, that is—

HALSEY Yankees are right up t th minute in tellin folk how t turn a trick. They always were good at talkin.

KABNIS Well, anyway, they should be stopped.

LAYMAN Thats right. Thats true. An its th worst ones in th community that comes int th church t shout. I've sort a made a study of it. You take a man what drinks, th biggest licker-head around will come int th church an yell th loudest. An th sister whats done wrong, an is always doin wrong, will sit down in th Amen corner an swing her arms an shout her head off. Seems as if they cant control themselves out in th world; they cant control themselves in church. Now dont that sound logical, Professor?

HALSEY Reckon its as good as any. But I heard that queer cuss over younder—y know him, dont y, Kabnis? Well, y ought t. He had a run-in with your boss th other day—same as you'll have if you dont walk th chalk-line. An th quicker th better. I hate that Hanby. Ornery bastard. I'll mash his mouth in one of these days. Well, as I was sayin, that feller, Lewis's name, I heard him sayin somethin about a stream whats dammed has got t cut loose somewheres. An that sounds good. I know th feelin myself. He strikes me as knowin a bucketful bout most things, that feller does. Seems like he doesnt want t talk, an does, sometimes, like Layman here. Damn queer feller, him.

LAYMAN Cant make heads or tails of him, an I've seen lots o queer possums in my day. Everybody's wonderin about him. White folks too. He'll have t leave here soon, thats sho. Always askin questions. An I aint seed his lips move once. Pokin round an notin somethin. Noted what I said th other day, an that werent fer notin down.

KABNIS What was that?

LAYMAN Oh, a lynchin that took place bout a year ago. Th worst I know of round these parts.

HALSEY Bill Burnam?

LAYMAN Na. Mame Lamkins.

HALSEY *grunts but says nothing. The preacher's voice rolls from the church in an insistent chanting monotone. At regular intervals it rises to a crescendo note. The sister begins to shout. Her voice, high-pitched and hysterical, is almost perfectly attuned to the nervous key of* KABNIS. HALSEY *notices his distress and is amused by it.* LAYMAN'*s face is expressionless.* KABNIS *wants to hear the story of Mame Lamkins. He does not want to hear it. It can be no worse than the shouting.*

KABNIS (*his chair rocking faster*) What about Mame Lamkins?

HALSEY Tell him, Layman.

The preacher momentarily stops. The choir, together with the entire congregation, sings an old spiritual. The music seems to quiet the shouter. Her heavy breathing has the sound of evening winds that blow through pinecones. LAYMAN'*s voice is uniformly low and soothing. A canebrake, murmuring the tale to its neighbor-road would be more passionate.*

LAYMAN White folks know that niggers talk, an they dont mind jes so long as nothing comes of it, so here goes. She was in th family-way, Mame Lamkins was. They killed her in th street, an some white man seein th risin in her stomach as she lay there soppy in her blood like any cow, took an ripped her belly open, an th kid fell out. It was living; but a nigger baby aint supposed t live. So he jabbed his knife in it an stuck it t a tree. An then they all went away.

KABNIS Christ no! What had she done?

LAYMAN Tried t hide her husband when they was after him.

A shriek pierces the room. The bronze pieces on the mantel hum. The sister cries frantically: "Jesus, Jesus, I've found Jesus. O Lord, glory t God, one mo sinner is acomin home." At the height of this, a stone, wrapped round with paper, crashes through the window. KABNIS *springs to his feet, terror-stricken.* LAYMAN *is worried.* HALSEY *picks up the stone. Takes off the wrapper, smooths it out, and reads: "You northern nigger, its time fer y t leave. Git along now."* KABNIS *knows that the command is meant for him. Fear squeezes him. Caves him in. As a violent external pressure would. Fear flows inside him. It fills him up. He bloats. He saves himself from bursting by dashing wildly from the room.* HALSEY *and* LAYMAN *stare stupidly at each other. The stone, the crumpled paper are things, huge things that weight them. Their thoughts are vaguely concerned with the texture of the stone, with the color of the paper. Then they remember the words, and begin to shift them about in sentences.* LAYMAN *even construes them grammatically. Suddenly the sense of them comes back to* HALSEY. *He grips* LAYMAN *by the arm and they both follow after* KABNIS.

A false dusk has come early. The countryside is ashen, chill. Cabins and roads and canebrakes whisper. The church choir, dipping into a long silence, sings:

My Lord, what a mourning,
My Lord, what a mourning,
My Lord, what a mourning,
When the stars begin to fall.

Softly luminous over the hills and valleys, the faint spray of a scattered star . . .

III

A splotchy figure drives forward along the cane- and corn-stalk hemmed-in road. A scarecrow replica of KABNIS, *awkwardly animate. Fantastically plastered with red Georgia mud. It skirts the big house whose windows shine like mellow lanterns in the dusk. Its shoulder jogs against a sweet-gum tree. The figure caroms off against the cabin door and lunges in. It slams the door as if to prevent some one entering after it.*

KABNIS God Almighty, theyre here. After me. On me. All along the road I saw their eyes flaring from the cane. Hounds. Shouts. What in God's name did I run here for? A mud-hole trap. I stumbled on a rope. O God, a rope. Their clammy hands were like the love of death playing up and down my spine. Trying to trip my legs. To trip my spine. Up and down my spine. My spine . . . My legs . . . Why in hell didnt they catch me?

(KABNIS *wheels around, half defiant, half numbed with a more immediate fear.*) Wanted to trap me here. Get out o there. I see you. (*He grabs a broom from beside the chimney and violently pokes it under the bed. The broom strikes a tin wash-tub. The noise bewilders. He recovers.*) Not there. In the closet. (*He throws the broom aside and grips the poker. Starts towards the closet door, towards somewhere in the perfect blackness behind the chimney.*) I'll brain you. (*He stops short. The barks of hounds, evidently in pursuit, reach him. A voice, liquid in distance, yells, "Hi! Hi!"*) O God, theyre after me. Holy Father, Mother of Christ—hell, this aint no time for prayer—

Voices, just outside the door: "Reckon he's here." "Dont see no light though." The door is flung open.

KABNIS Get back or I'll kill you. (*He braces himself, brandishing the poker.*)

HALSEY (*coming in*) Aint as bad as all that. Put that thing down.

LAYMAN Its only us, Professor. Nobody else after y.

KABNIS Halsey. Layman. Close that door. Dont light that light. For godsake get away from there.

HALSEY Nobody's after y, Kabnis, I'm tellin y. Put that thing down an get yourself together.

KABNIS I tell you they are. I saw them. I heard the hounds.

HALSEY These aint th days of hounds an Uncle Tom's Cabin, feller. White folks aint in fer all them theatrics these days. Theys more direct than that. If what they wanted was t get y, theyd have just marched right in an took y where y sat. Somebodys down by th branch chasin rabbits an atreein possums.

A shot is heard.

HALSEY Got him, I reckon. Saw Tom goin out with his gun. Tom's pretty lucky most times.

He goes to the bureau and lights the lamp. The circular fringe is patterned on the ceiling. The moving shadows of the men are huge against the bare wall boards. HALSEY *walks up to* KABNIS, *takes the poker from his grip, and without more ado pushes him into a chair before the dark hearth.*

Youre a mess. Here, Layman. Get some trash an start a fire.

LAYMAN *fumbles around, finds some newspapers and old bags, puts them in the hearth, arranges the wood, and kindles the fire.* HALSEY *sets a black iron kettle where it soon will be boiling. Then takes from his hip-pocket a bottle of corn licker which he passes to* KABNIS.

Here. This'll straighten y out a bit.

KABNIS *nervously draws the cork and gulps the licker down.*

KABNIS Ha. Good stuff. Thanks. Thank y, Halsey.

HALSEY Good stuff! Youre damn right. Hanby there dont think so. Wonder he doesn't come over t find out whos burnin his oil. Miserly bastard, him. Th boys what made this stuff—are y listenin t me, Kabnis? th boys what made this stuff have got th art down like I heard you say youd like t be with words. Eh? Have some, Layman?

LAYMAN Dont think I care for none, thank y jes th same, Mr. Halsey.

HALSEY Care hell. Course y care. Everybody cares around these parts. Preachers an school teachers an everybody. Here. Here, take it. Dont try that line on me.

LAYMAN *limbers up a little, but he cannot quite forget that he is on school ground.*

LAYMAN Thats right. Thats true, sho. Shinin is th only business what pays in these hard times.

He takes a nip, and passes the bottle to KABNIS. KABNIS *is in the middle of a long swig when a rap sounds on the door. He almost spills the bottle but manages to pass it to* HALSEY *just as the door swings open and* HANBY *enters. He is a well-dressed, smooth, rich, black-skinned Negro who thinks there is no one quite so suave and polished as himself. To members of his own race he affects the manners of a wealthy white planter. Or, when he is up North, he lets it be known that his ideas are those of the best New England tradition. To white men he bows, without ever completely humbling himself. Tradesmen in the town tolerate him because he spends his money with them. He delivers his words with a full consciousness of his moral superiority.*

HANBY Hum. Erer, Professor Kabnis, to come straight to the point: the progress of the Negro race is jeopardized whenever the personal habits and examples set by its guides and mentors fall below the acknowledged and hard-won standard of its average member. This institution, of which I am the humble president, was founded, and has been maintained at a cost of great labor and untold sacrifice. Its purpose is to teach our youth to live better, cleaner, more noble lives. To prove to the world that the Negro race can be just like any other race. It hopes to attain this aim partly by the salutary examples set by its instructors. I cannot hinder the progress of a race simply to indulge a single member. I have thought the matter out beforehand, I can assure you. Therefore, if I find your resignation on my desk by to-morrow morning, Mr. Kabnis, I shall not feel obliged to call in the sheriff. Otherwise . . .

KABNIS A fellow can take a drink in his own room if he wants to, in the privacy of his own room.

HANBY His room, but not the institution's room, Mr. Kabnis.

KABNIS This is my room while I'm in it.

HANBY Mr. Clayborn (the sheriff) can inform you as to that.

KABNIS Oh, well, what do I care—glad to get out of this mud-hole.

HANBY I should think so from your looks.

KABNIS You neednt get sarcastic about it.

HANBY No, that is true. And I neednt wait for your resignation either, Mr. Kabnis.

KABNIS Oh, you'll get that all right. Dont worry.

HANBY And I should like to have the room thoroughly aired and cleaned and ready for your successor by to-morrow noon, Professor.

KABNIS (*trying to rise*) You can have your godam room right away. I dont want it.

HANBY But I wont have your cursing.

HALSEY *pushes* KABNIS *back into his chair.*

HALSEY Sit down, Kabnis, till I wash y.

HANBY (*to* HALSEY) I would rather not have drinking men on the premises, Mr. Halsey. You will oblige me—

HALSEY I'll oblige you by stayin right on this spot, this spot, get me? till I get damned ready t leave.

He approaches HANBY. HANBY *retreats, but manages to hold his dignity.*

HALSEY Let me get you told right now, Mr. Samuel Hanby. Now listen t me. I aint no slick and span slave youve hired, an dont y think it for a minute. Youve bullied enough about this town. An besides, wheres that bill youve been owin me? Listen t me. If I dont get it paid in by tmorrer noon, Mr. Hanby (*he mockingly assumes* HANBY'*s tone and manner*), I shall feel obliged t call th sheriff. An that sheriff'll be myself who'll catch y in th road an pull y out your buggy an rightly attend t y. You heard me. Now leave him alone. I'm takin him home with mc. I got it fixed. Before you came in. He's goin t work with me. Shapin shafts and buildin wagons'll make a man of him what nobody, y get me? what nobody can take advantage of. Thats all . . .

HALSEY *burrs off into vague and incoherent comment. Pause. Disagreeable.* LAYMAN'*s eyes are glazed on the spurting fire.* KABNIS *wants to rise and put both* HALSEY *and* HANBY *in their places. He vaguely knows that he must do this, else the power of direction will completely slip from him to those outside. The conviction is just strong enough to torture him. To bring a feverish, quick-passing flare into his eyes. To mutter words soggy in hot saliva. To jerk his arms upward in futile protest.* HALSEY, *noticing his gestures, thinks it is water that he desires. He brings a glass to him.* KABNIS *slings it to the floor. Heat of the conviction dies. His arms crumple. His upper lip, his mustache, quiver. Rap! rap, on the door. The sounds slap* KABNIS. *They bring a hectic color to his cheeks. Like huge cold finger tips they touch his skin and goose-flesh it.* HANBY *strikes a commanding pose. He moves toward* LAYMAN. LAYMAN'*s face is innocently immobile.*

HALSEY Whos there?

VOICE Lewis.

HALSEY Come in, Lewis. Come on in.

LEWIS *enters. He is the queer fellow who has been referred to. A tall wiry copper-colored man, thirty perhaps. His mouth and eyes suggest purpose guided by an adequate intelligence. He is what a stronger* KABNIS *might have been, and in an odd faint way resembles him. As he steps towards the others, he seems to be issuing sharply from a vivid dream.* LEWIS *shakes hands with* HALSEY. *Nods perfunctorily to* HANBY, *who has stiffened to meet him. Smiles rapidly at* LAYMAN, *and settles with real interest on* KABNIS.

LEWIS Kabnis passed me on the road. Had a piece of business of my own, and couldnt get here any sooner. Thought I might be able to help in some way or other.

HALSEY A good baths bout all he needs now. An somethin t put his mind t rest.

LEWIS I think I can give him that. That note was meant for me. Some Negroes have grown uncomfortable at my being here—

KABNIS You mean, Mr. Lewis, some colored folks threw it? Christ Amighty!

HALSEY Thats what he means. An just as I told y. White folks more direct than that.

KABNIS What are they after you for?

LEWIS Its a long story, Kabnis. Too long for now. And it might involve present company. (*He laughs pleasantly and gestures vaguely in the direction of* HANBY.) Tell you about it later on perhaps.

KABNIS Youre not going?

LEWIS Not till my month's up.

HALSEY Hows that?

LEWIS I'm on a sort of contract with myself. (*Is about to leave.*) Well, glad its nothing serious—

HALSEY Come round t th shop sometime why dont y, Lewis? I've asked y enough. I'd like t have a talk with y. I aint as dumb as I look. Kabnis an me'll be in most any time. Not much work these days. Wish t hell there was. This burg gets to me when there aint. (*In answer to* LEWIS' *question.*) He's goin t work with me. Ya. Night air this side th branch aint good fer him. (*Looks at* HANBY. *Laughs.*)

LEWIS I see . . .

His eyes turn to KABNIS. *In the instant of their shifting, a vision of the life they are to meet.* KABNIS, *a promise of a soil-soaked beauty; uprooted, thinning out. Suspended a few feet above the soil whose touch would resurrect him. Arm's length removed from him whose will to help . . . There is a swift intuitive interchange of consciousness.* KABNIS *has a sudden need to rush into the arms of this man. His eyes call, "Brother." And then a savage, cynical twistabout within him mocks his impulse and strengthens him to repulse* LEWIS. *His lips curl cruelly. His eyes laugh. They are glittering needles, stitching. With a throbbing ache they draw* LEWIS *to.* LEWIS *brusquely wheels on* HANBY.

LEWIS I'd like to see you, sir, a moment, if you dont mind.

HANBY'*s tight collar and vest effectively preserve him.*

HANBY Yes, erer, Mr. Lewis. Right away.

LEWIS See you later, Halsey.

HALSEY So long—thanks—sho hope so, Lewis.

As he opens the door and HANBY *passes out, a woman, miles down the valley, begins to sing. Her song is a spark that travels swiftly to the near-by cabins. Like purple tallow flames, songs jet up. They spread a ruddy haze over the heavens. The haze swings low. Now the whole countryside is a soft chorus. Lord. O Lord . . .* LEWIS *closes the door behind him. A flame jets out . . .*

The kettle is boiling. HALSEY *notices it. He pulls the wash-tub from beneath the bed. He arranges for the bath before the fire.*

HALSEY Told y them theatrics didn't fit a white man. Th niggers, just like I told y. An after him. Aint surprisin though. He aint bowed t none of them. Nassur. T nairy a one of them nairy an inch nairy a time. An only mixed when he was good an ready—

KABNIS That song, Halsey, do you hear it?

HALSEY Thats a man. Hear me, Kabnis? A man—

KABNIS Jesus, do you hear it.

HALSEY Hear it? Hear what? Course I hear it. Listen t what I'm tellin y. A man, get me? They'll get him yet if he dont watch out.

KABNIS *is jolted into his fear.*

KABNIS Get him? What do you mean? How? Not lynch him?

HALSEY Na. Take a shotgun an shoot his eyes clear out. Well, anyway, it wasnt fer you, just like I told y. You'll stay over at th house an work with me, eh, boy? Good t get away from his nobs, eh? Damn big stiff though, him. An youre not th first an I can tell y. (*Laughs.*)

He bustles and fusses about KABNIS *as if he were a child.* KABNIS *submits, wearily. He has no will to resist him.*

LAYMAN (*his voice like a deep hollow echo*) Thats right. Thats true, sho. Everybody's been expectin that th bust up was comin. Surprised um all y held on as long as y did. Teachin in the South aint th thing fer y. Nassur. You ought t be way back up North where sometimes I wish I was. But I've hung on down this way so long—

HALSEY An there'll never be no leavin time fer y.

IV

A month has passed.

HALSEY'*s workshop. It is an old building just off the main street of Sempter. The walls to within a few feet of the ground are of an age-worn cement mixture. On the outside they are considerably crumbled and peppered with what looks like musket-shot. Inside, the plaster has fallen away in great chunks, leaving the laths, grayed and cobwebbed, exposed. A sort of loft above the shop proper serves as a breakwater for the rain and sunshine which otherwise would have free entry to the main floor. The shop is filled with old wheels and parts of wheels, broken shafts, and wooden litter. A double door, midway the street wall. To the left of this, a workbench that holds a vise and a variety of woodwork tools. A window with as many panes broken as whole, throws light on the bench. Opposite, in the rear wall, a second window looks out upon the back yard. In the left wall, a rickety smoke-blackened chimney, and hearth with fire blazing. Smooth-worn chairs grouped about the hearth suggest the village meetingplace. Several large wooden blocks, chipped and cut and sawed on their upper surfaces are in the middle of the floor. They are the supports used in almost any sort of wagonwork. Their idleness means that* HALSEY *has no worthwhile job on foot. To the right of the central door is a junk heap, and directly behind this, stairs that lead down into the cellar. The cellar is known as "The Hole." Besides being the home of a very old man, it is used by* HALSEY *on those occasions when he spices up the life of the small town.*

HALSEY, *wonderfully himself in his work overalls, stands in the doorway and gazes up the street, expectantly. Then his eyes grow listless. He slouches against the smooth-rubbed frame. He lights a cigarette. Shifts his position. Braces an arm against the door.* KABNIS *passes the window and stoops to get in under* HALSEY'S *arm. He is awkward and ludicrous, like a schoolboy in his big brother's new overalls. He skirts the large blocks on the floor, and drops into a chair before the fire.* HALSEY *saunters towards him.*

KABNIS Time f lunch.

HALSEY Ya. (*He stands by the hearth, rocking backward and forward. He stretches his hands out to the fire. He washes them in the warm glow of the flames. They never get cold, but he warms them.*)

KABNIS Saw Lewis up th street. Said he'd be down.

HALSEY's eyes brighten. He looks at KABNIS. *Turns away. Says nothing.* KABNIS *fidgets. Twists his thin blue cloth-covered limbs. Pulls closer to the fire till the heat stings his shins. Pushes back. Pokes the burned logs. Puts on several fresh ones. Fidgets. The town bell strikes twelve.*

KABNIS Fix it up f tnight?
HALSEY Leave it t me.
KABNIS Get Lewis in?
HALSEY Tryin t.

The air is heavy with the smell of pine and resin. Green logs spurt and sizzle. Sap trickles from an old pine-knot into the flames. Layman enters. He carries a lunch-pail. KABNIS, *for the moment, thinks that he is a day laborer.*

LAYMAN Evenin, gen'lemun.
BOTH Whats say, Layman.

LAYMAN *squares a chair to the fire and droops into it. Several town fellows, silent unfathomable men for the most part, saunter in. Overalls. Thick tan shoes. Felt hats marvelously shaped and twisted. One asks* HALSEY *for a cigarette. He gets it. The blacksmith, a tremendous black man, comes in from the forge. Not even a nod from him. He picks up an axle and goes out.* LEWIS *enters. The town men look curiously at him. Suspicion and an open liking contest for possession of their faces. They are uncomfortable. One by one they drift into the street.*

LAYMAN Heard y was leavin, Mr. Lewis.
KABNIS Months up, eh? Hell of a month I've got.
HALSEY Sorry y goin, Lewis. Just getting acquainted like.
LEWIS Sorry myself, Halsey, in a way—
LAYMAN Gettin t like our town, Mr. Lewis?
LEWIS I'm afraid its on a different basis, Professor.
HALSEY An I've yet t hear about that basis. Been waitin long enough, God knows. Seems t me like youd take pity on a feller if nothin more.
KABNIS Somethin that old black cockroach over yonder doesnt like, whatever it is.

LAYMAN Thats right. Thats right, sho.

HALSEY A feller dropped in here tother day an said he knew what you was about. Said you had queer opinions. Well, I could have told him you was a queer one, myself. But not th way he was driftin. Didnt mean anything by it, but just let drop he thought you was a little wrong up here—crazy, y'know. (*Laughs.*)

KABNIS Y mean old Blodson? Hell, he's bats himself.

LEWIS I remember him. We had a talk. But what he found queer, I think, was not my opinions, but my lack of them. In half an hour he had settled everything: boll weevils, God, the World War. Weevils and wars are the pests that God sends against the sinful. People are too weak to correct themselves: the Redeemer is coming back. Get ready, ye sinners, for the advent of Our Lord. Interesting, eh, Kabnis? but not exactly what we want.

HALSEY Y could have come t me. I've sho been after y enough. Most every time I've seen y.

KABNIS (*sarcastically*): Hows it y never came t us professors?

LEWIS I did—to one.

KABNIS Y mean t say y got somethin from that celluloid-collar-eraser-cleaned old codger over in th mud hole?

HALSEY Rough on th old boy, aint he? (*Laughs.*)

LEWIS Something, yes. Layman here could have given me quite a deal, but the incentive to his keeping quiet is so much greater than anything I could have offered him to open up, that I crossed him off my mind. And you—

KABNIS What about me?

HALSEY Tell him, Lewis, for godsake tell him. I've told him. But its somethin else he wants so bad I've heard him downstairs mumblin with th old man.

LEWIS The old man?

KABNIS What about me? Come on now, you know so much.

HALSEY Tell him, Lewis. Tell it t him.

LEWIS Life has already told him more than he is capable of knowing. It has given him in excess of what he can receive. I have been offered. Stuff in his stomach curdled, and he vomited me.

KABNIS' *face twitches. His body writhes.*

KABNIS You know a lot, you do. How about Halsey?

LEWIS Yes . . . Halsey? Fits here. Belongs here. An artist in your way, arent you, Halsey?

HALSEY Reckon I am, Lewis. Give me th work and fair pay an I aint askin nothin better. Went overseas an saw France an I come back. Been up North; an I come back. Went t school; but there aint no books whats got th feel t them of them there tools. Nassur. An I'm atellin y.

A shriveled, bony white man passes the window and enters the shop. He carries a broken hatchet-handle and the severed head. He speaks with a flat, drawn voice to HALSEY, *who comes forward to meet him.*

MR. RAMSAY Can y fix this fer me, Halsey?

HALSEY (*looking it over*) Reckon so, Mr. Ramsay. Here, Kabnis. A little practice fer y.

HALSEY *directs* KABNIS, *showing him how to place the handle in the vise, and cut it down. The knife hangs.* KABNIS *thinks that it must be dull. He jerks it hard. The tool goes deep and shaves too much off.* MR. RAMSAY *smiles brokenly at him.*

MR. RAMSAY (*to* HALSEY) Still breakin in the new hand, eh, Halsey? Seems like a likely enough faller once he gets th hang of it.

He gives a tight laugh at his own good humor. KABNIS *burns red. The back of his neck stings him beneath his collar. He feels stifled. Through* RAMSAY, *the whole white South weighs down upon him. The pressure is terrific. He sweats under the arms. Chill beads run down his body. His brows concentrate upon the handle as though his own life was staked upon the perfect shaving of it. He begins to out and out botch the job.* HALSEY *smiles.*

HALSEY He'll make a good un some of these days, Mr. Ramsay.

MR. RAMSAY Y ought t know. Yer daddy was a good un before y. Runs in th family, seems like t me.

HALSEY Thats right, Mr. Ramsay.

KABNIS *is hopeless.* HALSEY *takes the handle from him. With a few deft strokes he shaves it. Fits it. Gives it to* RAMSAY.

MR. RAMSAY How much on this?

HALSEY No charge, Mr. Ramsay.

MR. RAMSAY (*going out*) All right, Halsey. Come down an take it out in trade. Shoe-strings or something.

HALSEY Yassur, Mr. Ramsay.

HALSEY *rejoins* LEWIS *and* LAYMAN. KABNIS, *hangdog-fashion, follows him.*

HALSEY They like y if y work fer them.

LAYMAN Thats right, Mr. Halsey. Thats right, sho.

The group is about to resume its talk when HANBY *enters. He is all energy, bustle, and business. He goes direct to* KABNIS.

HANBY An axle is out in the buggy which I would like to have shaped into a crow-bar. You will see that it is fixed for me.

Without waiting for an answer, and knowing that KABNIS *will follow, he passes out.* KABNIS, *scowling, silent, trudges after him.*

HANBY (*from the outside*) Have that ready for me by three o'clock, young man. I shall call for it.

KABNIS (*under his breath as he comes in*) Th hell you say, you old black swamp-gut.

He slings the axle on the floor.

HALSEY Wheeee!

LAYMAN, *lunch finished long ago, rises, heavily. He shakes hands with* LEWIS.

LAYMAN Might not see y again befo y leave, Mr. Lewis. I enjoys t hear y talk. Y might have been a preacher. Maybe a bishop some day. Sho do hope t see y back this away again sometime, Mr. Lewis.

LEWIS Thanks, Professor. Hope I'll see you.

LAYMAN *waves a long arm loosely to the others, and leaves.* KABNIS *goes to the door. His eyes, sullen, gaze up the street.*

KABNIS Carrie K's comin with th lunch. Bout time.

She passes the window. Her red girl's-cap, catching the sun, flashes vividly. With a stiff, awkward little movement she crosses the doorsill and gives KABNIS *one of the two baskets which she is carrying. There is a slight stoop to her shoulders. The curves of her body blend with this to a soft rounded charm. Her gestures are stiffly variant. Black bangs curl over the forehead of her oval-olive face. Her expression is dazed, but on provocation it can melt into a wistful smile. Adolescent. She is easily the sister of* FRED HALSEY.

CARRIE K. Mother says excuse her, brother Fred an Ralph, fer bein late.

KABNIS Everythings all right an O.K., Carrie Kate. O.K. an all right.

The two men settle on their lunch. CARRIE, *with hardly a glance in the direction of the hearth, as is her habit, is about to take the second basket down to the old man, when* LEWIS *rises. In doing so he draws her unwitting attention. Their meeting is a swift sunburst.* LEWIS *impulsively moves toward her. His mind flashes images of her life in the southern town. He sees the nascent woman, her flesh already stiffening to cartilage, drying to bone. Her spirit-bloom, even now touched sullen, bitter. Her rich beauty fading . . . He wants to— He stretches forth his hands to hers. He takes them. They feel like warm cheeks against his palms. The sunburst from her eyes floods up and haloes him. Christ-eyes, his eyes look to her. Fearlessly she loves into them. And then something happens. Her face blanches. Awkwardly she draws away. The sin-bogies of respectable southern colored folks clamor at her: "Look out! Be a* good *girl. A* good *girl. Look out!" She gropes for her basket that has fallen to the floor. Finds it, and marches with a rigid gravity to her task of feeding the old man. Like the glowing white ash of burned paper,* LEWIS' *eyelids, wavering, settle down. He stirs in the direction of the rear window. From the back yard, mules tethered to odd trees and posts blink dumbly at him. They too seem burdened with an impotent pain.* KABNIS *and* HALSEY *are still busy with their lunch. They havent noticed him. After a while he turns to them.*

LEWIS Your sister, Halsey, whats to become of her? What are you going to do for her?

HALSEY Who? What? What am I goin t do? . . .

LEWIS What I mean is, what does she do down there?

HALSEY Oh. Feeds th old man. Had lunch, Lewis?

LEWIS Thanks, yes. You have never felt her, have you, Halsey? Well, no, I guess not. I dont suppose you can. Nor can she . . . Old man? Halsey, some one lives down there? I've never heard of him. Tell me—

KABNIS (*takes time from his meal to answer with some emphasis*) Theres lots of things you aint heard of.

LEWIS Dare say. I'd like to see him.

KABNIS You'll get all th chance you want tnight.

HALSEY Fixin a little somethin up fer tnight, Lewis. Th three of us an some girls. Come round bout ten-thirty.

LEWIS Glad to. But what under the sun does he do down there?

HALSEY Ask Kabnis. He blows off t him every chance he gets.

KABNIS *gives a grunting laugh. His mouth twists.* CARRIE *returns from the cellar. Avoiding* LEWIS, *she speaks to her brother.*

CARRIE K. Brother Fred, Father hasnt eaten now goin on th second week, but mumbles an talks funny, or tries t talk when I put his hands ont th food. He frightens me, an I dunno what t do. An oh, I came near fergettin, brother, but Mr. Marmon—he was eatin lunch when I saw him—told me t tell y that th lumber wagon busted down an he wanted y t fix it fer him. Said he reckoned he could get it t y after he ate.

HALSEY *chucks a half-eaten sandwich in the fire. Gets up. Arranges his blocks. Goes to the door and looks anxiously up the street. The wind whirls a small spiral in the gray dust road.*

HALSEY Why didnt y tell me sooner, little sister?

CARRIE K. I fergot t, an just remembered it now, brother.

Her soft rolled words are fresh pain to LEWIS. *He wants to take her North with him. What for? He wonders what* KABNIS *could do for her. What she could do for him. Mother him.* CARRIE *gathers the lunch things, silently, and in her pinched manner, curtsies, and departs.* KABNIS *lights his after-lunch cigarette.* LEWIS, *who has sensed a change becomes aware that he is not included in it. He starts to ask again about the old man. Decides not to. Rises to go.*

LEWIS Think I'll run along, Halsey.
HALSEY Sure. Glad t see y any time.
KABNIS Dont forget tnight.
LEWIS Dont worry. I wont. So long.
KABNIS So long. We'll be expectin y.

LEWIS *passes* HALSEY *at the door.* HALSEY'*s cheeks form a vacant smile. His eyes are wide awake, watching for the wagon to turn from Broad Street into his road.*

HALSEY So long.

His words reach LEWIS *halfway to the corner.*

V

Night, soft belly of a pregnant Negress, throbs evenly against the torso of the South. Night throbs a womb-song to the South. Cane and cotton fields, pine forests, cypress swamps, sawmills, and factories are fecund at her touch. Night's womb-song sets them singing. Night winds are the breathing of the unborn child whose calm throbbing in the belly of a Negress sets them somnolently singing. Hear their song.

White-man's land.
Niggers, sing.
Burn, bear black children

Till poor rivers bring
Rest, and sweet glory
In Camp Ground.

Sempter's streets are vacant and still. White paint on the wealthier houses has the chill blue glitter of distant stars. Negro cabins are a purple blur. Broad Street is deserted. Winds stir beneath the corrugated iron canopies and dangle odd bits of rope tied to horse- and mule-gnawed hitching-posts. One store window has a light in it. Chesterfield cigarette and Chero-Cola cardboard advertisements are stacked in it. From a side door two men come out. Pause, for a last word and then say good night. Soon they melt in shadows thicker than they. Way off down the street four figures sway beneath iron awnings which form a sort of corridor that imperfectly echoes and jumbles what they say. A fifth form joins them. They turn into the road that leads to HALSEY'S *workshop. The old building is phosphorescent above deep shade. The figures pass through the double door. Night winds whisper in the eaves. Sing weirdly in the ceiling cracks. Stir curls of shavings on the floor.* HALSEY *lights a candle. A good-sized lumber wagon, wheels off, rests upon the blocks.* KABNIS *makes a face at it. An unearthly hush is upon the place. No one seems to want to talk. To move, lest the scraping of their feet . . .*

HALSEY Come on down this way, folks.

He leads the way. STELLA *follows. And close after her,* CORA, LEWIS, *and* KABNIS. *They descend into the Hole. It seems huge, limitless in the candle light. The walls are of stone, wonderfully fitted. They have no openings save a small iron-barred window toward the top of each. They are dry and warm. The ground slopes away to the rear of the building and thus leaves the south wall exposed to the sun. The blacksmith's shop is plumb against the right wall. The floor is clay. Shavings have at odd times been matted into it. In the right-hand corner, under the stairs, two good-sized pine mattresses, resting on cardboard, are on either side of a wooden table. On this are several half-burned candles and an oil lamp. Behind the table, an ir-*

regular piece of mirror hangs on the wall. A loose something that looks to be a gaudy ball costume dangles from a near-by hook. To the front, a second table holds a lamp and several whiskey glasses. Six rickety chairs are near this table. Two old wagon wheels rest on the floor. To the left, sitting in a high-backed chair which stands upon a low platform, the OLD MAN. *He is like a bust in black walnut. Gray-bearded. Gray-haired. Prophetic. Immobile.* LEWIS' *eyes are sunk in him. The others, unconcerned, are about to pass on to the front table when* LEWIS *grips* HALSEY *and so turns him that the candle flame shines obliquely on the* OLD MAN'*s features.*

LEWIS And he rules over—

KABNIS Th smoke an fire of th forge.

LEWIS Black Vulcan? I wouldnt say so. That forehead. Great woolly beard. Those eyes. A mute John the Baptist of a new religion—or a tongue-tied shadow of an old.

KABNIS His tongue is tied all right, an I can vouch f that.

LEWIS Has he never talked to you?

HALSEY Kabnis wont give him a chance.

He laughs. The girls laugh. KABNIS *winces.*

LEWIS What do you call him?

HALSEY Father.

LEWIS Good. Father what?

KABNIS Father of hell.

HALSEY Father's th only name we have fer him. Come on. Lets sit down an get t the pleasure of the evenin.

LEWIS Father John it is from now on . . .

Slave boy whom some Christian mistress taught to read the Bible. Black man who saw Jesus in the ricefields, and began preaching to his people. Moses- and Christ-words used for songs. Dead blind father of a muted folk who feel their way upward to a life that crushes or absorbs them. (Speak, Father!) Suppose your eyes could see, old man. (The years hold hands. O Sing!) Suppose your lips . . .

Halsey, does he never talk?

HALSEY Na. But sometimes. Only seldom. Mumbles. Sis says he talks—

KABNIS I've heard him talk.

HALSEY First I've ever heard of it. You dont give him a chance. Sis says she's made out several words, mostly one—an like as not cause it was "sin."

KABNIS All those old fogies stutter about sin.

CORA *laughs in a loose sort of way. She is a tall, thin, mulatto woman. Her eyes are deep-set behind a pointed nose. Her hair is coarse and bushy. Seeing that* STELLA *also is restless, she takes her arm and the two women move towards the table. They slip into chairs.* HALSEY *follows and lights the lamp. He lays out a pack of cards.* STELLA *sorts them as if telling fortunes. She is a beautifully proportioned, large-eyed, brown-skin girl. Except for the twisted line of her mouth when she smiles or laughs, there is about her no suggestion of the life she's been through.* KABNIS, *with great mock-solemnity, goes to the corner, takes down the robe, and dons it. He is a curious spectacle, acting a part, yet very real. He joins the others at the table. They are used to him.* LEWIS *is surprised. He laughs.* KABNIS *shrinks and then glares at him with a furtive hatred.* HALSEY, *bringing out a bottle of corn licker, pours drinks.*

HALSEY Come on, Lewis. Come on, you fellers. Heres lookin at y.

Then, as if suddenly recalling something, he jerks away from the table and starts towards the steps.

KABNIS Where y goin, Halsey?

HALSEY Where? Where y think? That oak beam in the wagon—

KABNIS Come ere. Come ere. Sit down. What in hell's wrong with you fellers? You with your wagon. Lewis with his Father John. This aint th time fer foolin with wagons. Daytime's bad enough f that. Ere, sit down. Ere, Lewis, you too sit down. Have a drink. Thats right. Drink corn licker, love th girls, an listen t th old man mumblin sin.

There seems to be no good-time spirit to the party. Something in the air is too tense and deep for that. LEWIS, *seated now so that his eyes rest upon the* OLD MAN, *merges with his source and lets the pain and beauty of the South meet him there. White faces, pain-pollen, settle downward through a cane-sweet mist and touch the ovaries of yellow flowers. Cotton-bolls bloom, droop. Black roots twist in a parched red soil beneath a blazing sky. Magnolias, fragrant, a trifle futile, lovely, far off . . . His eyelids close. A force begins to heave and rise . . .* STELLA *is serious, reminiscent.*

STELLA Usall is brought up t hate sin worse than death—

KABNIS An then before you have y eyes half open, youre made t love it if y want t live.

STELLA Us never—

KABNIS Oh, I know your story: that old prim bastard over yonder, an then old Calvert's office—

STELLA It wasnt them—

KABNIS I know. They put y out of church, an then I guess th preacher came around an asked f some. But thats your body. Now me—

HALSEY (*passing him the bottle*) All right, kid, we believe y. Here, take another. Wheres Clover, Stel?

STELLA You know how Jim is when he's just out th swamp. Done up in shine an wouldnt let her come. Said he'd bust her head open if she went out.

KABNIS Dont see why he doesnt stay over with Laura, where he belongs.

STELLA Ask him, an I reckon he'll tell y. More than you want.

HALSEY Th nigger hates th sight of a black woman worse than death. Sorry t mix y up this way, Lewis. But y see how tis.

LEWIS' *skin is tight and glowing over the fine bones of his face. His lips tremble. His nostrils quiver. The others notice this and smile knowingly at each other. Drinks and smokes are passed around. They pay no neverminds to him. A real party is being worked up. Then* LEWIS *opens his eyes and looks at them. Their smiles disperse in hot-cold tremors.* KABNIS *chokes his laugh. It sputters, gurgles. His eyes flicker and turn away. He tries to pass the thing off by taking a long drink which he makes considerable fuss over. He is drawn back to* LEWIS. *Seeing* LEWIS' *gaze still upon him, he scowls.*

KABNIS Whatsha lookin at me for? Y want t know who I am? Well, I'm Ralph Kabnis—lot of good its goin t do y. Well? Whatsha keep lookin for? I'm Ralph Kabnis. Aint that enough f y? Want th whole family history? Its none of your godam business, anyway. Keep off me. Do y hear? Keep off me. Look at Cora. Aint she pretty enough t look at? Look at Halsey, or Stella. Clover ought t be here an you could look at her. An love her. Thats what you need. I know—

LEWIS Ralph Kabnis gets satisfied that way?

KABNIS Satisfied? Say, quit your kiddin. Here, look at that old man there. See him? He's satisfied. Do I look like him? When I'm dead I dont expect t be satisfied. Is that enough f y, with your godam nosin, or do you want more? Well, y wont get it, understand?

LEWIS The old man as symbol, flesh, and spirit of the past, what do you think he would say if he could see you? You look at him, Kabnis.

KABNIS Just like any done-up preacher is what he looks t me. Jam some false teeth in his mouth and crank him, an youd have God Almighty spit in torrents all around th floor. Oh, hell, an he reminds me of that black cockroach over yonder. An besides, he aint my past. My ancestors were Southern bluebloods—

LEWIS And black.

KABNIS Aint much difference between blue an black.

LEWIS Enough to draw a denial from you. Cant hold them, can you? Master; slave. Soil; and the overarching heavens. Dusk; dawn. They fight and bastardize you. The sun tint of your cheeks, flame of the great season's multicolored leaves, tarnished, burned. Split, shredded: easily burned. No use . . .

His gaze shifts to STELLA. STELLA'*s face draws back, her breasts come towards him.*

STELLA I aint got nothin f y, mister. Taint no use t look at me.

HALSEY You're a queer feller, Lewis, I swear y are. Told y so, didnt I, girls? Just take him easy though, an he'll be ridin just th same as any Georgia mule, eh, Lewis? (*Laughs.*)

STELLA I'm goin t tell y somethin, mister. It aint t you, t the Mister Lewis what noses about. Its t somethin different, I dunno what. That old man there—maybe its him—is like m father used t look. He used t sing. An when he could sing no mo, they'd allus come f him an carry him t church an there he'd sit, befo th pulpit, aswayin an aleadin every song. A white man took m mother an it broke th old man's heart. He died; and then I didnt care what become of me, an I dont now. I dont care now. Dont get it in y head I'm some sentimental susie askin for yo sop. Nassur. But theres somethin t yo the others aint got. Boars an kids an fools—thats all I've known. Boars when their fever's up. When their fever's up they come t me. Halsey asks me over when he's off th job. Kabnis—it ud be a sin t play with him. He takes it out in talk.

HALSEY *knows that he has trifled with her. At odds things he has been inwardly penitent before her tasking him. But now he wants to hurt her. He turns to* LEWIS.

HALSEY Lewis, I got a little licker in me, an thats true. True's what I said. True. But th stuff just seems t wake me up an make my mind a man of me. Listen. You know a lot, queer as hell as y are, an I want t ask y some questions. Theyre too high fer them, Stella an Cora an Kabnis, so we'll just excuse em. A chat between ourselves. (*Turns to the others.*) You-all cant listen in on this. Twont interest y. So just leave th table t this gen'lemun an myself. Go long now.

KABNIS *gets up, pompous in his robe, grotesquely so, and makes as if to go through a grand march with* STELLA. *She shoves him off, roughly, and in a mood swings her body to the steps.* KABNIS *grabs* CORA *and parades around, passing the* OLD MAN, *to whom he bows in mock curtsy. He sweeps by the table, snatches the licker bottle, and then he and* CORA *sprawl on the mattresses. She meets his weak approaches after the manner she thinks* STELLA *would use.*

HALSEY *contemptuously watches them until he is sure that they are settled.*

HALSEY This aint th sort o thing f me, Lewis, when I got work upstairs. Nassur. You an me has got things t do. Wastin time on common low-down women—say, Lewis, look at her now—Stella—aint she a picture? Common wench—na she aint, Lewis. You know she aint. I'm only tryin t fool y. I used t love that girl. Yassur. An sometimes when the moon is thick an I hear dogs up th valley barkin an some old woman fetches out her song, an the winds seem like the Lord made them fer t fetch an carry th smell o pine an cane, an there aint no big job on foot, I sometimes get t thinkin that I still do. But I want t talk t y, Lewis, queer as y are. Y know, Lewis, I went t school once. Ya. In Augusta. But it wasnt a regular school. Na. It was a pussy Sunday-school masqueradin under a regular name. Some goody-goody teachers from th North had come down t teach the niggers. If you was nearly white, they liked y. If you was black, they didnt. But it wasnt that—I was all right, y see. I couldnt stand em messin an pawin over m business like I was a child. So I cussed em out an left. Kabnis there ought t have cussed out th old duck over yonder an left. He'd a been a better man today. But as I was sayin, I couldnt stand their ways. So I left an came here an worked with my father. An been here ever since. He died. I set in f myself. An its always been; give me a good job an sure pay an I aint far from being satisfied, so far as satisfaction goes. Prejudice is everywheres about this country. An a nigger aint in much standin anywheres. But when it comes t pottin round an doin nothing, with nothin bigger'n an ax-handle t hold a feller down, like it was a while back befo I got this job—that beam ought t be—but tmorrow mornin early's time enough f that. As I was sayin, I gets t thinkin. Play dumb naturally t white folks. I gets t thinkin. I used to subscribe t the *Literary Digest* an that helped along a bit. But there werent nothing I could sink m teeth int. Theres lots I want t ask y,

Lewis. Been askin y t come around. Couldnt get y. Cant get in much tnight. (*He glances at the others. His mind fastens on* KABNIS.) Say, tell me this, whats on your mind t say on that feller there? Kabnis' name. One queer bird ought t know another, seems like t me.

Licker has released conflicts in KABNIS *and set them flowing. He pricks his ears, intuitively feels that the talk is about him, leaves* CORA, *and approaches the table. His eyes are watery, heavy with passion. He stoops. He is a ridiculous pathetic figure in his showy robe.*

KABNIS Talkin bout me. I know. I'm th topic of conversation everywhere theres talk about this town. Girls an fellers. White folks as well. An if its me youre talkin bout, guess I got a right t listen in. Whats sayin? Whats sayin bout his royal guts, the Duke? Whats sayin, eh?

HALSEY (*to* LEWIS) We'll take it up another time.

KABNIS No nother time bout it. Now. I'm here now an talkin's just begun. I was born an bred in a family of orators, thats what I was.

HALSEY Preachers.

KABNIS Na. Preachers hell. I didnt say wind-busters. Y misapprehended me. Y understand what that means, dont y? All right then, y misapprehended me. I didn't say preachers. I said orators. O R A T O R S. Born one an I'll die one. You understand me, Lewis. (*He turns to* HALSEY *and begins shaking his finger in his face.*) An as f you, youre all right f choppin things from blocks of wood. I was good at that th day I ducked the cradle. An since then, I've been shapin words after a design that branded here. Know whats here? M soul. Ever heard o that? Th hell y have. Been shapin words t fit m soul. Never told y that before, did I? Though I couldnt talk. I'll tell y. I've been shapin words; ah, but sometimes theyre beautiful an golden an have a taste that makes them fine t roll over with y tongue. Your tongue aint fit f nothin but t roll an lick hog meat.

STELLA *and* CORA *come up to the table.*

HALSEY Give him a shove there, will y, Stel?

STELLA *jams* KABNIS *in a chair.* KABNIS *springs up.*

KABNIS Cant keep a good man down. Those words I was tellin y about, they wont fit int th mold thats branded on m soul. Rhyme, y see? Poet, too. Bad rhyme. Bad poet. Somethin else youve learned tnight. Lewis dont know it all, an I'm atellin y. Ugh. Th form thats burned int my soul is some twisted awful thing that crept in from a dream, a godam nightmare, an wont stay still unless I feed it. An it lives on words. Not beautiful words. God Almighty no. Misshapen, split-gut, tortured, twisted words. Layman was feedin it back there that day you thought I ran out fearin things. White folks feed it cause their looks are words. Niggers, black niggers feed it cause theyre evil an their looks are words. Yallar niggers feed it. This whole damn bloated purple country feeds it cause its goin down t hell in a holy avalanche of words. I want t feed th soul—I know what that is; th preachers dont—but I've got t feed it. I wish t God some lynchin white man ud stick his knife through it an pin it to a tree. An pin it to a tree. You hear me? Thats a wish f y, you little snot-nosed pups who've been makin fun of me, an faltin that I'm weak. Me, Ralph Kabnis weak. Ha.

HALSEY Thats right, old man. There, there. Here, so much exertion merits a fittin reward. Help him t be seated, Cora.

HALSEY *gives him a swig of shine.* CORA *glides up, seats him, and then plumps herself down on his lap, squeezing his head into her breasts.* KABNIS *mutters. Tries to break loose. Curses.* CORA *almost stifles him. He goes limp and gives up.* CORA *toys with him. Ruffles his hair. Braids it. Parts it in the middle.* STELLA *smiles contemptuously. And then a sudden anger sweeps her. She would like to lash* CORA *from the place. She'd like to take* KABNIS *to some distant pine grove and nurse and mother him. Her eyes flash. A quick tensioning throws her breasts and neck into a poised strain. She starts towards them.* HALSEY *grabs her arm and pulls her to him. She struggles.* HALSEY *pins her arms and kisses her. She settles, spurting like a pine-knot afire.*

LEWIS *finds himself completely cut out. The glowing within him subsides. It is followed by a dead chill.* KABNIS, CARRIE, STELLA, HALSEY, CORA, *the* OLD MAN, *the cellar, and the workshop, the southern town descend upon him. Their pain is too intense. He cannot stand it. He bolts from the table. Leaps up the stairs. Plunges through the workshop and out into the night.*

VI

The cellar swims in a pale phosphorescence. The table, the chairs, the figure of the old man are amœba-like shadows which move about and float in it. In the corner under the steps, close to the floor, a solid blackness. A sound comes from it. A forcible yawn. Part of the blackness detaches itself so that it may be seen against the grayness of the wall. It moves forward and then seems to be clothing itself in odd dangling bits of shadow. The voice of HALSEY, *vibrant and deepened, calls.*

HALSEY Kabnis. Cora. Stella. (*He gets no response. He wants to get them up, to get on the job. He is intolerant of their sleepiness.*) Kabnis! Stella! Cora! (*Gutturals, jerky and impeded, tell that he is shaking them.*) Come now, up with you.

KABNIS (*sleepily and still more or less intoxicated*) Whats th big idea? What in hell—

HALSEY Work. But never you mind about that. Up with you.

CORA Oooooo! Look here, mister, I aint used t bein thrown int th street befo day.

STELLA Any bunk whats worked is worth in wages moren this. But come on. Taint no use t arger.

KABNIS I'll arger. Its preposterous—

The girls interrupt him with none too pleasant laughs.

Thats what I said. Know what it means, dont y? All right, then. I said its preposterous t root an artist out o bed at this ungodly hour, when there aint no use t it. You can start your damned old work. Nobody's stoppin y. But what we got t get up for? Fraid somebody'll see th girls leavin? Some sport, you are. I hand it t y.

HALSEY Up you get, all th same.

KABNIS Oh, th hell you say.

HALSEY Well, son, seeing that I'm th kind-hearted father, I'll give y chance t open your eyes. But up y get when I come down. (*He mounts the steps to the workshop and starts a fire in the hearth. In the yard he finds some chunks of coal which he brings in and throws on the fire. He puts a kettle on to boil. The wagon draws him. He lifts an oak beam, fingers it, and becomes abstracted. Then comes to himself and places the beam upon the workbench. He looks over some newly cut wooden spokes. He goes to the fire and pokes it. The coals are red-hot. With a pair of long prongs he picks them up and places them in a thick iron bucket. This he carries downstairs. Outside, darkness has given way to the impalpable grayness of dawn. This early morning light, seeping through the four barred cellar windows, is the color of the stony walls. It seems to be an emanation from them.* HALSEY'*s coals throw out a rich warm glow. He sets them on the floor, a safe distance from the beds.*) No foolin now. Come. Up with you.

Other than a soft rustling, there is no sound as the girls slip into their clothes. KABNIS *still lies in bed.*

STELLA (*to* HALSEY) Reckon y could spare us a light?

HALSEY *strikes a match, lights a cigarette, and then bends over and touches flame to the two candles on the table between the beds.* KABNIS *asks for a cigarette.* HALSEY *hands him his and takes a fresh one for himself. The girls, before the mirror, are doing up their hair. It is bushy hair that has gone through some straightening process. Character, however, has not all been ironed out. As they kneel there, heavy-eyed and dusky, and throwing grotesque moving shadows on the wall, they are two princesses in Africa going through the early-morning ablutions of their pagan prayers. Finished, they come forward to stretch their hands and warm them over the glowing coals. Red dusk of a Georgia sunset, their heavy, coal-lit faces . . .* KABNIS *suddenly recalls something.*

KABNIS Th old man talked last night.

STELLA An so did you.

HALSEY In your dreams.

KABNIS I tell y, he did. I know what I'm talkin about. I'll tell y what he said. Wait now, lemme see.

HALSEY Look out, brother, th old man'll be getting in t you by way o dreams. Come, Stel, ready? Cora? Coffee an eggs f both of you. (*He goes upstairs.*)

STELLA Gettin generous, aint he?

She blows the candles out. Says nothing to KABNIS. *Then she and* CORA *follow after* HALSEY. KABNIS, *left to himself, tries to rise. He has slept in his robe. His robe trips him. Finally, he manages to stand up. He starts across the floor. Half-way to the* OLD MAN, *he falls and lies quite still. Perhaps an hour passes. Light of a new sun is about to filter through the windows.* KABNIS *slowly rises to support upon his elbows. He looks hard, and internally gathers himself together. The side face of Father John is in the direct line of his eyes. He scowls at him. No one is around. Words gush from* KABNIS.

KABNIS You sit there like a black hound spiked to an ivory pedestal. An all night long I heard you murmurin that devilish word. They thought I didnt hear y, but I did. Mumblin, feedin that ornery thing thats livin on my insides. Father John. Father of Satan, more likely. What does it mean t you? Youre dead already. Death. What does it mean t you? To you who died way back there in th 'sixties. What are y throwin it in my throat for? Whats it goin t get y? A good smashin in th mouth, thats what. My fist'll sink in t y black mush face clear t y guts—if y got any. Dont believe y have. Never seen signs of none. Death. Death. Sin an death. All night long y mumbled death. (*He forgets the* OLD MAN *as his mind begins to play with the word and its associations.*) Death . . . these clammy floors . . . just like the place they used t stow away th worn-out, no-count niggers in th days of slavery . . . that was long ago; not so long ago . . . no windows (*he rises higher on his elbows to verify this assertion; he looks around, and, seeing no one but the* OLD MAN, *calls.*) Halsey! Halsey! Gone an left me. Just like a nigger. I thought he was a nigger all th time. Now I know it. Ditch y when it comes right down t it. Damn him anyway. Godam him. (*He looks and re-sees the* OLD MAN.) Eh, you? T hell with you too. What do I care whether you can see or hear? You know what hell is cause youve been there. Its a feelin an its ragin in my soul in a way that'll pop out of me an run you through, an scorch y, an burn an rip your soul. Your soul. Ha. Nigger soul. A gin soul that gets drunk on a preacher's words. An screams. An shouts. God Almighty, how I hate that shoutin. Where's th beauty in that? Gives a buzzard a windpipe an I'll bet a dollar t a dime th buzzard ud beat y to it. Aint surprisin th white folks hate y so. When you had eyes, did you ever see th beauty of the world? Tell me that. Th hell y did. Now dont tell me. I know y didnt. You couldnt have. Oh, I'm drunk an just as good as dead, but no eyes that have seen beauty ever lose their sight. You aint got no sight. If you had, drunk as I am, I hope Christ will kill me if I couldnt see it. Your eyes are dull and watery, like fish eyes. Fish eyes are dead eyes. Youre an old man, a dead fish man, an black at that. Theyve put y here t die, damn fool y are not t know it. Do y know how many feet youre under ground? I'll tell y. Twenty. An do y think you'll ever see th light of day again, even if you wasnt blind? Do y think youre out of slavery? Huh? Youre where they used t throw the worked-out, no-count slaves. On a damp clammy floor of a dark scum-hole. An they called that an infirmary. Th sons-a . . . Why I can already see you toppled off that stool an stretched out on th floor beside me—not beside me, damn you, by yourself, with th flies buzzin an lickin God knows what they'd find on a dirty, black, foul-breathed mouth like yours . . .

Someone is coming down the stairs. CARRIE, *bringing food for the* OLD MAN. *She is lovely in her fresh energy of the morning, in the calm untested confidence and nascent maternity which rise from the purpose of her present mission. She walks to within a few paces of* KABNIS.

CARRIE K. Brother says come up now, Brother Ralph.

KABNIS Brother doesnt know what he's talkin bout.

CARRIE K. Yes he does, Ralph. He needs you on th wagon.

KABNIS He wants me on th wagon, eh? Does he think some wooden thing can lift me up? Ask him that.

CARRIE K. He told me t help y.

KABNIS An how would you help me, child, dear sweet little sister?

CARRIE K. (*moves forward as if to aid him*) I'm not a child, as I've more than once told you, Brother Ralph, an as I'll show you now.

KABNIS Wait, Carrie. No, thats right. Youre not a child. But twont do t lift me bodily. You dont understand. But its th soul of me that needs th risin.

CARRIE K. Youre a bad brother an just wont listen t me when I'm tellin y t go t church.

KABNIS *doesn't hear her. He breaks down and talks to himself.*

KABNIS Great God Almighty, a soul like mine cant pin itself onto a wagon wheel an satisfy itself in spinnin round. Iron prongs an hickory sticks, an God knows what all . . . all right for Halsey . . . use him. Me? I get my life down in this scum-hole. Th old man an me—

CARRIE K. Has he been talkin?

KABNIS Huh? Who? Him? No. Dont need to. I talk. An when I really talk, it pays th best of them t listen. The old man is a good listener. He's deaf; but he's a good listener. An I can talk t him. Tell him anything.

CARRIE K. He's deaf an blind, but I reckon he hears, an sees too, from th things I've heard.

KABNIS No. Cant. Cant I tell you. How's he do it?

CARRIE K. Dunno, except I've heard that th souls of old folks have a way of seein things.

KABNIS An I've heard them call that superstition.

The OLD MAN *begins to shake his head slowly.* CARRIE *and* KABNIS *watch him, anxiously. He mumbles. With a grave motion his head nods up and down. And then, on one of the downswings—*

OLD MAN (*remarkably clear and with great conviction*) Sin.

He repeats this word several times, always on the downward nodding. Surprised, indignant, KABNIS *forgets that* CARRIE *is with him.*

KABNIS Sin! Shut up. What do you know about sin, you old black bastard. Shut up, an stop that swayin an noddin your head.

OLD MAN Sin.

KABNIS (*tries to get up*) Didn't I tell y t shut up?

CARRIE *steps forward to help him.* KABNIS *is violently shocked at her touch. He springs back.*

KABNIS Carrie! What . . . how . . . Baby, you shouldnt be down here. Ralph says things. Doesnt mean to. But Carrie, he doesnt know what he's talkin about. Couldnt know. It was only a preacher's sin they knew in those old days, an that wasnt sin at all. Mind me, th only sin is whats done against th soul. Th whole world is a conspiracy t sin, especially in America, an against me. I'm th victim of their sin. I'm what sin is. Does he look like me? Have you ever heard him say th things youve heard me say? He couldnt if he had th Holy Ghost t help him. Dont look shocked, little sweetheart, you hurt me.

OLD MAN Sin.

KABNIS Aw, shut up, old man.

CARRIE K. Leave him be. He wants t say somethin. (*She turns to the* OLD MAN.) What is it, Father?

KABNIS Whatsha talkin t that old deaf man for? Come away from him.

CARRIE K. What is it, Father?

The OLD MAN*'s lips begin to work. Words are formed incoherently. Finally, he manages to articulate—*

OLD MAN Th sin whats fixed . . . (*Hesitates.*)

CARRIE K. (*restraining a comment from* KABNIS) Go on, Father.

OLD MAN . . . upon th white folks—

KABNIS Suppose youre talkin about that bastard race thats roamin round th country. It looks like sin, if thats what y mean. Give us somethin new an up t date.

OLD MAN —f tellin Jesus—lies. O th sin th white folks 'mitted when they made the Bible lie.

Boom. Boom. BOOM! *Thuds on the floor above. The* OLD MAN *sinks back into his stony silence.* CARRIE *is wet-eyed.* KABNIS, *contemptuous.*

KABNIS So thats your sin. All these years t tell us that the white folks made th Bible lie. Well, I'll be damned. Lewis ought t have been here. You old black fakir—

CARRIE K. Brother Ralph, is that your best Amen?

She turns him to her and takes his hot cheeks in her firm cool hands. Her palms draw the fever out. With its passing, KABNIS *crumples. He sinks to his knees before her, ashamed, exhausted. His eyes squeeze tight.* CARRIE *presses his face tenderly against her. The suffocation of her fresh starched dress feels good to him.* CARRIE *is about to lift her hands in prayer when* HALSEY, *at the head of the stairs, calls down.*

HALSEY Well, well. Whats up? Aint you ever comin? Come on. Whats up down there? Take you all mornin t sleep off a pint? Youre weakenin, man, youre weakenin. Th axle an th beam's all ready waitin f y. Come on.

KABNIS *rises and is going doggedly towards the steps.* CARRIE *notices his robe. She catches up to him, points to it, and helps him take it off. He hangs it, with an exaggerated ceremony, on its nail in the corner. He looks down on the tousled beds. His lips curl bitterly. Turning, he stumbles over the bucket of dead coals. He savagely jerks it from the floor. And then, seeing* CARRIE'*s eyes upon him, he swings the pail carelessly and with eyes downcast and swollen, trudges upstairs to the workshop.*

CARRIE'*s gaze follows him till he is gone. Then she goes to the* OLD MAN *and slips to her knees before him. Her lips murmur, "Jesus, come."*

Light streaks through the iron-barred cellar window. Within its soft circle, the figures of CARRIE *and the* OLD MAN.

Outside, the sun arises from its cradle in the tree-tops of the forest. Shadows of pines are dreams the sun shakes from its eyes. The sun arises. Gold-glowing child, it steps into the sky and sends a birth-song slanting down gray dust streets and sleepy windows of the southern town.

CURTAIN

A SEASON IN THE CONGO

by Aimé Césaire

Translated by Ralph Manheim

Aimé Césaire, the renowned Afro-Caribbean poet, was born in Martinique in 1913 and studied at the École Normale in Paris. His first major work, *Cahier d'un retour au pays natal,* was published in fragments in 1938, the complete transcript published in 1956 by Présence Africaine. Aimé Césaire has published many other books of poetry and has written two plays, the last of which is *A Season in the Congo.* He is Mayor of Fort de France and a deputy in the French National Assembly, representing the Independent Revolutionary Party of Martinique. He is active in the cause of Caribbean and African emancipation.

CAST OF CHARACTERS

SALESMAN (LUMUMBA)
MOKUTU
MAMA MAKOSI
BASILIO, *King of Belgium*
GENERAL MASSENS
KALA LUBU, *President of the Congolese Republic*
MPOLO
DAG HAMMARSKJÖLD
CROULARD
ISAAC KALONJI
HÉLÈNE JEWEL
PAULINE LUMUMBA
OKITO
TZUMBI
TRAVÉLÉ
MSIRI
MATTHEW CORDELIER
SANZA PLAYER
TWO BELGIAN COPS
VOICE
MAN
FIRST WOMAN
SECOND WOMAN
TWO JAILERS
WARDEN
FIVE BANKERS
BAKONGO TRIBESMAN
FOUR RADIO VOICES
ZIMBWÉ
THREE SENATORS
AMBASSADOR OF THE GRAND OCCIDENT
VOICE OF CIVIL WAR
THREE MINISTERS
BISHOP
PILOT
GHANA
MERCENARY
ONLOOKERS
SOLDIERS
GIRLS

ACT I

SCENE 1

African quarter of Leopoldville . . . Natives are gathered around the SALESMAN *who is making a speech. Beer is being dispensed from a stand. Two* BELGIAN COPS *are looking on rather suspiciously.*

SALESMAN Friends, the white men have invented a lot of things and brought them here to our country, good things and bad things. I won't stop to talk about the bad things today. But take it from me, friends, one of the good things is beer. My advice to you is to drink. Drink and drink some more. Come to think of it, do they leave us free to do anything else? If we get together, we end in jail. Hold a meeting? Jail. Write an article? Jail. Try to leave the country? Jail. And more of the same. But you don't have to take my word for it. Use your own eyes. I've been talking to you now for a good fifteen minutes, and their cops don't interfere . . . I've been doing the country from Stanleyville to Katanga, and their cops haven't bothered me! Why? Because I'm selling beer. Yes, you could say that here in the Congo a mug of beer is the symbol of all our rights and liberties.

But not so fast. Same as there are different races in one and the same country—that's right, even in Belgium they have their Flemings and their Walloons, and everybody knows there's nothing worse than the Flemish—there are different kinds of beer. Different races and families of beer. And I've come here to tell you about the best of the lot: Polar Beer.

Polar, the freshness of the poles in the heat of the tropics.

Polar, the beer of Congolese freedom! Polar, the beer of Congolese friendship and brotherhood!

ONLOOKER Sure! But I've heard that Polar makes a man impotent. Takes away your *ngolo.* What do you say to that?

SALESMAN That's a mean crack, citizen. If I wanted to give you a mean answer I'd tell you to lend me your wife or sister for a few minutes.

Laughter in the crowd.

ONLOOKER Ho, ho! He's got what it takes.

SALESMAN But why not ask those girls over there, those lovely little girls; we'll put it up to them. What about it, girls? You with the beaming smiles, you with the smooth snake bellies: you tell us what's what.

GIRLS (*singing*)

Women smooth as mirrors
Bodies without guile
Honey fritters,
Hair a shimmering water.
Two ripe and flawless
Papayas for breasts.

Applause in the crowd.

FIRST BELGIAN COP Not bad, his spiel. He's got a tongue in his head.

SECOND BELGIAN COP I suppose so. But it's got me worried. That beer mug of his is a grab bag. You never know what he's going to pull out of it next. I've got a mind to ask him a question or two.

FIRST BELGIAN COP Watch your step. We can't interfere with the sales of Polar Beer. Don't you know who owns Polar?

SECOND BELGIAN COP How should I? All I know is that that nigger's dangerous.

FIRST BELGIAN COP You're young. Just listen to me. The Minister's behind Polar . . . That's right . . . The Minister for the Congo! Knocks you for a loop, eh? But that's how it is. So now you see what's what. Come on, let's have a glass.

SECOND BELGIAN COP Suits me. But let's take that salesman's name . . . Something tells me we're going to need it.

FIRST BELGIAN COP Don't worry. We've got it. It's on file. His name is Patrice Lumumba.

SECOND BELGIAN COP And what about him over there? Is he on file too?

FIRST BELGIAN COP Oh, he's only a sanza player. Harmless. But a nuisance. He's everywhere all at once. Like a fly. And always buzzing.

SANZA PLAYER (*sings*)

Ata-ndele . . . [Sooner or later . . .]

SCENE 2

Waiters and customers moving about. They are setting up an African bar. Meanwhile a voice rises off-stage, growing louder and louder.

VOICE Hear, hear! The buffalo is wounded. Plugged full of bullets, he's at the end of his strength. He's gone mad. Who's the buffalo? The buffalo is the Belgian government. And now that the buffalo's wounded, he's threatening us right and left, What do you say? You going to let his threats get you down? The buffalo is a brute. Are you afraid of his brutality? Of his heavy tread? This is the song of our ancestors:

The buffalo has a heavy tread,
A heavy tread, a heavy tread.
If you see him, don't be afraid of his heavy tread,
His heavy tread, his heavy tread.

The bar has been set up. Glaring light. Small tables. Men and prostitutes are moving about.

FIRST WOMAN (*singing*)

Come, don't be afraid.
I'm not a married woman.
I married too soon.
I thought there was nobody else.
Oh, if I'd only known!

(*Approaching a table full of men.*) Really, Congolese have no manners. Men drinking beer all by themselves while a poor girl dies of thirst.

MAN (*whistles*) And what a girl! Say, boys, she's high octane. Move over, friends, there's plenty of room. Sit down, baby, sit down.

SECOND WOMAN (*approaching*) Hey, girls, help! Help! I've had an accident. I'm losing my *jikita.* Those Belgian waistbands are no good. Rotten cork, that's all they are. Damn Belgians, they cheat us every way they can.

MAN They cheat us, they exploit us; that's right, lady-o, they exploit us. Black people are just too trusting.

FIRST WOMAN (*stripping*) I've solved the problem. I've given up the *jikita.* The *jibula*'s the dress for me.

MAN (*laughing*) More like undress. Take it easy, sister. The slightest move in that get-up unveils the thighs. And plenty more. Hee, hee! Plenty more.

SECOND WOMAN Is that any way to talk to a lady? It's free, isn't it, so why complain? Ah, men are getting stingy and mean. Anyway, I'm sick of it all. (*Singing.*)

Listen, friends,
God gave us mothers,
Mothers who kill us for money,
For money and more money.

Enter MOKUTU *in European dress. He looks like a pimp.*

MOKUTU Boys and girls, howdy! I've got news for you. The Belgians have arrested Patrice. They wouldn't listen to reason. They've taken him to Elisabethville in handcuffs, and meanwhile the politicians are sitting around the table in Brussels, deciding the fate of the Congo. If those African politicians had any guts they'd boycott the conference until Patrice is released.

MAN Well, that's one way of looking at it. But isn't the fate of the country more important than the fate of one man?

MOKUTU Oh, oh! Have we got Belgians around here? Black Belgians? Tell me, friend, did you ever stop to think that the fate of the country might depend on the fate of one man?

MAN Okay, okay. But what are we going to do? Do you want us to storm the Elisabethville prison with our bare hands?

MOKUTU Christ, how do I know? Just do something. Anything you can do in the Congo today is a step toward the revolution. Do what you like. As long as you do something.

SANZA PLAYER (*his voice rises off-stage and sings the hymn of the Kibanguists*)

We are the orphan children,
Dark is the night, hard is the way.
Almighty God, who's going to help us?
Father Congo, who's going to give us a hand?

FIRST WOMAN I suggest we go into mourning for six months. That's what you do when you lose a member of the family, and I call Patrice a member of the family.

MOKUTU Don't make me laugh. Is that any skin off the Belgians' ass?

SECOND WOMAN I say we go on strike and parade with our banners. All our organizations, the Lolita Club, the Dollar Association, the Free Woman, marching up and down with our flags—yellow, green, and red—that'll put their eye out.

MAMA MAKOSI [*the Mighty Madame*] Baloney. No mourning, no strike. Work is work. We'll work. Harder than ever. We'll raise bail. The buffalo likes money. He feeds on money. And Patrice will sit at the table in Brussels with the rest of them. I have spoken.

MOKUTU Friends, I've got to leave you now. Do what your hearts tell you. Anything you do for Patrice is good. Thank you.

SANZA PLAYER (*stands up and sings; the song is taken up by the crowd*)

When the rainy season comes,
War will come too,
The season of red blood.
The buffalo's strong and the elephant's strong.
Where can we hide?
Their science doesn't tell us.
The buffalo will fall,
The elephant will fall,
They'll feel the heavy hand of God.
The blood-red season's coming.
The season of our freedom.

SCENE 3

Elisabethville prison.

FIRST JAILER (*on the phone*) Hello, yes sir . . . Certainly, sir . . .

SECOND JAILER What is it, boss? Bad news?

FIRST JAILER It's the warden. He's on his way over. Something about Mister Patrice Lumumba.

SECOND JAILER What a pest he turned out to be! I've seen a lot of prisoners in my time, but take it from me, there's nothing worse than an egghead nigger.

FIRST JAILER You can say that again. Who does he think he is? He's even started writing poetry. Since when do baboons write poetry? All right, bring him in, we'll get him into shape to see the warden.

While the SECOND JAILER *goes out and returns with* LUMUMBA, *the* FIRST JAILER *reads.*

Get a load of this!

"Congo, and then the white men came
Raping your women and making
Your warriors drunk.
But the future will bring deliverance.
The banks of the great river will be yours,
Yours this land and all its riches,
Yours the sun in the sky."

Where does he get that stuff about the sun? I knew they wanted our houses and our women. Now they even want our sun . . . Oh, so there you are, you bastard. Ungrateful dog! So His Nibs writes poetry. Just tell me this, you baboon, who taught you how to read? Couldn't have been the no-good Belgians, could it? All right, I'm going to give you a little poetry in the ribs. (*He hits* LUMUMBA.)

SECOND JAILER You don't know the half of it. Look what I found in his cell. The manuscript of an article protesting his imprisonment. Claims it's illegal—that's what they all say. Demands to be set free so he can attend the Round Table conference in Brussels. Signed: Patrice Lumumba, President of the NCM.

FIRST JAILER That's rich. (*He hits* LUMUMBA *again.*) So His Blackness wants to go to Brussels, eh? And what would you say to the king if you saw him? What would you say to the Bwana Kitoko?

SECOND JAILER (*hitting* LUMUMBA) I guess he wants to be a minister! (*He laughs.*) His Excellency, the baboon! . . . His Excellency.

FIRST JAILER Maybe so. But he'll have to eat King Kala first. Easy there, son. Don't rough him up too much. The warden'll be here any minute. Hm. Here he comes.

Enter THE WARDEN.

WARDEN Mr. Lumumba, I bring you good news. Yes, believe it or not, occasionally a warden has good news for a prisoner: I've just received word from Brussels. His Excellency the Minister for the

Congo has decided to release you. He wishes you, as President of the NCM—the National Congo Movement, as you call it—to attend the Round Table conference. I have been instructed to do everything in my power to help you prepare for the trip. There's a Sabena plane for Brussels tomorrow. You are free, Mr. Lumumba. Bon voyage, Your Excellency!

JAILERS Good grief! (*They bow.*) Bon voyage, Your Excellency!

The SANZA PLAYER *passes, singing:*

Kongo Mpaka Dima [Be watchful, brothers, the Congo is moving.]

SCENE 4

A sign is lowered from the grid, reading: BRUSSELS, CONFERENCE ROOM. *The antechamber of a room in the palace. Four or five men, caricatures of bankers—dinner jacket, top hat, big cigar—are pacing about. Indignation and panic; they have just heard through indiscretion that at* LUMUMBA'*s request the Belgian government has set the date for Congolese independence at June 30, 1960.*

FIRST BANKER We're screwed. A government of traitors has given away our empire.

SECOND BANKER They've set the date for independence.

THIRD BANKER They've knuckled under to that baboon.

FIFTH BANKER Chin up, gentlemen. Chin up, I say. You've got to wed the spirit of the times. I don't say love her, it's enough to wed her. There's nothing so frightening about this independence.

FIRST BANKER

What's this? You shrug your shoulders at a blow
That will disrupt the state and dam the flow
Of our finances. Good Lord, this will make
Belgium a third-rate power, a Liechtenstein!

FOURTH BANKER

Your attitude is dangerous. Do you mean
It, or is that a sample of your wit?
I'm a plain man, and I'll speak straight
From the shoulder. When ruin threatens a great state,
It's not the time for liberal ideas.

FIFTH BANKER

My friend, when ruin threatens a great state,
The only good ideas are bold ideas.

FIRST BANKER

We've heard enough of your obscurities.
Come to the point. If you have got some plan,
Let's hear it. Speak up. Make some suggestion, man.
Don't stand there looking wise.

SECOND BANKER That's telling him. Have you a policy?

FIFTH BANKER

Policy? Hm. That's maybe too much said,
But some ideas have shaped up in my head.
No credit due. It's normal after twenty
Years in the tropics, time to find out plenty.
To handle savages, there are two ways:
One is the club, but that's seen better days.
The other is the purse.

FIRST BANKER Go on.

FIFTH BANKER

All right, I'll spell it out. Just pay attention.
What do their leaders want? They want to be
Presidents, ministers, living in luxury.
In short, the purse! High-powered cars,
Villas, high wages, cushy bank accounts.
Spare no expense. Just grease their palms and stuff
Them. The investment will pay off.
You'll see, their hearts will melt. And presently

Those smirking, smiling politicians will be
A special class between us and their people.
They'll hold the people down provided we
Tie them with bonds—well, maybe not of friendship,
That's out of date in this sad century—
But knots and tangles of complicity.

FIRST BANKER Bravo! Good man! We're with you.

CHORUS OF BANKERS Hurrah! Hurrah! Three cheers for independence.

SCENE 5

Leopoldville. The crowd is celebrating independence. Atmosphere of friendly good nature. The "Independence Hot-cha-cha" is heard.

A WOMAN How's Dependa going to get here? By car? By boat? Or by airplane?

FIRST MAN She's coming with the little white king, Bwana Kitoko. He's bringing her.

SANZA PLAYER Listen to me, citizens. Nobody's bringing us Dependa. We're taking her.

BAKONGO TRIBESMAN It's all the same. Maybe they're giving us Dependa and maybe we're taking her, but one thing is sure: Now that we've got her, we're going to send all those Bengalas back to their villages. The Bengalas are wrecking the country.

FIRST MAN Watch your step, sir. Don't try to provoke us. If you ask me, it's pretty nice of us to put up with a Bakongo president, to let a Bakongo rule us. By rights a river man should have the job. Jean Bolikango! That's the man! Hurrah for Jean Bolikango!

MPOLO That's enough, gentlemen. Calm down. Let's not have tribal quarrels. That's just what the colonialists want. Divide and rule, that's their motto. We've got to stop being Bengalas, Bakongos, and Batetelas. From now on we're all just plain Congolese, free, united, and organized. Let's all drink a good glass of beer to our unity. Be my guests, gentlemen.

FIRST MAN Good idea. But the question is: what kind of beer? I only drink Polar.

SECOND MAN Primus is my brand.

THIRD MAN Primus, the queen of beers. That's King Kala's brand.

FIRST MAN It's Polar for me: the freshness of the poles in the heat of the tropics.

MPOLA Let's drink to peace. To every kind of peace, peace in our hearts, peace between tribes, peace between tribes, peace between the different brands of beer. Drink, gentlemen, Polar or Primus, it's all the same. So long as we drink to the Congo!

ALL Here's to the Congo! (*They sing the "Independence Hotcha-cha."*)

SCENE 6

Somewhere in Leopoldville, BASILIO, *King of Belgium, and* GENERAL MASSENS, *Commander of the Congolese Militia, standing before the curtain.*

BASILIO Not so long ago this barbarous people lay stunned beneath the heavy fist of Stanley, of Boula Matari, the Rock Crusher, as they call him out here. We took them in hand. Yes, Providence entrusted them to our care, we fed them, cared for them, educated them. The independence I am granting them today will show whether we have succeeded in bettering their nature, whether our efforts have been rewarded. Freedom will put them to the test. Either they will set all Africa an example, as we ourselves have done in Europe: the example of a united, self-respecting, hard-working people. In that case the emancipation of our wards will redound to the eternal glory of Belgium. Or else the barbaric root, nurtured in the moldering depths, will regain its noxious vigor and stifle the good seed sown for the last fifty years by the untiring devotion of our missionaries. In that case . . .

GENERAL MASSENS In that case?

BASILIO We'll see about that when the time comes, Massens. Meanwhile, let's put our trust in human nature.

GENERAL MASSENS Your Majesty, these experiments bear witness to your generosity, your genius. But you know how I feel about it. I have my doubts . . .

However, if such is your sovereign will, I have only one recommendation. Make it clear to them that you have given them this freedom—this hashish that intoxicates them with such deplorable visions—and that they haven't conquered it. Perhaps they are not too obtuse to grasp the big difference between a right they have earned and the gift of your Royal Munificence.

BASILIO Don't worry, Massens. I will make that very clear. But here they are.

The curtain rises. LUMUMBA, KALA, *other Congolese delegates, and, in the background, the Congolese crowd are on stage.*

KALA LUBU (*President of the Congolese Republic, to* LUMUMBA): Mr. Mayor, oh, I beg your pardon, Mr. Prime Minister, I mean. The essential thing, in my opinion, is that this ceremony should pass off smoothly, that we observe the proprieties. The rules of good manners demand it, the rules of politics as well. This is no time for complaints and recriminations, for high-sounding—or low-sounding—words. Childbirth is never painless; that's the law of nature. But when the child is born, everyone smiles. Today I want to see a Congo wreathed in smiles. But here's the King. (*Addressing the crowd.*) All together now, Long live the King!

CROWD Long live the King! Hurrah for Bwana Kitoko! Hurrah for King Kala!

The crowd waves little flags with the sign of the kodi, *a shell pierced with a sword, emblem of the Abako,* KALA's *political organization. Firecrackers are set off. A group of black children led by a bearded missionary, sing a song in the style of the Vienna* Sängerknaben.

BASILIO I shall be brief. A word in pious recollection of my predecessors who were the guardians of this country before me, and first of all of Leopold, the founder, who came here not to take, not to dominate, but to give and to bring civilization. And a word of gratitude to all those who built up this country day by day—at the cost of untold hardships. Glory to the founders! And glory to those who carried on their work. And now, gentlemen, I give you this State, the work of our hands. We are a nation of engineers and manufacturers. I can say without boasting that we are putting an excellent machine into your hands; take good care of it, that's all I ask of you. But since it is a machine, mechanical difficulties can reasonably be foreseen, and it goes without saying that you can come to us with your problems, that you can count on our assistance; our disinterested assistance, gentlemen. And now, men of the Congo, take over the controls, the eyes of the whole world are upon you!

KALA LUBU Sire! Your august Majesty's presence at the ceremonies of this memorable day is new and striking proof of your solicitude for this people that you have loved and protected. The people of the Congo have received your message of friendship with respect and fervent devotion. They will long bear in their hearts the words you have just addressed to them in this solemn hour. They will never cease to prize the friendship which the Belgian government has offered them and will unstintingly do their part to maintain a sincere collaboration between our two nations. People of the Congo, my brothers, I want you to know, to understand, that independence has not come to our country to abrogate law or tribal custom; it has come to complete them, to fulfill and harmonize them. Nor has independence come to us to undo the work of civilization. Independence comes to us under the twofold guidance of custom and civilization. Independence has come to reconcile the old and the new, the nation and its tribes. If we keep faith with civilization and with custom, God will protect the Congo.

Uncertain applause.

LUMUMBA As for me, Sire, my thoughts are for those who have been forgotten. We are the people who have been dispossessed, beaten, mutilated; the people whom the conquerors treated as inferiors, in whose faces they spat. A people of kitchen boys, house boys, laundry boys, in short, a people of boys, of yes-bwanas, and anyone who wanted to prove that a man is not necessarily a man could take us as an example.

Sire, whatever suffering, whatever humiliation could be known, we have known it.
But comrades, they were not able to dull our taste for life, and we resisted.
We didn't have much to fight with, but we fought, we fought for fifty years.
And today we have won.
Today our country is in the hands of its children.
This sky, this river, these lands are ours.
Ours the lake and the forest,
Ours Karissimbi, Nyiragongo, Niamuragira, Mikeno, Ehu, mountains sprung from the word of fire.
People of the Congo, this is a great day.
It is the day when the nations of the world welcome Congo our mother,
and still more Congo our child,
child of our sleepless nights, of our sufferings, of our struggles.
Comrades and brothers in combat, it is up to us to transform each of our wounds into a nurturing breast,
each of our thoughts, our hopes, into a fountain of change.
Kongo! Watch me. I raise him above my head;
I put him back on my shoulder;
Three times I spit in his face;
I set him down on the ground, and I ask you; tell me the truth, do you know this child? And you all answer: it's Kongo, our king.
I wish I were a toucan, that wonderful bird, to cross the skies an-

nouncing to races and tongues that Kongo has been born to us, our king. Long live Kongo!

Kongo, late born, may he follow the sparrow hawk!

Kongo, late born, let him have the last word!

Comrades, everything remains to be done, or done over, but we will do it, we will do it over. For Kongo.

We will remake all the laws, one by one, for Kongo.

We will revise all the customs, one by one, for Kongo.

Uprooting injustice, we will rebuild the old edifice piece by piece, from cellar to attic, for Kongo.

That which is bowed shall be raised, and that which is raised shall be raised higher—for Kongo!

I demand the union of all.

I demand the devotion of every man. For Kongo!

Uhuru! Freedom!

A moment of ecstasy.

Congo! These are great days!
When this day's rags and this day's tinsel have been burned,
Let us advance rejoicing to my unanimous step
Into the new day! Into the solstice!

Stupor. Enter the first FOUR BANKERS.

FIRST BANKER Terrible, terrible! It was bound to end this way.

SECOND BANKER That speech! This time we're through. We can pack our bags.

THIRD BANKER (*with great dignity*) Obviously. Where order breaks down, the banker packs his bags.

FOURTH BANKER Poor Congo, drifting on uncharted seas!

MOKUTU *passes. He is preoccupied and sees no one.*

MOKUTU And I picked him for a winner. Who could have written that speech of his? And to think I thought I could make a statesman out of him! Well, if he wants to break his neck, it's his funeral. Too bad! Too bad! Knife oversharpened cuts its sheath. *He spits.*)

SANZA PLAYER (*perplexed*) Let's not be too quick to judge the boss. He must have had his reasons even if we can't see them.

Enter LUMUMBA.

LUMUMBA Well, did you like what I said? Or are you one of those people who think the sky is going to fall because a black man has the audacity to give a king a piece of his mind with the whole world listening in? No, you don't like it. I can see it in your eyes.

MOKUTU Since you're asking me, let me tell you a little story.

LUMUMBA I hate stories.

MOKUTU Just to save time. When I was a boy, I went hunting with my grandfather. One day I found myself face to face with a leopard. I lost my head. I threw my javelin and wounded him. My grandfather was furious. He made me go in and retrieve the spear. That day I understood, once and for all, that you don't attack a beast unless you're sure of killing him.

LUMUMBA (*very coldly*) You're wrong if you're against what I said. There was a taboo that needed breaking. I broke it. As for your story, if it means that you hate the beast—colonialism—and that you're determined to hunt it down to a finish with me . . . everything will be all right.

MOKUTU Did you ever doubt it, Patrice?

LUMUMBA (*brusquely*) Good. That's enough for me. Let's make up.

They go out. The SANZA PLAYER *comes in and sings the lupeto song.*

SANZA PLAYER

Nobody's better
At sniffing the wind.
They haven't the mugs
Of murdering thugs,
But noses to sniff out the wind.
They're the lupeto boys.

Those boys like to eat,
They don't care where they get it

As long as they can eat it.
They're the lupeto boys.

You ask me what's lupeto.
You haven't understood.
Lupeto's money, lucre, dough,
They're neither bad nor good.
They're the lupeto boys.

Enter the FIFTH BANKER.

FIRST BANKER Congratulations for your shrewd advice!

FIFTH BANKER

Colleague and friend, I think you're being unfair.
Risks are the price of politics, the price
Of any action.

SECOND BANKER

Phrases, words, hot air.
Your plan goes wrong, and you stand there and gas.

FIFTH BANKER

Phrases, why, not at all. Chin up, my friends!
Shall we lie down like bathmats at the first
Love tap? No, listen. Follow my idea (*He whispers in their ears.*)
If self-determination is the style,
It can't be helped. But then, why not for all?
For you and me, it's only logical.
You catch my drift, you read between the lines?
Then self-determination for our mines!

FIRST BANKER

Hush, hush! Let's listen, please.
Our colleague often gets some good ideas.

FIFTH BANKER

Friends, when I see this turmoil, this commotion,
I realize there's only one solution.
Yes, when I see this Congo, this immense
Chaotic mass, it simply doesn't make sense
That our Katanga, our beloved nation,
Shouldn't cast loose. That's self-determination.

FIRST BANKER

Ah, now you're talking, pal. I love you. Self-
Determined uranium? That's the ticket, eh?

FIFTH BANKER

And not just uranium. Diamonds, copper, cobalt.
All Katanga. Shining, clinking, gilt-edged Katanga.

CHORUS OF BANKERS Hurrah! Hurrah! Three cheers for Katanga!

SCENE 7

A night club. A record is playing "Franco de Mi Amor." When it stops, a woman's voice is heard over the radio.

FIRST VOICE This is the voice of African Moral Rearmament. Get to work, citizens. To work! And when I say "to work," it's the same as if I were saying "to arms." We are at war, citizens, at war for the future of the Congo. The mobilization of the working classes must be total, unconditional, deliberate, voluntary. The Congo has been living in prehistoric times. With independence we have acceded to the historical age, and that means the age of hard work. To work, citizens! To work!

Another voice is heard.

SECOND VOICE People of the Congo, wake up. Don't let yourselves be brainwashed! Come out of your holes, your workshops, your factories. Make yourselves heard, demand your rights. Independence, yes! But don't let it be an empty word. Take it from me, citizens, it's not empty for everybody. Ask the members of parliament, ask the ministers. Who gets the cars? Who gets the women? The ministers, the members of parliament! Who gets Santa Claus? The eggheads. We demand Santa Claus for everybody! That's what we mean by independence. Hurrah for independence!

The stage is invaded by Congolese SOLDIERS, *half drunk, swinging their belts.*

SOLDIERS (*shouting rhythmically*) Down with the politicians! Down with Lumumba, Lumumba *pamba,* Lumumba *pamba!* . . .

SCENE 8

Leopoldville, the Prime Minister's office.

LUMUMBA Get me Makessa. Where's Kangolo? Absent. Some office manager. No use looking for Sissoko. He's asleep. He never gets up in the daytime. Maybe you think things can go on like this? No, goddammit, they can't. Gentlemen, who are we? Well, I'm going to tell you who we are. We're slaves. I'm a slave, a voluntary slave. You're all slaves, or you ought to be, and by slaves I mean men condemned to work without rest. You have no right to rest. You're here to serve the Congo twenty-four hours a day. Private life is out. But at least you're free from material worries . . . because you won't have time for any. I know, I know. They say I ask too much, they say I'm adventurous, foolhardy and so on. Is that it? They say I'm trying to go too fast. Well, you no-good snails, let me tell you this. We've got to go fast, we've got to go too fast. Do you know how much time I have to catch up with fifty years of history? Three months, gentlemen. And you think I can afford to take it easy?

MPOLO Mr. President, the soldiers! The soldiers are coming.

LUMUMBA Soldiers? What in hell do they want? What are they squawking about?

MPOLO They're yelling, "Kill Lumumba. Lumumba *pamba*!"

LUMUMBA (*flying into a rage*) Is that all? The bastards, the traitors. Belgians, that's what they are. Lousy Flemish bastards! When I think that for fifty years they crawled for the Belgians. And the minute we settle our African asses to give them an African government they come around snapping at our ankles.

MINISTER Well, if you ask me, independence is getting off to a lovely start.

LUMUMBA Idiot! How did you expect it to start? And how do you expect it to go on? What did you think? When I picked you as my ministers, did you think I was inviting you to a picnic? I won't try to fool you, gentlemen. There's going to be trouble, every kind of trouble before you can say Jack Sprat: mutiny, sabotage, threats, slander, blackmail, and treason. You look surprised. That's what power means: betrayal, maybe death. Yes, death and no maybe. That's the Congo. The Congo, you see, is a country where things go fast. A seed in the ground today, tomorrow a bush, no, tomorrow a forest. In any case, the things that move quickly will keep on moving quickly. Don't count on me to slow them down. Mpolo, let those loudmouthed bastards in, I'll speak to them . . . I'll move them. I'll turn their hearts.

Enter the soldiers' delegation.

Come in, gentlemen. Ah, it's too bad you haven't brought your civilian friends, those union leaders, who've suddenly got so brave when it comes to holding the knife to our throats. For fifty years they've kept their mouths shut and trembled at the sight of a Belgian. And now they refuse to give a Congolese government, a government of their brothers, the few months' time it needs to get its bearings. As for you soldiers, I won't beat about the bush. Your demands are legitimate. I understand them and I intend to meet them. When you were the militia, your officers were Belgians; now that you're the National Army, you want to be commanded by Congolese. That's perfectly reasonable. And if we hesitated a moment before Africanizing the Army, it was because our good will was blocked by the ill will and the prejudices of General Massens. That shows you what to expect of the colonialists. They're obstinate, gentlemen, and they're underhanded. But we have dismissed Massens.

SOLDIERS Down with Massens!

LUMUMBA Massens is gone and the government will meet your demands. Each one of you is being promoted to the next higher rank: every private will be a corporal, every corporal a sergeant . . .

SOLDIERS No! No! Colonels! Generals!

MOKUTU Mr. Prime Minister, the troops demand the total and immediate Africanization of the officers' corps. The way things stand, there isn't a moment to lose.

LUMUMBA The government is not unaware of the problem. As of the present moment I am in a position to inform you that the government is considering . . . no, that the government has decided to appoint a Congolese general and a Congolese colonel immediately. The general is Lundula, the colonel is our secretary of state for youth problems, Mpolo, here present.

SOLDIERS No! We don't want Mpolo. He's not a soldier, he's a politician. We want Mokutu. To hell with Mpolo. We want Mokutu. He was in the militia for seven years. He's a soldier.

LUMUMBA You want Mokutu? Good. I ratify your choice. It's true, Mokutu's a soldier. And Mokutu's my friend, my brother. I know that Mokutu will never betray me. Mpolo was appointed by the government. Well, I appoint Mokutu. That settles it. But the question isn't whether you're going to be officers or not, because you are officers right now. The question is what kind of officers you choose to be: parade officers? Bakshish officers? A new caste? The government wants you to be officers of the Congolese people, fired with the spirit of the Congolese people and determined to fight like tigers to safeguard our Congolese independence. What do you say?

SOLDIERS Yes! Yes! Hurrah for Lumumba!

LUMUMBA Congolese soldiers and officers, if the enemy attacks us, and that may be sooner than we think, it's up to you . . . I expect him to burn his claws like a hawk that tries to steal meat from the villagers' fire. Long live the Congolese Army. Long live the Congo!

SOLDIERS Hurrah! Hurrah!

SANZA PLAYER (*enters and sings*)

Pollen of fire
Drunken springtime
A little bird is flitting
Forgetful of snares
Forgetting the blowpipe.
Birdbrain, says the trap.
The bird has forgotten the trap,
The trap remembers the bird.

SCENE 9

In the darkness white refugees cross the stage, carrying what few belongings they have been able to save. Suddenly red lights illumine an immense map of the Congo. On a balcony in the half-darkness two shadows: BASILIO *and* MASSENS.

FIRST RADIO VOICE Marigold calling Gardenia, Marigold calling Gardenia. Answer, Gardenia.

SECOND RADIO VOICE Betty calling Angela. Two cars full of women and children are headed for Kitona base. You will send troops to meet them.

THIRD RADIO VOICE Marigold calling Gardenia. Latest news from Luluabourg, Kasai province. Twelve hundred Europeans barricaded in Immokasai building besieged by Congolese troops armed with mortars and machine guns. Send troops immediately. Urgent. Out.

FOURTH RADIO VOICE Phoenix, do you read me, Phoenix? Dispatch received from Juba. Watsa troops in revolt. Forty Belgian officers with their families taken prisoner. They are being tortured. Urge immediate action. Out.

Enter BASILIO *and* MASSENS *in uniform.*

MASSENS Well, your Majesty. Now we know. They've wrecked our Congo.

BASILIO Alas!

MASSENS Majesty, they're savages. Order must be restored, and I see only one way.

BASILIO I know, Massens. But unfortunately international law doesn't allow it.

MASSENS Your Majesty, this is no time to tie our hands with juridical scruples. Human lives are at stake, European lives. That's more important than any law.

BASILIO You're right, Massens. That's more important than any law. Very well. I give you carte blanche.

MASSENS (*in a thundering voice*) Forward march!

A vision of Belgian paratroopers in action. Darkness.

LUMUMBA'S VOICE (*shouting the Congolese war cry*) People of the Congo! *Luma! Luma!*

The war tomtoms sound in the night, spreading the news of the Belgian attack.

SCENE 10

LUMUMBA, KALA, *and a* PILOT *in a plane over Elisabethville. Wind, rain, lightning.*

LUMUMBA Damn weather! Look! Look! The wind's uprooting the trees. And the rain! The weather's as bad as the situation in the Congo, and that's something. Looks like a herd of phantom elephants stampeding through a bamboo forest. Isn't it a little early for the rainy season to be starting?

KALA Yes, the weather's bad. Definitely . . . But when God is perplexed, we ignorant mortals call it fog.

LUMUMBA Pilot, aren't we going to land soon? This trip is interminable. Where are we?

PILOT We'll be over Elisabethville in a moment. Have patience, your Excellency. We're in the middle of a tropical hurricane. Wait. The radio operator's trying to tell me something. (*A paper is handed him. He reads it aloud.*) Isn't that nice! Msiri and Tzumbi in person in the control tower. The Katanga authorities won't let us land.

LUMUMBA Msiri? Tzumbi? The Katanga authorities? Are we or are we not the Congo authorities? Does Katanga belong to the Congo, or doesn't it? Pilot, I order you to land. Immediately.

PILOT It can't be done, sir. Not in this weather. They've turned out the lights on the airstrip. Look, you can see for yourself.

LUMUMBA Traitor! Flemish dog! You disobey me? Are you in cahoots with the secessionists?

As the plane regains altitude.

PILOT Where do we head for, Mr. President?

KALA Leopoldville.

LUMUMBA No. It's arms that we need! Arms! To Moscow! To Moscow!

SCENE 11

At the Congolese parliament in Leopoldville. As the SENATORS *take their places, the* SANZA PLAYER *passes, singing:*

Palm wine man climbing the palm tree,
Come down, little ant,
Come down, little sparrow,
The good souls sing at the foot of the palm tree.
Up you go, palm wine man, up you go,
Sparrow drunk with freedom.

FIRST SENATOR Honorable colleagues: The Congo has become a vast cemetery; the Belgians have been conducting themselves like the Roman legions.

SECOND SENATOR I wish to call the attention of the government to our finances—yes, our finances. The Congolese treasury has evaporated, the north wind has blown it away. Where are we going to find money now? The Bank of the Congo has been transferred to Katanga. Are we going to sleep while Rome burns? That is the question I ask the government. I for my part intend to die in the toga of a senator.

THIRD SENATOR Fellow senators! We haven't come here to discourage each other. But there are some things that cannot be passed over in silence. Our prime minister and our president are never here. We must have the courage to look the facts in the face. When we think they are in Leo, they are in Matadi; when they are supposed to be in Matadi, they are in Banana; in Banana the word is that they've gone off to Moanda or Boma. They fly right and left, all over the place, and always the two of them. Gentlemen, it's customary in a civilized country that when the husband goes out the wife stays home.

LUMUMBA I for my part, gentlemen, assure you that we don't travel enough. Ah, I wish I could multiply and divide myself, so as to be everywhere at once. In Matadi, in Boma, in Elisabethville, in Luluabourg, to crush the enemy's many-headed plot. For the plot is everywhere. Ever since the very first day of our independence, I've seen the Belgians, men ravaged by hatred and eaten by resentment, hatching their plot. General Massens stirring up the militia against the government, representing us as a gang of politicians and unscrupulous profiteers. The Belgian ambassador, Mynher Van den Putt, doing everything in his power to sabotage, to undermine, to disorganize our republic, putting pressure on all Belgian technicians and civil servants to leave the country. From the very first day General Massens has been setting the scene for his raids, working up a pretext for his mercenaries to step in. That's the Belgian plot, gentlemen. Their treaty of friendship with us? As far as they are concerned, it's a scrap of paper. We let them maintain staging areas on our territory. They turn them into armed camps from which to attack us. That's the Belgian plot. They've shelled Kabalo, Boma, and Matadi! But the worst was yet to come. Today, July 11, 1960, Tzumbi, our brother Abraham Tzumbi, seconded by Msiri, incited, advised, and financed by the Belgians, has proclaimed the independence of Katanga, our richest province, without consulting the population. And what is the first act of this independent state? To conclude a treaty of military assistance and economic cooperation with Belgium. That's the Belgian plot. Have I made myself clear? People of the Congo, we've got to smash that plot. People of the Congo, we have paid dearly for our independence. Are we going to let them throttle it now? And you, my brother Africans, Mali, Guinea, Ghana, we cry out to you across our borders. (*Shouting.*) Africa! Do they think Africa is deaf? Or faint-hearted? Or do they think Africa is too feeble to deliver us? I know the colonialists are powerful. But I swear to you by Africa: All of us united, together, will subdue the monster. Brothers, already the Congo has won a great victory. We sent out an appeal to the United Nations and the United Nations has sent a favorable reply. Tomorrow Mr. Hammarskjöld, Secretary General of the United Nations, whose integrity and impartiality are recognized by all, will be with us in Leopoldville. We trust him. The United Nations will see to it that justice is done. Full justice.

Gentlemen, I have finished. In a word, our independence, our existence as a nation, our freedom, and everything that Dependa means to our people are at stake.

Brothers, I stand here before you, and through you I look every single Congolese straight in the eye. And what I have to tell him is best said by our Kikongo song:

Brother, in your hand
You hold what belongs to you.
Are you going to let another
Take it away?

You all know the answer. *Kizola ko.* I won't allow it.

SENATORS (*rising and shouting*) *Kizola ko. Kizola ko.*

SCENE 12

Darkness, then light. In the background a group of European experts take their places around HAMMARSKJÖLD. *They have just landed in Leopoldville after ferrying across the Congo from Brazzaville. The* SANZA PLAYER *crosses the stage, singing:*

Father Congo
river of flowers and islands.
What swells your gray heart
and shakes it with sobs?

HAMMARSKJÖLD (*to his experts*) Gentlemen, as we set foot for the first time on the soil of the Congo, I am sure that you all share my feeling that this is a profoundly significant moment. The Congo is not only a country, a state, an unhappy state that needs and has asked for our help and protection, it is also a proving ground for the international action that is the aim and ideal of our organization. The work that awaits you here is a great deal more than academic fact-finding. We shall be working for the future of the world.

Gentlemen, in this hour I wish not to sum up my instructions to you, but to define the spirit in which I want you to confront your task here in the Congo. And I believe that there is no better way of doing so than to cite the words of the poet:

I recognize no quarrel. I say, let us live,
torch in the wind, flame in the wind,
And in us let all men be so mingled with the flame
  and so consumed
that in the mounting torch a greater light is
  born within us . . .
Tingling the flesh in which the itching soul keeps
  us still rebellious

And it is a time of high fortune when the great
adventurers of the soul
seek passage on the high road of mankind, questioning
the whole threshing floor of the earth, trying to
discover
the meaning of this vast disorder, questioning
the bed, the waters of the sky, and the tide-
marks of the river of shadow on the earth,
perhaps even rebelling at finding no answer . . .

But here come our hosts. Meditate on those words, gentlemen, meditate on them and find strength in them as you go forth like a new order of chivalry upon the high road of humanity.

The Congolese delegation enters and advances toward the Europeans.

Gentlemen of the Congolese government, I am glad to be here in the Congo at a time when the United Nations, at your request, has undertaken to help you, by all the means at its disposal, to lay the foundations of a happy and prosperous future. Seeing me for the first time, you must wonder what sort of man I am. That is only natural. And it's a question I want to answer. I am a neutral. A good many people think there's no such animal. But there is, thank the Lord. I am a *neutral,* and I'm here to prove it. The problems confronting the Congo must be solved by conciliation and diplomacy. They cannot be solved by force and intimidation, but only in a spirit of peace and justice. And that is why neutrals can make themselves useful here in the Congo, why they can help to find a satisfactory solution to your problems. For come to think of it, what does the word "neutral" mean? It means "fair," it means "just." And when I say "just," I take the word in the most exacting sense. The just, said Meister Eckhart, "are those who have left their selves behind; who look for nothing above or below or alongside of themselves; who seek neither wealth nor glory nor comfort nor pleasure nor interest nor sanctity nor reward, but have made themselves free from all that."

In short, those who give God their due and through whom God is glorified.

That, gentlemen, is the spirit in which we have come among you. To help you to overcome your passions, to bring appeasement to your hearts. To help you to achieve justice and peace. Justice and peace. Those are my words of greeting to the Congo. Long live the Congo!

SCENE 13

As the Congolese crowd demonstrates, dancing and singing the "Independence Hot-cha-cha," the AMBASSADOR OF THE GRAND OCCIDENT *steps forward.*

AMBASSADOR I know my country is getting a bad reputation. They say we're trigger-happy. But is there any room for rockingchair politics when the world is off its rocker? With people going berserk all over the world, somebody's got to make them behave. And, praise the Lord, Providence has picked us for the job . . . You heard what the man said. "To Moscow! To Moscow!" That's what he said. Well, I've got news for you folks. They call us the policemen of the world. Okay. But we're the fire department, too. And it's our job to check the flames of incendiary Communism. Wherever it shows its ugly head. And that includes the Congo. A word to the wise!

ACT II

SCENE 1

The same African bar as in Act I; the GIRLS *and* MAMA MAKOSI *moving about.* LUMUMBA, MOKUTU, *and friends take seats.*

LUMUMBA I like these places . . . I know it upsets the Pharisees, but . . .

MOKUTU All the same, it's not going to help our reputation any. Especially abroad. They'll say we're a lot of sex-crazed apes. Yes, I know. The scenes of your youth, and all that. But things have changed. We're ministers and top brass now. You're a *Mbota Mutu,* a big shot, and don't forget it.

LUMUMBA Don't make me laugh. Let the ladies' betterment societies turn up their noses. It gives me a kick. Vice was the only freedom the white men left us. And then they complain about our morals. Same as the Americans complain about Harlem . . .

MOKUTU Maybe so, but you're not seriously thinking of coming here to discuss affairs of state? Hasn't the Congo got a bad enough reputation as it is?

LUMUMBA (*ironically*) Not a bad idea. I'll think it over . . . but now let's talk about something serious. When the Europeans came, the Congo started to disintegrate. It began to rot, piece by piece, and to stink. The state, the family, the people. So maybe this dive with its shady mixed fauna is a faithful reflection of our Congo today. Garbage rotting in the sun. But here and there you see something fresh and new sprouting through the compost. And that's ground for encouragement. (*To* MAMA MAKOSI, *who approaches.*) Well, Mama Makosi, how you doing?

MAMA MAKOSI Hello, Patrice. Say, we're giving a big freedom

ball. Can I count on you? It's going to be terrific: we've rented the Elite Bar.

MOKUTU Don't be unreasonable, Mama Makosi. Your old friend Patrice is Prime Minister now. You can't expect . . .

MAMA MAKOSI Oh, come off it. He'll always be the same Patrice for us. Wherever he goes, we'll go. And vice versa. He's not ashamed of his friends.

GIRL Oh yes, it would be so sweet. I'm the union song leader, and you know what? We're working up a beautiful song. (*She sings.*)

When I wear my green bandana . . .

Enter the SANZA PLAYER *disguised as a madman. He passes between the tables, humming.*

MOKUTU Who's that character?

MAMA MAKOSI He's just a crazy man. Been coming around for the last few days and we can't get rid of him.

MOKUTU Can't you call the police?

LUMUMBA Leave the poor man alone. He isn't bothering anybody.

SANZA PLAYER (*declaiming*) Ah, God of the Christians! Why did you let the white men go away . . . ?

MOKUTU Get a load of that. He can't live without his daily ration of kicks. He's an addict.

LUMUMBA No, Mokutu, it's worse than that . . . It takes a lot of thinking to face the truth that God is dead. Our country people . . .

SANZA PLAYER Oh God, why did you make black men so wicked?

MOKUTU Good grief!

SANZA PLAYER I came down the river, looking for the white men who left my village, and I didn't find them; the white men left our village and the black men are wicked. The black men are cursed . . .

LUMUMBA See, Mokutu? It's useful to hang around these places. That's the bitter truth of our Congo. That's the disease we've got to cure our people of. Mama Makosi, I want to thank you and your bar for this lesson. And don't worry, you can count on me,

I'll come to your ball, and I'll bring my Cabinet. (*They exit.*)

SANZA PLAYER Let's throw off this mask. I've said enough. I've done enough. Even if a man has good eyes, you've got to show him certain things. But he'll see the rest for himself. And it's plain enough to see. It doesn't take a hurricane to a part a chicken's tail feathers.

SCENE 2

A meeting of the Congolese Cabinet. LUMUMBA, MPOLO, MOKUTU, CROULARD (LUMUMBA'*s Belgian secretary*), *and others.*

LUMUMBA Gentlemen, that is the situation. There's no time to lose. We're in the midst of a battle. On every front. The survival of the Congo is at stake.

CROULARD I beg your pardon, Your Excellency, but Mr. Bunche, the Assistant Secretary of the United Nations, wants to see you. He says it's urgent.

LUMUMBA Who told him to come here? Who sent for him? But never mind, Croulard, as long as you've interrupted us, pass me the file on the district chiefs . . . And another thing, gentlemen, we've got to take up the question of visas. All sorts of people are coming in without visas. Or worse, with Belgian visas.

CROULARD Your Excellency, Mr. Bunche is very insistent. He says . . .

LUMUMBA Croulard! Will you kindly let us work? (*He rushes to the phone.*) Hello. Stanleyville? Is that you, Jean? . . . All right, arrange the meeting. I'll speak . . . I can tell you right now, there's going to be some excitement. We're going to abolish the district militias and mobilize the unemployed. Hello? Oh yes, I'd forgotten. Don't forget to order beer . . . by the carload . . . Enough for the whole population . . . Good-bye. (*He hangs up.*)

Enter ISAAC KALONJI.

ISAAC Howdy! Howdy, everybody . . . All that's fine and dandy, my dear Prime Minister. But when are we going into Katanga? What are we waiting for? All you've got to do is make a beeline for Bakwanga! Our partisans will rise up . . . Albert Kalonji has taken it on the lam . . . Tzumbi is saying his prayers . . .

MPOLO I agree with Isaac. We need Bakwanga. That's where the diamonds are. And what's a crown without diamonds?

LUMUMBA We need. We need. Just get me some planes. But don't worry, Isaac, I'm attending to it.

MOKUTU Not just planes, Mr. Prime Minister . . . troops . . . no money, no troops. That's the way soldiers are, and they haven't been paid in two months.

LUMUMBA All right, all right. We'll give you money.

MOKUTU Thank you. But you haven't heard the last of my complaints. I won't stand for amateurishness. You made me a colonel, I'm going to be a real colonel.

LUMUMBA What's on your mind?

MOKUTU Well, I hear that Mpolo has been going around with a colonel's cap and a swagger stick . . . The government will have to choose between us. It's either him or me.

LUMUMBA Come, come, Mokutu, there's nothing to get excited about . . . you were away on a tour of inspection. We thought it wise to appoint Mpolo a colonel too. In this situation two of you aren't too many. If you're not satisfied, we can appoint you general and Mpolo can be chief of staff.

Hubbub among the ministers.

SANZA PLAYER That's it . . . A good compromise. Now everybody will be happy.

MOKUTU I'm sorry. I'm telling you plainly. The army isn't an operetta. I'd rather resign.

LUMUMBA All right. Mokutu remains chief of staff. As for you, Mpolo, we'll see later on. Meanwhile, take off that uniform. Well, Croulard, what about that file on the district chiefs? All those petty potentates, those police dogs who helped the Belgians to crush our people. If we want real leaders, we've got to get rid of them first. And where do you find real leaders except among the common people? Well, Croulard, how about that file?

CROULARD I can't find it, Your Excellency . . . This place is such a mess. Well, here at least is a big bundle I wasn't looking for . . . I open it, and what do I see? Guess. A bundle of telegrams. Messages from twenty nations or more, recognizing the Republic of the Congo. And nobody's read them. Been here for two weeks. It's a mess, I tell you. A mess.

LUMUMBA Luckily we have you, Croulard, to make a little order.

MOKUTU (*grumbling*) And to poke his nose into a lot of things that are none of his business.

MPOLO Comrade Prime Minister, we were speaking of Katanga just now. Maybe if we can't take Katanga for the moment, we could at least take Leopoldville. The Abako youth organization are acting as if they owned the streets. Agitating against us under our own windows.

MOKUTU Careful, gentlemen. A blow at the Abako is a blow at the President.

LUMUMBA Mpolo, you're the youth minister, aren't you? Why can't you set up your own youth organization? The NCM Youth Brigade. Every time the Abako demonstrates, you stage a counter-demonstration. That'll do it. You don't need government intervention for that.

MPOLO Okay, chief!

Enter the CHIEF OF POLICE.

Well, well, here comes my police force. What news?

CHIEF OF POLICE Excellency, another article by Gabriel Makoso in *Christian Conscience.* A diatribe by Monsignor Malula . . . and leaflets, millions of leaflets!

LUMUMBA Never mind the leaflets. I know them by heart: Lumumba has mortgaged the Congo to the Russians, Lumumba has sold his soul to the Devil, Lumumba has received millions from the Czech Ambassador. (*Taking the newspaper.*) This is more serious. (*He glances through it.*) Oh, oh! Monsignor doesn't pull his punches. Hmm. Read it to us, Mpolo.

MPOLO (*reading*) "And first and foremost we must denounce anticlericalism, that waste-product of the Occident, imported into the Congo by unworthy rulers. To arms against the enemies of religion wherever they may be, the Freemasons like Makessa, the self-styled atheists like the ignominious Lumumba!"

LUMUMBA Not bad for a bishop. The ignominious Lumumba! Well, he's going to hear from the ignominious Lumumba. They want war? All right, they'll get it.

Mr. Police Chief, do your duty. You will arrest Makoso and shut his paper down.

MOKUTU I beg your pardon, Mr. Prime Minister. Isn't that unwise? Won't it make for unrest?

LUMUMBA Watch your step, Mokutu . . . stick to your own department. You're in charge of the army. I've agreed to that. Politics is my business. And don't worry about the unrest, I'll know how to deal with it . . . Gentlemen, we can strike, or we can let ourselves be struck down. I have made up my mind: We will strike.

I demand that Lundula be given full powers: the army will arrest everyone, white or black, who attempts to stir up trouble. No half-measures. No hesitation. Which reminds me, the Abako is making too much noise. They've scheduled a congress in Thysville. They're talking secession. Another secession. Well, there's not going to be any congress. Their congress is cancelled. Come to think of it, they haven't a leg to stand on. The law requires two weeks' notice. They didn't give it . . . Agreed, gentlemen?

MPOLO Agreed. The law is the law. No special privileges.

LUMUMBA As for Katanga, Isaac is right. That's our main problem . . . the key to all our other problems . . . I'll see Hammarskjöld . . . The United Nations is here to help us . . . You'll get your planes, Mokutu, you'll get your planes. As Isaac says, Tzumbi had better say his prayers.

The SANZA PLAYER *passes, singing:*

Sun and rain
Driving rain
Rising sun
The elephant
Begets a son.

SCENE 3

LUMUMBA'*s office.*

LUMUMBA Mr. Secretary General, I appealed to the United Nations. I was the first chief of state to put full trust in your organization. Who would have thought that my first words to you would be words not of thanks but of reproach and recrimination. Please believe that I deeply regret it. But unfortunately you have put a very personal interpretation on the resolutions of the Security Council: the Belgians are still in the Congo. And the United Nations is holding diplomatic conversations with the traitor Tzumbi.

HAMMARSKJÖLD I am the Secretary General of the United Nations Organization. I am responsible solely to the General Assembly. I owe you no accounts. But I can tell you this much: I have no orders to massacre the people of Katanga.

LUMUMBA You have called off the military operations that would have enabled us to enter Elisabethville without striking a blow.

HAMMARSKJÖLD If I called them off, or postponed them, it was because Bunche's reports left no room for doubt: it would have been necessary to fight for every street, for every house in Elisabethville.

LUMUMBA Nonsense. The population of Katanga are only waiting to throw off Tzumbi's yoke. They would have welcomed you as a liberator. But you saw fit to confer with the rebel . . .

HAMMARSKJÖLD Mr. Prime Minister, I followed the dictates of my conscience. It is a point of doctrine, a point of my doctrine, that the UN must not participate in an internal conflict, constitutional or otherwise, and that its armed forces cannot be utilized in such conflicts. I am not saying there is no problem. There is. But it is a problem that I do not despair of solving. President

Tzumbi has impressed me as a sensible man. I shall make every effort to reason with him and convince him. In any case, this country has suffered enough. I have no desire to add a full-scale war to its misfortunes.

LUMUMBA I appreciate your solicitude. But tell me, what greater misfortune can there be for this country than the secession of its richest province? You speak of resistance in Katanga. Tzumbi and Msiri must have had a good laugh. They had already rented houses for themselves in Rhodesia. Your Bunche is as gullible as a child. He misjudged the situation. Unless . . . After all, Bunche is an American . . .

HAMMARSKJÖLD That has nothing to do with it. I permit no one to cast aspersions on the honesty and impartiality of my co-workers. I am a neutral, surrounded by neutrals who put the interest of the world at large before any consideration deriving from their own personal nationality.

LUMUMBA I leave it to history to judge that. In any event, since the UN has failed to meet its obligations, to carry out its mission, the government of the Congolese Republic will assume its responsibilities. We will reduce the secession of Katanga by force. Our troops are ready. The campaign must be concluded before the rainy season. I trust that the UN will not refuse to lend me a certain number of planes to transport our armed forces.

HAMMARSKJÖLD Planes? I thought I had made it clear to you that the United Nations troops are by definition a peace force, not a force of aggression.

LUMUMBA There you have it, that's the impartiality of the UN. Every day Belgian arms and mercenaries pour into the Congo. And you just look on.

HAMMARSKJÖLD You are unjust. I have addressed a strong note of protest on the subject to the Brussels government.

LUMUMBA A note! Yes, a note. And meanwhile the secessionists are building up their forces. Everybody knows it, and what do you do? You not only refuse to take action, but you prevent us from acting. Very well! The Congo will do without your help. We still have a few friends in the world. We will manage without you neutrals.

HAMMARSKJÖLD I wish to remind you that all foreign aid to the Congo must pass through United Nations channels.

LUMUMBA You don't do things by halves, Mr. Secretary General. Very well, but permit me in turn to remind you that it is a point of doctrine, a point of my doctrine, that the Congo is an independent country and that we haven't shaken off Belgian rule in order to accept the rule of the United Nations. Good day, Mr. Secretary General. The Russians will lend me the planes that you refuse me. In a few days we shall be in Elisabethville. As for you, whatever may happen, I hope you will not one day pay too dearly for your illusions.

HAMMARSKJÖLD Mr. Lumumba, I learned one thing long ago: to say yes to Destiny, whatever it may be. But since we are exchanging good wishes, I hope that whatever may befall, you will not one day have to pay too dearly for your imprudence and impulsiveness . . . Good-bye.

The SANZA PLAYER *passes, singing:*

A magpie on a cherry tree
Preens himself and plays the peacock,
Saying "This tree belongs to me."
Oh, let me die in poverty
If riches means a magpie's tree.

SCENE 4

Darkness, then half-light. Alarming noises. Gradually, as in a nightmare, groups appear: women, witches, warriors armed with spears and blowguns. A voice rises, the VOICE OF CIVIL WAR.

VOICE OF CIVIL WAR

Boy, pour the palm wine.
Hot and spicy,
Thick muddy dregs.

Pour the palm wine. When I'm drunk, I ask
For my sword, my sharpened sword that hangs
On the wall with buffalo horn and *assegai.*
Pour the palm wine, boy!
When I'm drunk, I take down my bow that hangs
On the wall with my war horn and *assegai.*
Boy, by day I'll fight
And at night, I'll praise my bow,
I'll honor it with a branch of wild grape.
I'll rub it with oil at night,
At night it deserves to shine like a mirror.
Boy! My machete!
A brave man isn't made to die in his bed,
A brave man is an elephant,
A spitting serpent.
Palm wine man, pour the wine, color of enemy
blood.
When the day returns, we'll face
The enemy eye to eye.
Boy! Pour the palm wine.
I'm drunk! On wine? On enemy blood? I don't know.
The spear is in my hands. Eiii!
The spear strikes and bends in the wound!
Enemy head, I'll display you in every village.

SCENE 5

Meeting of the Congolese Cabinet.

LUMUMBA Gentlemen, I've got big news for you. Our troops have taken Bakwanga. The traitor Kalonji has fled.

KALA A victory, unfortunately, that may cost us more than a defeat.

FIRST MINISTER I see what you mean, and I share your sentiments. We've got to admit that our army has had a heavy hand.

Six thousand Balubas killed. In the church of Saint-Jean of Bakwanga forty Baluba families massacred with the most atrocious cruelty.

SECOND MINISTER I demand that the army be recalled.

THIRD MINISTER Our army has dishonored us in the eyes of the world.

LUMUMBA Poor Balubas! Massacred by our soldiers in Kasai! Exterminated by Tzumbi's police in Katanga! They've been called the Jews of Africa. But a military campaign is never a battle of flowers.

KALA We're in a pretty mess all the same. The world press is up in arms against us. Especially the Belgian papers. And Hammarskjöld is raising hell in the UN. He accuses us of genocide.

LUMUMBA He does, does he? And where was Hammarskjöld when the Belgians were massacring our men and raping our women?

And now we're the savages!

So the Belgians are complaining? That's a good one. And who stirred up the Luluas against the Balubas? Who made the Balubas think the Luluas were getting ready to murder them? Who invented Chief Kalamba Mangole and started him plugging for a Lulua kingdom that would drive out the Balubas unless they submitted to the laws and customs of the Luluas? Who persuaded the Balubas and Luluas that they couldn't coexist anymore? In 1959. You remember? And what did the Belgian police do while they were cutting each other's throats? They looked on and smiled. And where was Lumumba then? In prison. And what about the Christian, civilized world press? What did it have to say then? And the world conscience? No! Do they think I'm going to let the Congo be torn limb from limb for fear of their hypocritical protests? Gentlemen, I reject your authority. (*He laughs.*) I reject your law, your morality, your whole system! Yes, my friends, let us celebrate. I want every Congolese citizen to drink a glass of beer to the capture of Bakwanga.

Tonight I'm going to make a speech on the radio to celebrate the taking of Bakwanga. Mpolo, we'll go to the Elite Bar tonight. No, to Cassian's. I know a Lulua girl. She's beautiful. Her name is Hélène Jewel. And she certainly is a jewel. Get in touch with her. I'm going to dance with her tonight. With a Lulua girl. In the eyes of the whole world.

And you, gentlemen of the press and pulpit, champions of the world conscience, I expect you to light up the dance floor with your grimaces.

SCENE 6

Cassian's Bar. LUMUMBA *and* HÉLÈNE JEWEL, *dancing in a pink and green half-light.*

HÉLÈNE

I dance things of cavernous darkness
blood's fire, keen snakes
caught in the brambles of exile.

LUMUMBA

I dance the sprouting of man and his saliva, salt.
And alone in the depths of his aloneness man sickens at the taste of his flesh, insipid cassava.

HÉLÈNE

I dance the pavonia flower that wheels around the sun, when every flick of the planet's lashes brightens the smooth purple of the living blood.

LUMUMBA

I dance the high vessel that with its blazoned prow governs the panic of Desire; the pavonia bird and its pavan.

HÉLÈNE

I dance the joy, sown by the sun, of the incongruous small rain planting its dispersed copper laughter in the briny flesh of the sea.

LUMUMBA

I dance the insect, more beautiful than any name, which in the core of the ripe fruit established its glutted weariness, gold and jade and obsidian.

HÉLÈNE

And now our dance is danced, the refrain closes its corolla as, proud to have sustained the unsustainable, ablaze and slaked with fire, the pavonia flower closes.

LUMUMBA

We have danced the dance of my life! When I am gone, when I
am spent like the blinding blind meteor in the night sky,
when the Congo is no more than a season seasoned with blood,
be beautiful, still beautiful, keeping
of the terrible days no more
than the few drops of dew that make
the hummingbird's plumes more beautiful
for having traversed the storm.
No sadness, darling. Dance with me till dawn
and give me heart
to go on to the end of the night.

SCENE 7

A room in the President's palace. KALA *is alone.*

KALA All I hear about is blood. Blood and horror. The Luluas killing the Balubas. The Balubas exterminating the Luluas. And our army, the National Army of the Congo, massacring everybody in sight.

Oh, this war! this war!

Yes, yes, I gave my consent. But do you think it's easy to say no to that goateed devil? Anyway, it was his decision. Let him take the consequences.

He's too highhanded.

That incident with the UN soldiers, for instance. Bunche wants to see him about it, Lumumba refers him to some undersecretary. Naturally—what would you expect—Bunche ends up in my office. What could I say? Nobody tells me anything, I said. And it's true. He doesn't tell me anything . . . What does he take me for? A figurehead? To tell the truth, he's a strange man. I'll never get used to him. Sometimes he's so sensitive, so full of fine feeling. I remember what he said to me before leaving for New York. "President, I leave you my heart."

"I leave you my heart." There was real friendship in those words. They came from the heart . . . Ah, what a man!

Maybe that's what I hold against him most, his impulsiveness. Always so agitated, so excited. A ball of fire! A hammerbird, always looking for somebody to ram his head into.

Our ancestors were right, a real chief doesn't get excited. He doesn't run around in circles. He is immobile and enduring. He concentrates. He is the concentrated essence of the country. And by concentrating, he emanates a gentle persuasive light . . . This fellow's a hothead. He doesn't emanate, he just sets everything on fire. He's a *Kintu-Kintu!* He'd turn the whole country upside down if I let him. He'd set the Congo on fire and the world with it. But I am here and I won't let him. I'm here to save the Congo and to save him from himself. Easy does it, Patrice. Go easy. Old Kala's here. He's here all right. And here to stay. They call me the old man. I'm not old. I'm slow. They say the tortoise is full of guile. Full of good sense would be more like it. I make my way slowly; slowly, *Kukutu Bvem, Kukutu Bvem.** And he's impetuous, a hothead.

I don't like hotheads even when they're right. They make me dizzy. And besides, sooner or later, they wear themselves out . . . But that's enough daydreaming. I've got to write this speech.

Actually I don't see why they all hound him so. But whom

* Onomatopoeia for the slow, deliberate movement of a turtle.

don't they hound? Ah, it's a bad world nowadays. They say Patrice leads me by the nose. They say I betrayed the Bakongo by accepting the presidency. They even dare to write: "Kala is Lumumba's woman." "Kala is Lumumba's wife."

That's stupid. A president is the chief. He's the king. Besides, I can dismiss him whenever I please. The constitution says so. The president makes the decisions, the ministers carry them out. Of course I don't mean to make use of my power. Patrice is intelligent, energetic, popular. Oh yes, he's popular all right. They can slander him all they like, they can't stop him from being popular. And there's strength in popularity.

And I've got to take it into consideration . . . But why in God's name are they all out to get him? Look what they've thought up now: Patrice is a communist. And by protecting him, I'm giving aid and comfort to the Communist International.

That's nonsense. Patrice a communist! I remember the look on his face that time, in the midst of our worst trouble with the Belgians, when I suggested a telegram to Khrushchev. Do you know what he said? "It's impossible, Mr. President. They're already saying that I've sold out to the communists. That would clinch it. You're a Christian, you can do it if you want to. And even so, they'll say I maneuvered you."

Hm . . . Maneuvered me? That would take quite a man. Quite a man. But it's true. He is quite a man. The American ambassador said to me last week: "If Lumumba went into a meeting of Congolese politicians with a tray, disguised as a waiter, he'd be Prime Minister by the time he left." But do they think it's so easy to fool old Kala . . . Do they really? . . . I'd better consult Bishop Malula. He's got a head on his shoulders . . . And I'll ask Mokutu to go with me . . . (*He laughs.*) I could have been a bishop myself . . . Why . . . we were at the seminary together . . . As a bishop I'd have had fewer worries, that's sure . . . But no man chooses his fate . . . Oh Lord, oh Lord. Oh, this presidency! . . . Well, how about it? Am I going to write that speech? Come along, Kala. Make a little effort. (*He starts to work.*)

The SANZA PLAYER *enters, singing:*

Thoughts come in sudden flashes
I see the croaking frog
The chameleon on his branch
Waiting with darting tongue.

SCENE 8

LUMUMBA'*s apartment.* LUMUMBA *and his wife,* PAULINE.

PAULINE Patrice, I'm afraid. Oh God! I can feel the knives of hatred in the darkness, and everywhere I see termites, toads, spiders, the crawling vermin of envy. Patrice, I can see their filthy plots tightening around you . . .

LUMUMBA What is there to be afraid of? It's true I have enemies . . . but the people are for me. The people are my shield. I speak to them and they understand me, they follow me. This is a revolution, Pauline, and in a revolution it's the people that count.

PAULINE The people, yes. But the people are weak and disarmed. They're credulous. And your enemies are sly and patient, and they've got the whole world behind them.

LUMUMBA Don't exaggerate . . . I have friends, too . . . faithful friends. We stick together . . . We're like a dog's hairs, all in the same bed.

PAULINE Friends, friends! . . . I can think of a dozen of them who owe you everything. They dance attendance, but they're only waiting for the chance to knife you. Some of them would sell you for a mess of pottage. I feel it in my bones.

LUMUMBA Oh, you women. So cynical. Always fearing the worst.

PAULINE And you men? And you yourself? So innocent and so trusting. You're a child, Patrice . . . For instance, I don't trust your Mokutu . . . I don't have to tell you that he was an informer for the Belgians . . .

LUMUMBA I know, I know that, Pauline . . . But I also know what the situation was in those days. A lot of people had no other choice than to starve and let their children starve or to play the stoolpigeon. It's not pretty, no, it's not pretty. But some of the people who disgraced themselves in those days can be saved . . . And Mokutu is one of them . . . He's intelligent, shrewd . . . not much character, but he's grateful to me for my confidence in him . . . My confidence helps him to redeem himself in his own eyes . . . I can answer for his loyalty.

PAULINE God protect you, Patrice. God protect you.

LUMUMBA And besides, what can he do to me? . . . Stop worrying . . . They can't hurt me as long as Kala and I stick together, and we always will.

PAULINE Are you so sure, Patrice? I have an idea that he's jealous of you . . .

PATRICE I repeat: never have two men seen more eye to eye than Kala and I . . . He has his faults, but he's a patriot . . . He's the chief of a powerful tribe, an excellent tribe, the Bakongo! And remember the proverb: Look at the cock's beak and you'll see the whole cock.

PAULINE All the same. So many people are trying to make trouble between you . . . He's secretive . . . sly . . . You just be careful. Sitting on his throne as rigid and serene as a copper god, all he seems to think of right now is holding his scepter up. But when the time comes, he's perfectly capable, if you ask me, of bringing it down on your head—without a word of warning.

LUMUMBA And you think I'm so easy to crush? You think I have no weapons, no friends . . . But we've talked enough, Pauline . . . I'm tired, give me my guitar. (*She gives him the guitar.*) I don't know why . . . I've got this sad tune running through my head . . . It's a Swahili song. Ever heard it, Pauline?

The lights are slowly dimmed as he sings.

Would you lean
Even your finger

On a rotting tree?
Life is a rotting tree.
Don't lean, don't lean
Even a finger
On the rotting tree.

LUMUMBA (*yawning*) Ah! Dependa wears you out! (*He dozes off, then wakes with a start.*) What's this?

In his nightmare a BISHOP, KALA, *and* MOKUTU *appear stage front.* KALA *and* MOKUTU *are kneeling.*

BISHOP My children, the time has come to prove your love for the Church and to chastise the enemies of our holy religion. The Church is relying on you. In the name of the Father, the Son, and the Holy Ghost, amen.

PAULINE Poor Patrice. Wake up. It's almost time for the news. (*She turns the radio dial, a speech by* KALA LUBU *is heard.*)

KALA My dear compatriots, I have an important announcement to make: The Mayor, I beg your pardon, the Prime Minister, I mean, who was appointed by the King of Belgium in accordance with the provisional constitution, has betrayed his trust. He has taken arbitrary measures which have provoked dissension among the government and the people. He has deprived many citizens of their basic liberties. He has plunged the country into an abominable civil war. In view of all this, I have esteemed it necessary to dissolve the government. I have appointed Joseph Ileo Prime Minister and empowered him to form a new government. I have already assured myself of the total and wholehearted support of our glorious Congolese Army and of its commander, Colonel Mokutu. I hope and trust that I can also count on the discipline and patriotism of the entire Congolese people. God protect the Congo!

SCENE 9

LUMUMBA's *office that same evening. Enter* MPOLO *in haste, a moment later* LUMUMBA.

LUMUMBA The bastard. But he hasn't heard the last of Patrice Lumumba. President of the Republic! Who made him President of the Republic?

But maybe it's all for the best, Mpolo. The Congo of the provisional constitution, the two-headed monster born of the fornications at the Round Table, was a compromise. I accepted it only as a temporary evil. And now King Kala, on his own initiative, has shown that the time for compromise has passed.

So much the better. The time has come to get rid of King Kala. Notify the radio station. I am going to address the nation.

MPOLO You're right. It's time for us to strike. But what about the UN? Will they be neutral?

LUMUMBA The UN? The UN is a fiction. What exists, regardless of the color of their helmets, is men, soldiers from all over Africa. And luckily for us, the radio station is in the hands of the Ghanaians. A soldier of Nkrumah isn't going to refuse aid and comfort to Lumumba. Send for Ghana!

SCENE 10

The Radio Building.

LUMUMBA I'm glad to see you, Colonel. Ghana is a great country, dear to the hearts of all true Africans. I for my part shall never forget that it was in Ghana—thanks to Nkrumah—that the African first threw off the chains of colonialism and stood up a free man.

GHANA Independence is one thing, disorder is another. And that is what I see in the Congo.

LUMUMBA We shall overcome it, Colonel, and you will help us. I trust that Mpolo has given you my message. The people are in need of explanations and directives. I will speak on the radio tonight.

GHANA So I have heard, Mr. Lumumba. Unfortunately, Monsieur Cordelier, the United Nations delegate in Leopoldville, has given strict orders: all political activity in the Congo is suspended until further notice, and no member of any political faction is to be given access to the radio.

LUMUMBA So now Cordelier is giving orders in the Congo! But let it pass . . . In any case, his orders don't apply to me. I shall address the country not as President of the National Congo Movement but as Prime Minister.

GHANA Mr. Lumumba, we have a proverb in our country: "The state is an egg. Squeeze it too tight and it will break; not tight enough, and it will fall and smash." I don't know whether you have squeezed too tight or not tight enough, but the fact is that there is no longer a Congolese state.

LUMUMBA Am I to understand that you, on your own responsibility, deny me the use of my country's radio?

GHANA I am only a soldier, sir. I carry out orders.

LUMUMBA Oh, oh! Perhaps you didn't realize, Colonel, that your president is my friend? That Ghana, more than an ally, is our brother country? That the government in Accra has promised me its total and unconditional support? Your cowardice and insolence leaves me aghast. And I warn you that I shall not fail to inform your president, my friend, Kwame Nkrumah.

GHANA Sir, here in the Congo I am not in the service of Ghana, but of the United Nations. I am a soldier, sir, not a politician. As for my relations with Nkrumah, the two of us will straighten that out when the time comes, without your help. You have enough to do in the Congo.

LUMUMBA I understand. You call yourself a soldier. No, I'll tell you what you are. You're just one more traitor.

Nkrumah wrote me: "Brother, you must keep as cool as a cucumber." He's right. Treason is worse than toad venom, worse than the scaly pangolin coiled around its branch. To keep calm in the presence of an African traitor I'd need to have water in my veins like a Ghanaian cucumber, not Congolese blood.

GHANA (*drawing his revolver*) Everybody knows that a man who sets foot in this lousy country has to be prepared for anything. But there's one thing I'll never put up with, less in this filthy Congo than anywhere else, and that's the insolence of a half-baked communist.

LUMUMBA Fire! Go ahead and fire! You see that I'm as cool as a cucumber.

GHANA (*returning his pistol to its holster*) Come to think of it, no . . . The Congolese will attend to it themselves.

Exit GHANA, *enter the* SANZA PLAYER *and* MOKUTU *with a detachment of paratroopers.*

SANZA PLAYER Fellow Africans, that's the tragedy. A hunter catches sight of a crowned stork in the treetop. Luckily the tortoise has seen the hunter. The stork is saved, you will say. And indeed, the tortoise tells the big leaf, who's supposed to tell the creeper, who's supposed to tell the bird. Oh no! It's everybody for himself. Result: the hunter kills the bird, takes the big leaf to wrap the bird in, and cuts the creeper to tie up the leaf . . . And oh yes, I forgot. He even walks off with the tortoise. Africans, my brothers! When will you understand?

SCENE 11

LUMUMBA'*s home, occupied by* MOKUTU'*s paratroopers.*

LUMUMBA Thank you for coming. I'm glad you recognize that I am entitled to an explanation.

MOKUTU There's nothing to explain. Civil war, foreign war, anarchy. Patrice, I'm afraid you're a luxury the Congo can't afford.

LUMUMBA Can you be sincere? Do you really think you're saving the Congo? Doesn't it occur to you that by wrecking our constitutional government before we've even had time to set it up, you are endangering the very life of your country?

MOKUTU You'd have made things easier for us by stepping down of your own accord. But that's too much to expect of a politician. I have no other course than to dismiss you. But the old man is mistaken. I'm dismissing him too . . . I've decided to neutralize the government.

LUMUMBA When I hear big words like that, I can't help smelling a rat. Exactly what are you driving at?

MOKUTU It's perfectly simple. The President fires the Prime Minister. The Prime Minister strikes back and fires the President. I'm firing both of you. We're sick of politicians.

LUMUMBA In other words, you've decided to seize power. Well, after all, you won't be the first colonel to stage a coup d'état. But watch your step, Mokutu. The day when every discontented officer feels entitled to make a grab for power, there won't be much left of our country. A gang of thieves is no substitute for a state.

MOKUTU Don't you dare to impugn my honesty. I am a soldier and always will be. I have appointed a committee of specialists to run the government until order is restored. Meanwhile I'm calling off the civil war. I have ordered the army to suspend operations against Kasai. There's plenty of work to do right here in Leopoldville.

LUMUMBA Mokutu, I won't remind you of our friendship, of the struggles we've been through together, but . . .

MOKUTU No, there's no point in talking about the past. Sure. I helped you to get out of prison. I was with you at the Round Table conference in Brussels. I campaigned for you day and night. Five years of friendship. But I refuse to let friendship interfere with my duty as a citizen and a Congolese patriot. This is the parting of the ways. It's my duty to neutralize you.

LUMUMBA You're right, this is no time for personal sentiment. But have you ever stopped to think about Africa? Look here. No need of a wall map, it's engraved in the palm of my hand.

Here's Northern Rhodesia; its heart is the Copper Belt. A silent country, except for a foreman's curses now and then, the bark of a police dog, the burbling of a Colt—they've gunned down a black man, who drops without a word. Look here, next door. Southern Rhodesia. Millions of Negroes robbed, dispossessed, herded into the so-called townships.

And here's Angola. What's its main article of export? Not sugar, not coffee, but slaves. Yes, Colonel, slaves. Two hundred thousand men a year sent to the mines of South Africa in exchange for good money to help replenish Papa Salazar's empty treasury.

And dangling from it like a rag, this little island, this rock, San Tomé, devouring niggers by the thousands, by the millions. Africa's penal colony. (*He sings.*)

They took our boy away,
Sent him to San Tomé
'Cause he had no card,
Aié
He never came back 'cause death
Took him away,
Aié
They sent him to San Tomé.

Funny you never heard that song. I'll teach it to you, Mokutu, if you give me time. Well, further down there's South Africa, the racist slave camp, with its tanks and planes, its Bible, its laws, its courts, its press, its hatred, its lies—its hard, cruel heart. That's our Africa, Mokutu. Prostrate, bound, trampled, a target for white men's guns. But there's hope, you'll say. They suffer, but they hope. And it's true. Because deep down in their dungeon, like a diver deep under the sea, they see a spot of light on the surface, a spot of light, growing, growing. Why shouldn't they hope? There's been Ghana, Guinea, Senegal, Mali . . . Dahomey, Cameroun. Not so long ago, Togoland. And now the Congo. And imprisoned Africa says to itself: "Tomorrow will be my turn. Tomorrow isn't so far off." And they clench their fists and breathe a little freer. The air of tomorrow, the good salt air of freedom.

Mokutu, do you know what you're doing? You're blacking out the little patch of light over the prisoner's cell. The great rainbow bird is wheeling over the cells of a hundred and fifty million men; at both ends of the horizon the double serpent is rearing up, bearing promise of life, a hope of life and sky. But with one stroke of your stupid club you strike it down, and the scaly coils of malignant darkness come down on the whole continent.

MOKUTU I won't follow you in your apocalypse. I'm not responsible for Africa but for the Congo. And in the Congo I mean to restore order. Order, do you understand? Order.

SOLDIERS *have come in silently and occupy the whole stage.*

ACT III
SCENE 1

Camp Hardy in Thysville. A prison cell. MPOLO, OKITO, *and* LUMUMBA *on narrow cots. Morning.* LUMUMBA *tossing and moaning in his sleep.*

LUMUMBA Oh! Oh!

OKITO He's got one of his nightmares again.

MPOLO Poor Patrice. He's struggling like a fly caught in syrup.

LUMUMBA (*waking up and rubbing his eyes*) There's no way out! What a dream! Big ferocious birds were attacking me from all directions, I was thrashing around like a madman trying to defend myself. It was awful.

OKITO The proverb says: We eat with the sun, not with the moon. I don't like dreams.

LUMUMBA I do, even when they're terrible. There's wisdom in them. We forget it too soon when we wake up.

MPOLO I know. I know. Our ancestors! You can have them. Right now they're kind of stingy with their favors.

OKITO Yes, they've forgotten us in the bitter savannah.

LUMUMBA Courage, friends. The people were taken by surprise, but they're pulling themselves together now. You know the legend. We'll sacrifice Lumumba, the gods will be appeased and smile on the Congo. Sure. Things will pick up . . . The Belgians will disarm, Tzumbi will return to the fold, the UN will pour in aid by the shipload, and so on. But friends, it doesn't work. Things are going from bad to worse. Waste, disorder, anarchy, corruption, humiliation. You'll see, it won't be long before they come begging us to take the reins again.

MPOLO Unless to eliminate that possibility they decide to do away with us first. Something tells me they're not going to stop halfway. We never do in the Congo.

OKITO The Congo, the Congo! The international bankers, you mean. They're touchy. At the slightest poke they go out of their minds. The buffalo, that's what it is, the buffalo.

MPOLO When the buffalo shits, the whole world stinks.

LUMUMBA All that is true; our life is at the mercy of the first killer on the payroll. Black or white, it's all the same. If he's black, a white man has sent him. Yes, they can destroy us, but they can't defeat us. It's too late. We've got the jump on them. History will leave them behind.

MPOLO You certainly are a prophet, Patrice. You march ahead and proclaim the future. That's your strength and your weakness.

LUMUMBA Part praise, part blame; I accept that verdict, Mpolo. Especially if it can infect you with my unshakable faith in the future.

MPOLO Yes, part praise and part blame. Sometimes I wonder if we weren't trying to go too fast.

LUMUMBA I regret nothing, Mpolo. Does an architect project half a house? No, he plans the whole house at once. When the sky was black and there was no horizon in sight, wasn't it necessary to show the way with one magic stroke?

And let's not underestimate our strength. It's enormous. We've just got to know how to use it. Look, here are two letters I've just received, that escaped the vigilance of Mokutu's thugs. One's from Van Laert, the other's from Luis. Isn't it marvelous? Luis, a Spaniard! Why should he be interested in the Congo? After all, those people have their own problems. And Van Laert. A Belgian. My friend, my brother in Brussels. I bet you he's thinking of me right now, this very minute, same as I'm thinking of him. Those people are with us. They're with us because they know that the battle we're fighting isn't for ourselves, or even for Africa, but for all mankind. And Africa. Yes, I know, it's divided, it seems to be weak, but it won't fail us. Wasn't it here in Africa, from the solemn encounter of muck, sun, and water, that man was born? What is man but a certain way of dispelling the mists of life, by standing erect and holding the head high?

All right, Mpolo, I'll talk to the soldiers, they're Congolese, I'll break their hearts. (*To the* JAILERS *and* SOLDIERS.) Well, comrade jailers, how about a glass of beer? But I'm sorry, all I've got is Polar.

JAILER Don't let that worry you, boss. Primus or Polar, it's all the same to us. We won't argue about the brand, we're too damn thirsty.

LUMUMBA Drink, friends. And how's the country getting along?

JAILER The country? Nothing's changed. People are beginning to wonder if Dependa isn't a swarm of grasshoppers come to ruin us.

LUMUMBA Let's not blame Dependa for what her enemies do. But never mind. How about the army? Have the men been paid?

JAILER Nobody's been paid for two months.

LUMUMBA Hmm. Maybe it's because there's no money left in the till. And what about Mokutu? And Kala? And the UN? What have they been doing?

SOLDIER That's what I'd like to know. If the treasury's empty, where's the money? Just tell me that. You ought to know, you were a minister. But hell, you're like all the rest of them, a nigger egghead.

LUMUMBA Take it easy, friend. Take it easy. You want to know where the money is. I'll tell you. It's in Katanga. Yes, sir, in Katanga. In Tzumbi's treasury. And I'll tell you something else. It's because I tried to get it back that I'm here!

SOLDIER That's the truth. That's what I've been telling the boys. Some believe me, some don't. Anyway, it's a mess. You say it's the Katanga police that get the money?

LUMUMBA Sure, the police. And Tzumbi. And Msiri. And the Belgians. But come along, men, why all these gloomy thoughts? Let's have another round.

The SOLDIERS *pour themselves beer. Glasses are passed around.*

Soldiers, I see that a lot of you are Batetelas. Glad to know it. I'm a Mutetela myself. We're the tribe that put up the last fight against the Belgians sixty years ago. We saved the honor of the whole Congo. And I'm doing my duty as a Mutetela by fighting the last battle maybe, to prevent our country from falling into the clutches of a new colonialism.

Soldiers of other tribes, I trust you no less; I know the army as a whole is loyal to me as its legitimate commander. The army had nothing to do with Mokutu's treachery. His tools were his hand-picked praetorians, his paratroopers. He puts them up at the Hotel Memling and stuffs them like geese. Where does he get the money? I'll tell you. Partly from the Americans. But mostly out of the funds the UN gave him to pay you with. You fellows aren't staying at the Memling. I know the life you lead. You do all the dirty work. No hope of promotion, no pay. Your ribs stick out so the top brass and their bodyguards can roll in fat. When I appointed the first black officers, how could I imagine that quicker than lava spurts from a volcano, a new caste would be born, the caste of colonels and new masters, and that those voracious, insatiable dogs would monopolize all the benefits of Congolese freedom.

SOLDIER To hell with Mokutu. We're letting you out. Go on home. Maybe you'll help us fill our bellies.

SECOND SOLDIER Hurray for Lumumba! When he talks, he says something.

SOLDIERS Down with Mokutu! Down with Mokutu!

SOLDIER If I catch him, I'll cut his gizzard out.

LUMUMBA I respect your opinions and I don't want to influence you. But I want you all to know that the situation is critical. Two months after independence the kid is walking into the gullet of a wild beast. If I, Lumumba, brace myself and hold on for dear life, it's to save the Congo from the claws of the beast. Will you help me?

SOLDIERS (*shouting*) We're with you. You're our chief. Down with Mokutu!

The SOLDIERS *open the gates of the prison and carry* LUMUMBA *out in triumph.*

SCENE 2

African bar. Men and women. Same atmosphere as in Act I, Scene 2. A woman sings.

WOMAN

Who's seen my husband?
Nobody's seen him.
A bamboo splinter
Has pierced my heart.

Suddenly the door opens. Enter LUMUMBA, MPOLO, *and* OKITO.

MAMA MAKOSI Patrice! You here?

LUMUMBA See for yourself.

MAMA MAKOSI I knew they couldn't hold you.

LUMUMBA It's a good thing to have faith. A lot of people wouldn't have given two cents for Lumumba's hide. Yes, here I am. Free. Freed by our Congolese soldiers. Go get my wife and children. This is my headquarters from now on.

MAMA MAKOSI You're right. They betrayed you, the whole lot of them. Kala. Mokutu. Your buddy Mokutu. I never did like him. He looks like a sneaky little girl. Here you're safe, the house is yours, and the people will protect you.

LUMUMBA You'll have to forgive me. My presence is likely to upset your routine around here.

MAMA MAKOSI Never mind about that. Just tell us what those scoundrels did to you.

WOMEN Yes, yes, tell us about it.

The SANZA PLAYER *sings*

Nut, nut
One cocoanut, just one,
Its oil is enough
To fill the bowl.

LUMUMBA Thank you, friend. You've given me the courage and strength to defy the whole world. But what do you want me to tell you? The details? What's the good of details? I've better things to tell you. I'll tell you about Africa. Yes, Africa! The eyes, the back, the flanks! Africa is like a man who wakes up in the morning and sees that he's being attacked on all sides.

Attacked by hawks and vultures. He hasn't hid from one before the next is on him with its dripping beak. Makes me think of our Mukongo dance of the twelve masks: we had riches, beauty, assurance, potent medicines, and then came the Spirit of Jealousy and Evil with its powerful fetishes, sullying the cheeks of our virgins, felling our warriors, bringing corruption and dissension. A hideous nightmare! In the end, thank God, the Spirit of Evil was defeated, and we brought back Prosperity. Do you hear me, all of you? We'll bring back Prosperity, and we'll keep her. Prosperity's coming back to the Congo, friends. Let's drink to her! But let's not be selfish. I'm going to pass on the good news to our foreign friends, to the whole world. Call in the gentlemen of the press.

MAN Yes, the press. Let them come. But we want them to know that you're our king! Our legitimate king! Put on the leopard skin.

CROWD Yes! Yes! The leopard skin!

LUMUMBA Friends, don't make me do that. One day in the bush I met my animal soul: it had the form of a bird. My sign is a bird, that's better than a leopard. To enter the new day, the bronze wings of the ibis.

MAN You're right. The chiefs and kings have all betrayed us. You're better than they are. You are our inspired guide, our Messiah. Glory be, Simon Kibangu is back again.

CROWD (*singing*)

We are the orphan children.
Dark is the night, hard is the way.
Almighty God, who's going to help us?
Father Congo, who's going to give us a hand?

The MAN *holds out to* LUMUMBA *a kind of stole which* LUMUMBA *waves away.*

LUMUMBA And what do I do but give you a hand? With all my strength. Beyond my strength. But I won't wear a stole any more than a leopard skin. It may come as a disappointment to you, but I'm not Simon Kibangu. He wanted to give you back your strength, our Congo *ngolo,* and for that he deserves to be remembered. He wanted to go see God all alone, all alone, as your ambassador, to demand your rights, and for that you have every reason to glorify him. The white men confiscated God for their own benefit, and Simon Kibangu tried to win him back. But they robbed us of more than God, they robbed Africa of herself. Africa is hungry for its own being. And that's why I don't want to be a Messiah or a prophet. My only weapon is my tongue; I speak, I awaken, I'm not a redresser of wrongs. I don't perform miracles, I'm a redresser of life. I speak, I give Africa back to herself. I speak, and I give Africa to the world.

Uncertainty in the crowd. Enter PAULINE LUMUMBA. *She and* LUMUMBA *embrace.*

PAULINE Oh God, how happy I am! I was so worried. Those people are brutes. They're capable of anything. But here you are! Saved! But you're not safe here in Leo. We're going away. To Stanleyville. I've arranged everything. In Stanleyville the whole population's behind you.

LUMUMBA Stanleyville? All I've been doing is fighting secession, and you want me to organize a new secession? No, I won't desert, I won't run away. And there's nothing to be afraid of here. My enemies have learned their lesson. They know the Congo can't get along without me.

PAULINE You've always been stubborn and intractable. A regular mule. Does that man even give me a thought? Patrice, I'm talking to you. And you look up above me.

LUMUMBA Above, below, I don't know. Both, I guess. Above I see Africa, and below, mingled with the muffled drum of my blood, the Congo.

PAULINE Admit, Patrice, that I never turned you aside from your duty, but Africa's not your wife. You have other responsibilities besides the weal and woe of Africa. Do you remember the day we were married, Patrice? My father poured the palm wine, you took a sip, you held out the glass for me, I took a sip, and so we drank together till the glass was empty. I haven't got the name of a country or a river, I've got the name of a woman: Pauline. That's all I have to say. Except one question: Do you want the people to see me with my head shaved, following a funeral procession? And the children? Do you want them to be orphans?

LUMUMBA It can't be helped. In my heart I've always called you Pauline Congo, and your double name has helped me doubly to control my weakness. And I'm prepared to defy the whole world if I know I can count on you. If I die, I leave the children the legacy of a great struggle. And you will help them, guide them, arm them. But let's not be pessimistic. I'm going to live through this struggle and win. Forgive me, Pauline. Go to Brazzaville, try to see Luis. Tell him what's been happening. And now I have to speak to the press.

PAULINE (*exits slowly, singing*)

Alas, alas, who's seen my husband?
Nobody's seen my husband.
A bamboo splinter
Has pierced my heart.

Enter the gentlemen of the press.

LUMUMBA Make yourselves as comfortable as you can, gentlemen. Excuse the surroundings. They don't mean a thing. No, as a matter of fact, they mean a great deal. They mean that I put my trust in the people. It's a humble place, but here at least the heart of the Congo beats in its own way, more freely than in any government palace. I've called you here to tell you, and for you to tell the world, that the Congo is taking up where it left off. I was deposed by a childish coup d'état, but now I'm back in the saddle. My government is the only legal government of the Congo. It intends to make itself respected, to restore and reinforce the unity of the Congo. We do not seek revenge. The era of hatred is ended. Now it is time to build the Republic in peace and dignity. Gentlemen, I am counting on you to inform world public opinion of our peaceful intentions. My government will do everything in its power to maintain friendly relations with all foreign countries. In return, I expect every foreign government to recognize that the Congo is an independent country and intends to preserve its full independence and sovereignty.

REPORTER Mr. Lumumba, that sounds like a Prime Minister's speech of investiture. But aren't you being unrealistic? Are you aware of the present political situation? Are you aware of your own situation?

LUMUMBA Thank you for your concern. Let me set your mind at rest. I am the Prime Minister of the Republic of the Congo. I have the support of the people, and the parliament has given me an overwhelming vote of confidence. I therefore have every legitimate right to speak in the name of the Congo. Gentlemen of the press, it is your noble mission to inform your readers. I call upon you to do so with scrupulous honesty.

Women rush in, in a panic.

MAMA MAKOSI Patrice, the paratroopers! They've surrounded the house.

MPOLO Don't worry about them, Patrice, our boys are ready. The people are with us. Mokutu's thugs will get more than they bargained for.

LUMUMBA No, Mpolo. There has been enough bloodshed.

MPOLO But we can't just sit here with our hands folded.

LUMUMBA I'm not a religious man, but I am convinced of this: that justice cannot be won by violence.

MPOLO In this situation non-violence is suicide.

LUMUMBA Exactly, Mpolo. If I have to die, I want to die like Gandhi. All right, show those people in. I grant them an audience.

Enter KALA, MOKUTU, *and a group of* PARATROOPERS.

MOKUTU (*to the* PARATROOPERS) Get rid of all these people. (*To the newspapermen.*) Excuse me, gentlemen, the show is over. Now we have work to do. I'll see you again in due time. Goodbye.

The NEWSPAPERMEN, GIRLS, *and* CUSTOMERS *are removed.*

KALA (*to* LUMUMBA) I come to you with an offer. It may seem surprising. But not if you bear in mind that for me the welfare of my country outweighs all other considerations. I hope I find you in the same frame of mind.

LUMUMBA I have never served any other interests than those of the Congo. Say your piece.

KALA Our government cannot function without an executive.

LUMUMBA I'm glad to hear you say that. I am the Prime Minister. I have not been overthrown by the parliament. Consequently there is no government crisis. If there seems to be, it is only because certain people have acted illegally.

KALA You don't seem to understand. No one can turn back the clock. Try to be realistic for once. Ileo is the man of the situation. He is level-headed, reassuring. The country is in flames. Let him put out the fire. Once that's done, we shall see . . . I'm only asking you to have a little patience. Just a little patience. The banana ripens slowly.

LUMUMBA I hate time. I detest your *slowly*. And why do you always want to reassure people? Give me a man who upsets them, who tells them what the bad shepherds are doing to us.

KALA I am offering you a place in the Cabinet. Choose any portfolio you wish. Vice-president, Minister of State, minister of anything you like. Do you or do you not accept?

LUMUMBA (*airily*) Say, that reminds me, how's Youlou getting along? Yes, Fulbert Youlou. I hear he's sent away to Paris for a new soutane. Pure nylon.

KALA (*shocked*) This is no time for jokes. I expect a serious answer.

LUMUMBA It's not a bad idea, come to think of it. Gives his wives less washing to do. But don't get hot and bothered. I'll give you your serious answer. Mr. President, I will not be your Quisling.

KALA What's that?

LUMUMBA I will not, by my presence, lend support to a policy that I disavow. And still less will I sponsor a government of corrupt traitors.

KALA Do you know what I came here for? To save your life. To give you a chance to save your skin. Don't tempt fate.

LUMUMBA Do you know what you're asking of me?

KALA Asking? Are you so sure that you're in a position to give?

LUMUMBA If I weren't, you wouldn't have honored me with your visit. You came here to ask me for the seal of legitimacy. Very well, in the name of the Congo, I refuse it.

MOKUTU Mr. President, there's no use arguing. You're talking to a lunatic. Never mind. I'll take him down a peg.

KALA You asked for it, Patrice. Good-bye. He's all yours Mokutu.

MOKUTU All right, Mr. Lumumba, it's your funeral, you ordered it. Soldiers. This man is your prisoner.

SCENE 3

Elisabethville, the seat of the Katanga government. The dominant characteristics of the Katangese leaders are hypocrisy and ecclesiastical unctuousness, except for MSIRI, *who is a savage.* ZIMBWÉ *and* TRAVÉLÉ *are slightly drunk. During the whole scene whiskey and champagne are poured generously.*

MOKUTU It is not a pleasant mission that has brought me here. You have violated your agreement with the Leopoldville government which I represent. You stated your conditions. They were reasonable and we subscribed to them. We have carried out our side of the bargain. And you? Katanga has not only maintained its secession but given the whole world to understand . . .

TZUMBI Come, come . . . An agreement. That's a big word. There has been no agreement . . . in the strict sense. Just friendly conversations among good friends . . .

ZIMBWÉ Tut, tut. Words. Let's not talk about words. Agreement, treaty, conversation. What difference does it make? The main thing, in my opinion, is to distinguish between the spirit and the letter. For the letter kills . . .

TRAVÉLÉ You took the words out of my mouth. And the spirit saves. (*He laughs idiotically.*)

TZUMBI Zimbwé and Travélé are right. The spirit of our conversations was that the elimination of Lumumba was the *sine qua non* . . .

MOKUTU Good Lord, man. Haven't we eliminated him?

MSIRI Don't be childish. Do we have to spell it out for you? A single blow isn't fatal to a snake like Lumumba. Lumumba is still a menace to Congo.

TZUMBI Forgive our good friend Msiri, he may be uncouth but he has a heart of gold. And plenty of wisdom. It's true that we don't care much for Leopoldville. The UN, your populace, your soldiery . . . Too much noise and agitation. And I don't want to be unkind, but you people in the government lead the life of Riley . . . Oh well, that's none of my business. The point is we think Lumumba would be better off in Katanga.

MOKUTU He's a troublesome prisoner. I'd be only too glad to get rid of him. But sending him to Katanga would raise certain delicate problems—both domestic and international. The people are devoted to Lumumba. And you know how world opinion feels about democratic forms, what a fetish they make of democracy.

ZIMBWÉ Tut tut. Democracy. That's a big word with you Leopoldville people. Well, my dear colleague, we're democrats too, here in Katanga, but in our opinion, democracy means only one thing: democracy is what serves the interests of the people. And this transfer, I am sure we all agree, will serve the interests of this country's people.

TRAVÉLÉ (*laughing*) Just as I said. It's the spirit that saves. The spirit.

MSIRI You spoke just now of an internal problem. There's no internal problem. The people! The people! Bah! The people obey the man with the biggest stick. If you know how to command, the rabble will crawl. That's the only question. Do you know how to command? Will you ever learn to be chiefs?

MOKUTU All right, all right, Msiri, don't get excited, we'll try. In any case I will submit your proposal to the government. Goodbye.

TZUMBI Au revoir. You mean au revoir. Because this time we can call it an agreement. We are bound by an agreement. Remember that. And don't forget to tell Kala that this time we'll let Lumumba land. (*He laughs.*)

ZIMBWÉ Land. Hee-hee. I get it.

TRAVÉLÉ (*laughing*) It's the spirit that saves . . . and the letter that kills . . . And when I say kill, I mean kill. Your health, Mokutu!

As the light fades, the SANZA PLAYER *passes, singing.*

Oh little sparrow hawk, oh! oh!
Oh little sparrow hawk, spread your wings.
The sun's drinking blood, oh oh!
Little sparrow hawk, little sparrow hawk,
What blood is the sun drinking?

SCENE 4

The United Nations in New York.

HAMMARSKJÖLD Have you heard the news? I've received a cable. They've taken Lumumba to Katanga; there's good reason to fear for his life . . . it's dreadful.

CORDELIER Yes, in view of the customs of that delightful country, the Lumumba question seems to be settled once and for all.

HAMMARSKJÖLD It doesn't seem to trouble you very much.

CORDELIER Since Mr. Lumumba is not a personal friend of mine, I can only take a professional view of the matter. You will admit that it simplifies the political situation of the Congo.

HAMMARSKJÖLD Tell the truth, Cordelier. You hated him. Why not admit it? And you people call yourselves neutrals. I should have kept my eyes open. You never stopped plotting against him.

CORDELIER The UN is an organization, no, an organism that doesn't take kindly to the foreign body known as sentimentality.

HAMMARSKJÖLD I have a strong case against you. You kept him

out of the radio station, you prevented him from defending himself when his enemies had every opportunity to spread their insidious propaganda. On pretext of reserving the Leopoldville air field for United Nations planes, you cut him off from the outside world while Belgian planes were landing in Katanga around the clock . . . In short, we pinned down his arms while his enemies struck him. Nice work!

CORDELIER Your sympathies are carrying you away. You sound like the Soviet delegate.

HAMMARSKJÖLD The worst part of it is that Zorine is right, thanks to you. You deceived me. The whole lot of you. And to think that I lent my name to your odious acts.

CORDELIER Mr. Secretary General, let me defend myself.

HAMMARSKJÖLD No, you can't expect me to say what Lord Jim said to Doramin: "I take it all on myself." No, I won't be silent. I've been silent long enough. Tell me, Cordelier, what do you think of Jesus Christ?

CORDELIER That's an odd question. I'm a Christian . . . a Methodist, and you know it.

HAMMARSKJÖLD What do I care if you're a Methodist and a Christian? Anybody can beat his breast and say "I'm a Christian" . . . What I'm asking you is not what Matthew Cordelier thinks of Christ—who cares?—but what side you, Matthew Cordelier, would have been on one thousand nine hundred and sixty-one years ago when in Judea, under the Roman occupation, one of your contemporaries, a certain Jesus, was arrested and put to death. And now get out of here, you murderer of Christ!

SCENE 5

A training camp in Katanga. A white MERCENARY, *in front of him a dummy representing a Negro. He cleans his revolver and sings.*

MERCENARY

In the south, in the tropics,
in the desert, in the jungle,
in the marshes of the deltas

rain, mosquitoes, fever
weather-beaten skin
knight of the new day
my heart swells in my breast
for liberty and justice.

(*He stands up, goes into position, and fires at the dummy.*) Swine, baboon, savage, magician, ungrateful bastard! Nun raper. Bing! Bing! Bing! (*He fires.*) Ah, the devils! They won't die. Look at him with his big white eyes and his big red face. Bing, bing, bing! Take that! (*He fires.*) I've seen them. Even when they're dead, they keep coming at you. We had to kill them ten times. They say their magicians promise to turn our bullets into water. Bing! Bing! Bing! (*He fires, the dummy topples over.*) I don't guess that one turned into water. (*He laughs.*) But Christ, I'm wringing wet! Oof! It's hot. Christ, am I thirsty! Stinking country! (*He wipes his forehead and pours himself a drink. He sings.*)

I had some trouble with my folks,
They didn't like my kind of jokes,
The fights, the debts, the broads, the junk,
I wasn't cut out for a monk.
My girl was cute, my girl had curves,
But she was getting on my nerves.
I hugged her tight, I packed my trunk,
And lit out for the Congo.

It grows dark. When the light goes on again, the white MERCENARY *is still holding his smoking revolver, but on the ground the dummy has been replaced by two corpses,* OKITO *and* MPOLO. *Enter* MSIRI *and a mercenary, pushing* LUMUMBA. *Suddenly* MSIRI *flings himself on* LUMUMBA *and strikes him in the face.*

MSIRI D'you see the way your buddies spat out the bullets? Ha ha ha. Well, that leaves just you and me. (*The* MERCENARY *tries to interfere.* MSIRI *snatches his bayonet.*) No, I've got a personal account to settle with our friend here. (*To* LUMUMBA.) I'm told you think you're invulnerable. Is that a fact? Will you answer when you're spoken to?

LUMUMBA It's Msiri all right. I was expecting this meeting. It had to be. We are the two opposing forces. You're the invention of the past. And I an inventor of the future.

MSIRI They tell me you Kasai people have powerful magic. Ocelot skin or some such thing. This is the time to show what it's worth.

LUMUMBA My magic is an invulnerable idea. As invincible as a people's hope, as the fire that spreads from bush to bush, as the pollen in the wind, as a root in the blind earth.

MSIRI (*prodding him with the bayonet*) How about this? or this? I suppose you don't feel it? Cutting into your hide . . . cutting, cutting . . . closer and closer to the heart!

LUMUMBA Careful. My heart has a hard pit, a flint that will break your blade. It's the honor of Africa.

MSIRI (*sneering*) Africa! Africa doesn't give a hoot in hell. Africa can't do a thing for you. Msiri is right here. And Msiri is man enough to drink your blood and eat your heart.

LUMUMBA All night I heard wailing and laughing, sighing and scolding . . . that was the hyena!

MSIRI You arrogant son-of-a-bitch! Can't you see death looking you in the eye? You're living your death and you don't even notice it.

LUMUMBA I'm dying my life, and that's good enough for me.

MSIRI Look! (*He thrusts in the blade.*) All right, prophet, what do you see now?

LUMUMBA

I will be field, I will be pasture,
I will be with the Wagenia fisherman
I will be with the Kivu drover
I will be on the mountain, I will be in the ravine.

MSIRI Let's get this over with. (*He presses the bayonet.*)

LUMUMBA Oh, the dew over Africa. Comrades, I see the flaming tree, I see Pygmies with axes busy around the precarious trunk, but the head grows, the head grows, and it calls out to the tumbling sky in the first foam of dawn.

MSIRI Bastard! (LUMUMBA *falls. To the* MERCENARY.) Dog, finish him off.

A shot. The MERCENARY *gives* LUMUMBA *the coup de grâce. Darkness. When the light goes on, a group of statuelike figures is seen in the background: the* BANKERS, KALA, TZUMBI, MOKUTU. *Slightly to one side,* HAMMARSKJÖLD. PAULINE LUMUMBA *enters.*

PAULINE

A cage, four clouds. Lycaon, Lycaon of the flashing eyes!
The alphabet of fear
Mumbled as the buzzards fly overhead.
Close to the ground treason nibbles its shadow.
Higher, a hovering batlike flight of premonitions.
Below, on the black-white that torpor
Pours unceasingly, shipwreck
Repeats with gentle beckonings its invitation
To the most beautiful marriage of disaster and the stars.

Giggling slightly, the SANZA PLAYER *steps forward, dressed like a Congolese sorcerer; straw skirt, bells on his wrists and ankles. He crosses the stage chanting.*

SANZA PLAYER

Hey you, the great god Nzambi,
What a big fool you are!
You eat our ribs, you eat our asses,
Hey, Nzambi, what a big fool you are!
You eat our hearts and livers!
Hey, Nzambi. You eat too much.

About to leave the stage, he turns back, faces the audience and twirls his mpiya, *a bundle of cock plumes, an instrument of divination.*

Sing, women! Men, give me song!
In the sand of falsehood I scratch.
Spur, I scratch! Down to the truth I scratch.
        Scratching spur!
I am the *nganga,*
        The cock of divination.

HAMMARSKJÖLD Congo!
Through the matrix of original sin
The logic of things past penetrates
To the black hearth of our selves,
The terrible inner fire that gives forth evil.
Oh, that the just should become unjust;
That sincerity should become a machine to crush sincerity!
Oh God, why did they choose me
To preside over their diabolical alchemy!
But Thy will be done! Thy will, not mine.
I await the order. I hear the order.
It's only the first step that's hard.

He takes a step.

It's only the first step that counts.

He goes out.

BANKER For my part, I see no ground for political speculation. A mere episode of folklore, as it were, an outcropping of that Bantu mentality which periodically, even in the best of them, bursts through the frail varnish of civilization.

In any case, and this is my main point, you've seen for yourselves that we had nothing to do with it. Nothing whatever. (*He goes out with great dignity.*)

TZUMBI (*stepping forward*) You'll see. You'll see. I'll be blamed for the whole business. I tell you in all sincerity: this crime is part of a plot against my person. (*He goes out.*)

KALA See for yourself: nobody obeys me in the Congo. I told them to prune the tree, not to pull it up by the roots. (*He goes out.*)

MOKUTU I had no personal animosity toward him. Everyone

knew that that's why the politicians of this country were so careful not to inform me of the plot against him. Oh yes, I know. I found it necessary to put a temporary stop to his career, to neutralize him, as I put it. And that will be held against me. But God himself has an eraser on his pencil. I fully expected that what political expediency had made me do, political expediency would make me undo. But crime foiled my plans.

Darkness, then light. A sign indicates: July, 1966. A public square in Kinshasa, Independence Day.

WOMAN Hurrah for Mokutu. Mokutu *uhuru!*

MAMA MAKOSI *Uhuru* Lumumba!

WOMAN Careful, citizen. *Uhuru* Mokutu is what you've got to say.

MAMA MAKOSI I say what I think. *Uhuru* Lumumba.

THE WOMAN In any case, down with colonialism! Boo! Boo! Here come the coffins!

MAMA MAKOSI The coffins? What coffins?

SANZA PLAYER Death butts into everything in the Congo!

WOMAN Why not? Death is life. The first coffin is for the Belgian Congo; the second is for daddy's Congo; the third is for tribal conflict. It's wonderful! Hurrah for Mokutu!

A VOICE Hush! Hush. The General is going to speak!

A VOICE Shut up. We want to listen.

MOKUTU (*in a leopard skin, haranguing the crowd*) Patrice, martyr, athlete, hero—I turn to you for the strength to carry on my task. (*Sensation.* MOKUTU *pauses for a moment with head bowed.*)

Congolese,
It is my wish that from this day on
The finest of our boulevards should bear his name;
That the place where he was struck down become the
  shrine of our nation;
and that a statue erected at the gate of what was
  formerly Leopoldville
signify to the world

that the piety of a nation will never cease
to make reparation for our crime,
the crime of which we are all guilty.
Congolese, may this day be the beginning of a new
era for the Congo!

As the curtain slowly falls, the SANZA PLAYER *steps forward and sings:*

The sorgho grows
The bird rises from the ground
Why shouldn't man
Have a right to change?

If a man is hungry
Do you deny him food?
So why say no to a country
That's thirsting for hope.

But just a minute! Let's not go off half-cocked.
A beginning is only a beginning
And if we're going to do this thing
Let's not do it by halves.

If you're going to grow
Then grow straight
And if you're going to rise from the ground
Then you must learn to soar.

Everyone's got a nose.
It grows, it shows, it blows.
Now that you're standing on feet of your own
Getting stronger and fatter
You'd better keep it clean.
This is the end of my chatter.

CURTAIN

GREAT GOODNESS OF LIFE

A Coon Show 1966

by Imamu Amiri Baraka

"For my father with love and respect"

Imamu Amiri Baraka (LeRoi Jones) can be described as the instigator of the new revolutionary black theater and as an originating force in the development of new black thought and literature. He was born in Newark, New Jersey, in 1934. As a boy in Newark he thought of entering the ministry. Upon graduation from Barringer High School, he began his college work at the Newark campus of Rutgers University. His college work was completed at Howard University in Washington, D.C., and after a stint in the Air Force he continued his studies at Columbia University and the New School for Social Research where he received his M.A. in German literature. A writer of great versatility, he is a poet, novelist, essayist, musicologist, critic, writer of short stories, and an editor as well as a dramatist. His more important plays include; *Dutchman* (awarded the Obie for Best American Play of the 1963–64 season), *The Slave, The Toilet, Black Mass,* and *Slaveship*. He has been both a Whitney and a Guggenheim fellow, and is a

CAST OF CHARACTERS

VOICE OF THE JUDGE

COURT ROYAL, *a middle-aged Negro man, gray haired, slight*

ATTORNEY BRECK, *middle-aged Negro man*

HOODS 1 & 2*

YOUNG WOMAN, *around 25 years old, colored*

HOODS 3 & 4

YOUNG VICTIM

scholar of the Yoruba Academy. Imamu founded the Black Arts Repertory Theater and School in Harlem during the early sixties, and later, moved from New York to Newark where he became founder and director of the Spirit House Movers and Players.

---

* HOODS 1 & 2 are KKK-like figures, HOODS 3 & 4 are more refined than the first two, wear business suits.

Outside an old log cabin, with morning frost letting up a little.

VOICE Court.

A man, COURT ROYAL, *comes out, gray but still young-looking. He is around fifty. He walks straight, though he is nervous. He comes uncertainly. Pauses.*

Come on.

He walks right up to the center of the lights.

Come on.

COURT ROYAL I don't quite understand.

VOICE Shutup, nigger.

COURT ROYAL What? (*Meekly, then trying to get some force up.*) Now what's going on? I don't see why I should . . .

VOICE I told you to shutup, nigger.

COURT ROYAL I don't understand. What's going on?

VOICE Black lunatic. I said shutup. I'm not going to tell you again!

COURT ROYAL But . . . Yes.

VOICE You are Court Royal, are you not?

COURT ROYAL Yes. I am. But I don't understand.

VOICE You are charged with shielding a wanted criminal. A murderer.

COURT ROYAL What? Now I know you have the wrong man. I've done no such thing. I work in the Post Office. I'm Court Royal. I've done nothing wrong. I work in the Post Office and have done nothing wrong.

VOICE Shutup.

COURT ROYAL But I'm Court Royal. Everybody knows me. I've always done everything . . .

VOICE Court Royal you are charged with harboring a murderer. How do you plead?

COURT ROYAL Plead? There's a mistake being made. I've never done anything.

VOICE How do you plead?

COURT ROYAL I'm not a criminal. I've done nothing . . .

VOICE Then you plead not guilty?

COURT ROYAL Of course I'm not guilty. I work in the Post Office. (*Tries to work up a little humor.*) You know me, probably. Didn't you ever see me in the Post Office? I'm a supervisor; you know me. I work at the Post Office. I'm no criminal. I've worked at the Post Office for thirty-five years. I'm a supervisor. There must be some mistake. I've worked at the Post Office for thirty-five years.

VOICE Do you have an attorney?

COURT ROYAL Attorney? Look you'd better check you got the right man. You're making a mistake. I'll sue. That's what I'll do.

The VOICE *laughs long and cruelly.*

COURT ROYAL I'll call my attorney right now. We'll find out just what's going on here.

VOICE If you don't have an attorney, the Court will assign you one.

COURT ROYAL Don't bother. I have an attorney. John Breck's my attorney. He'll be down here in a few minutes—the minute I call.

VOICE The Court will assign you an attorney.

COURT ROYAL But I have an attorney. John Breck. See, it's on this card.

VOICE Will the Legal Aid man please step forward.

COURT ROYAL No. I have an attorney. If you'll just call, or adjourn the case until my attorney gets here.

VOICE We have an attorney for you. Where is the Legal Aid man?

COURT ROYAL But I have an attorney. I want my attorney. I

don't need any Legal Aid man. I have money, I have an attorney. I work in the Post Office. I'm a supervisor; here, look at my badge.

A bald-headed smiling house slave in a wrinkled dirty tuxedo crawls across the stage; he has a wire attached to his back leading offstage. A huge key in the side of his head. We hear the motors "animating" his body groaning like tremendous weights. He grins, and slobbers, turning his head slowly from side to side. He grins. He makes little quivering sounds.

VOICE Your attorney.

COURT ROYAL What kind of foolishness is this? (*He looks at the man.*) What's going on? What's your name?

His "voice" begins some time after the question: the wheels churn out his answer, and the deliberating motors sound throughout the scene.

ATTORNEY BRECK Pul . . . lead . . . errr . . . (*As if the motors are having trouble starting.*) Pul . . . pul . . . lead . . . er . . . err . . . Guilty! (*Motors get it together and move in proper synchronization.*) Pul . . . Plead guilty, it's your only chance. Just plead guilty, brother. Just plead guilty. It's your only chance. Your only chance.

COURT ROYAL Guilty? Of what? What are you talking about? What kind of defense attorney are you? I don't even know what I'm being charged with, and you say plead guilty. What's happening here? (*At* VOICE.) Can't I even know the charge?

VOICE We told you the charge. Harboring a murderer.

COURT ROYAL But that's an obvious mistake.

ATTORNEY BRECK There's no mistake. Plead guilty. Get off easy. Otherwise *thrrrrit.* (*Makes throat-cutting gesture, then chuckles.*) Plead guilty, brother, it's your only chance. (*Laughs.*)

VOICE Plea changed to guilty?

COURT ROYAL What? No. I'm not pleading guilty. And I want my lawyer.

VOICE You have yr lawyer.

COURT ROYAL No, my lawyer is John Breck.

ATTORNEY BRECK Mr. Royal, look at me. (*Grabs him by the shoulders.*) I am John Breck. (*Laughs.*)Your attorney and friend. And I say plead guilty.

COURT ROYAL John Bre . . . what? (*He looks at* ATTORNEY BRECK *closely.*) Breck. Great God, what's happened to you? Why do you look like this?

ATTORNEY BRECK Why? Haha, I've always looked like this, Mr. Royal. Always.

Now another voice, strong, young, begins to shout in the darkness at COURT.

YOUNG VICTIM Now will you believe me stupid fool? Will you believe what I tell you or your eyes? Even your eyes. You're here with me, with us, all of us, and you can't understand. Plead guilty you are guilty stupid nigger. You'll die they'll kill you and you don't know why now will you believe me? Believe me, half-white coward. Will you believe reality?

VOICE Get that criminal out of here. Beat him. Shut him up. Get him.

Now sounds of scuffling come out of darkness. Screams. Of a group of men subduing another man.

YOUNG VICTIM You bastard. And you Court Royal you let them take me. You liar. You weakling, You woman in the face of degenerates. You let me be taken. How can you walk the eartttttt . . . (*He is apparently taken away.*)

COURT ROYAL Who's that? (*Peers into darkness.*) Who's that talking to me?

VOICE Shutup, Royal. Fix your plea. Let's get on with it.

COURT ROYAL That voice sounded very familiar. (*Caught in thought momentarily.*) I almost thought it was . . .

VOICE Since you keep your plea of not guilty you won't need a lawyer. We can proceed without your services, counselor.

ATTORNEY BRECK As you wish, your honor. Goodbye, Mr. Royal. (*He begins to crawl off.*) Goodbye, dead sucker! Hahahaha. (*Waving hands as he crawls off and laughing.*) Hahahaha, ain't I a bitch . . . I mean ain't I? (*Exits.*)

COURT ROYAL John, John. You're my attorney, you can't leave me here like this. (*Starts after him, shouts.*) JOHN!

A siren begins to scream, like in jailbreak pictures . . . "Arrrr-rrrrerrrr." The lights beat off, on, in time with the metallic siren shriek. COURT *is stopped in his tracks, bent in anticipation; the siren continues. Machine guns begin to bang bang as if very close to him, cell doors slamming, whistles, yells: "Break . . . Break!" The machine guns chatter,* COURT *stands frozen, half-bent arms held away from his body, balancing him in his terror. As the noise, din, continues, his eyes grow until he is almost going to faint.*

Ahhhhhhgggg. Please . . . please . . . don't kill me. Don't shoot me, I didn't do anything. I'm not trying to escape. Please . . . please pleeeeease . . .

The VOICE *begins to shriek almost as loud with laughter as all the other sounds and jumping lights stop as* VOICE *starts to laugh. The* VOICE *just laughs and laughs, laughs until you think it will explode or spit up blood; it laughs long and eerily out of the darkness. Still dazed and staggered, he looks around quickly, trying to get himself together. He speaks now very quietly, and shaken.*

Please. Please.

The other VOICE *begins to subside, the laughs coming in sharp cut-off bursts of hysteria.*

VOICE You donkey. (*Laughs.*) You piece of wood. You shiny shuffling piece of black vomit.

The laughter quits like the tide rolling softly back to silence. Now there is no sound, except for COURT ROYAL*'s breathing, and shivering clothes.*

COURT ROYAL (*whispering*) Please? (*He is completely shaken and defeated, frightened like a small animal, eyes barely rolling.*) Please. I won't escape. (*His words sound corny tinny stupid dropped in such silence.*) Please I won't try again. Just tell me where I am. (*The silence again. For a while no movement.* COURT *is frozen, stiff, with only eyes sneaking; now they stop, he's frozen, cannot move staring off into the cold darkness.*)

A chain, slightly, more, now heavier, dragged bent, wiggled slowly, light now heavily in the darkness, from another direction. Chains. They're dragged, like things are pulling them across the earth. The chains. And now low chanting voices, moaning, with incredible pain and despair, the voices press just softly behind the chains, for a few seconds, so very very briefly then gone. And silence. COURT *does not move. His eyes roll a little back and around. He bends his knees, dipping his head, bending. He moans.*

Just tell me where I am.

VOICE Heaven.

The VOICE *is cool and businesslike.* COURT'*s eyes and head raise an imperceptible trifle. He begins to pull his arms slowly to his sides, and claps them together. The lights dim, and only* COURT *is seen in dimmer illumination.*

VOICE Heaven. (*Pause.*) Welcome.

COURT ROYAL (*mumbling*) I never understood . . . these things are so confusing. (*His head jerks like he's suddenly heard Albert Ayler. It raises, his whole body jerks around like a suddenly animate ragdoll. He does a weird dance like a marionette jiggling and waggling.*) You'll wonder what the devil-meant. A jiggedy bobbidy fool. You'll wonder what the devil-sent. Diggedy dobbidy cool. Ah man. (*Singing.*) Ah man, you'll wonder who the devil-sent. And what was heaven heaven heaven. (*This is like a funny joke-dance, with sudden funniness from* COURT; *then suddenly as before he stops frozen again, eyes rolling, no other sound heard.*)

Now a scream, and white hooded men push a greasyhead nigger lady across in front of COURT. *They are pulling her hair, and feeling her ass. One whispers from time to time in her ear. She screams and bites occasionally, occasionally kicking.*

HOOD 1 (*to the* VOICE) She's drunk. (*Now to* COURT.) You want to smell her breath?

COURT ROYAL (*frightened, also sickened at the sight, embarrassed*) N-no. I don't want to. I smell it from here. She drinks and stinks and brings our whole race down.

HOOD 2 Ain't it the truth!

VOICE Grind her into poison jelly. Smear it on her daughter's head.

HOOD 1 Right, yr honor. You got a break, sister. (*They go off.*) Hey, uncle, you sure you don't want to smell her breath?

COURT ROYAL (*shivers*) No.

VOICE Royal, you have concealed a murderer, and we have your punishment ready for you. Are you ready?

COURT ROYAL What? No. I want a trial. Please a trial. I deserve that. I'm a good man.

VOICE Royal, you're not a man!

COURT ROYAL Please . . . (*Voice breaking.*) Your Honor, a trial. A simple one, very quick, nothing fancy . . . I'm very conservative . . . no frills or loud colors, a simple concrete black toilet paper trial.

VOICE And funeral.

Now two men in hoods, white work gloves, business suits, very sporty, come in with a stretcher. A black man is dead on it. There is long very piped applause. "Yea. Yea."

HOOD 1 It's the Prince, yr honor. We banged him down.

VOICE He's dead?

HOOD 2 Yes. A nigger did it for us.

VOICE Conceal the body in a stone. And sink the stone deep under the ocean. Call the newspapers and give the official history. Make sure his voice is in that stone too, or . . . (*Heavy nervous pause.*) Just go ahead.

HOOD 1 Of course, Your Honor. (*Looks to* COURT, *almost as an afterthought.*) You want to smell his breath? (*They go out.*)

COURT ROYAL (*mumbling, still very frightened*) No . . . no . . . I have nothing to do with any of this. I'm a good man. I have a car. A home. (*Running down.*) A club. (*Looks up, plead-*

ing.) Please there's some mistake. Isn't there? I've done nothing wrong. I have a family. I work in the Post Office, I'm a supervisor. I've worked for thirty-five years. I've done nothing wrong.

VOICE Shutup, whimpering pig. Shutup and get ready for sentencing. It'll be hard on you, you can bet that.

COURT ROYAL (*a little life; he sees he's faced with danger*) But tell me what I've done. I can remember no criminal, no murderer I've housed. I work eight hours, then home, and television, dinner, then bowling. I've harbored no murderers. I don't know any. I'm a good man.

VOICE Shutup, liar. Do you know this man?

An image is flashed on the screen behind him. It is a rapidly shifting series of faces. Malcolm. Patrice. Rev. King. Garvey. Dead nigger kids killed by the police. Medgar Evers.

COURT ROYAL What?

VOICE I asked you do you know this man? I'm asking again, for the last time. There's no need to lie.

COURT ROYAL But this is many men, many faces. They shift so fast I cannot tell who they are . . . or what is meant. It's so confusing.

VOICE Don't lie, Royal. We know all about you. You are guilty. Look at that face. You know this man.

COURT ROYAL I do? (*In rising terror.*) No. No. I don't, I never saw that man, it's so many faces, I've never seen those faces . . . never . . .

VOICE Look closer, Royal. You cannot get away with what you've done. Look more closely. You recognize that face . . . don't you? The face of the murderer you've sheltered all these years. Look, you liar, look at that face.

COURT ROYAL No, no, no . . . I don't know them. I can't be forced into admitting something I never did. Uhhh . . . I have worked. My God, I've worked. I've meant to do the right thing. I've tried to be a . . .

The faces shift, a long slow wail, like moan, like secret screaming, has underscored the flashing faces. Now it rises sharply to screaming point thrusts. COURT *wheels around to face the image on the screen, directly. He begins shouting loud as the voices.*

No, I've tried . . . please I never wanted anything but peace . . . please, I tried to be a man. I did. I lost my . . . heart . . . please it was so deep, I wanted to do the right thing, just to do the right thing. I wanted . . . everything to be . . . all right. Oh, please . . . please.

VOICE Now tell me, whether you know that murderer's face or not. Tell me before you die!

COURT ROYAL No, no. I don't know him. I don't. I want to do the right thing. I don't know them. (*Raises his hands in his agony.*) Oh, son . . . son . . . dear God, my flesh, forgive me . . . (*Begins to weep and shake.*) My sons. (*He clutches his body, shaken throughout by his ugly sobs.*) Dear God . . .

VOICE Just as we thought. You are the one. And you must be sentenced.

COURT ROYAL I must be sentenced. I am the one. (*Almost trance-like.*) I must be sentenced. With the murderer. I am the one.

VOICE The murderer is dead. You must be sentenced alone.

COURT ROYAL (*as first realization*) The murderer . . . is . . . dead?

VOICE And you must be sentenced. Now. Alone.

COURT ROYAL (*voice rising, in panic, but catching it up short*) The murderer . . . is dead.

VOICE Yes. And your sentence is . . .

COURT ROYAL I must be sentenced . . . alone. Where is the murderer? Where is his corpse?

VOICE You will see it presently.

COURT ROYAL (*head bowed*) God. And I am now to die like the murderer died?

VOICE No. (*Long pause.*) We have decided to spare you. We admire your spirit. It is a compliment to know you can see the clearness of your fate, and the rightness of it. That you love the beauty of the way of life you've chosen here in the anonymous world. No one beautiful is guilty. So how can you be? All the guilty have been punished. Or are being punished. You are absolved of your crime, at this moment, because of your infinite understanding of the compassionate God of the Cross. Whose head was cut off for you, to absolve you of your weakness. The murderer is dead. The murderer is dead.

Applause from the darkness

COURT ROYAL And I am not guilty now?

VOICE No you are free. Forever. It is asked only that you give the final instruction.

COURT ROYAL Final instruction . . . I don't understand . . .

VOICE Heroes! bring the last issue in.

The last two hooded men, HOODS 3 *and* 4, *return with a young black man of about twenty. The boy does not look up. He walks stiff-legged to the center in front of* COURT. *He wears a large ankh around his neck. His head comes up slowly. He looks into* COURT'*s face.*

YOUNG VICTIM Peace.

COURT ROYAL *looks at his face, begins to draw back. The hooded man comes and places his arms around* COURT'*s shoulders.*

VOICE Give him the instruction instrument.

HOODED MAN *takes a pistol out of his pocket and gives it with great show to* COURT.

HOOD 3 The silver bullet is in the chamber. The gun is made of diamonds and gold.

HOOD 4 You get to keep it after the ceremony.

VOICE And now, with the rite of instruction, the last bit of guilt falls from you as if it was never there, Court Royal. Now, at last, you can go free. Perform the rite, Court Royal, the final instruction.

COURT ROYAL What? No. I don't understand.

VOICE The final instruction is the death of the murderer. The murderer is dead and must die, with each gift of our God. This gift is the cleansing of guilt, and the bestowal of freedom.

COURT ROYAL But you told me the murderer was dead, already.

VOICE It *is* already. The murderer has been sentenced. You have only to carry out the rite.

COURT ROYAL But you told me the murderer was dead. (*Starts to back away.*) You told me . . . you said I would be sentenced alone.

VOICE The murderer *is dead.* This is his shadow. This one is not real. This is the myth of the murderer. His last fleeting astral projection. It is the murderer's myth that we ask you to instruct. To bind it forever . . . with death.

COURT ROYAL I don't . . . Why do . . . you said I was not guilty. That my guilt had fallen away.

VOICE The rite must be finished. This ghost must be lost in cold space. Court Royal, this is your destiny. This act was done by you a million years ago. This is only the memory of it. This is only a rite. You cannot kill a shadow, a fleeting bit of light and memory. This is only a rite, to show that you would be guilty but for the cleansing rite. The shadow is killed in place of the killer. The shadow for reality. So reality can exist beautiful like it is. This is your destiny, and your already lived-out life. Instruct, Court Royal, as the centuries pass, and bring you back to your natural reality. Without guilt. Without shame. Pure and blameless, your soul washed . . . (*Pause.*) White as snow.

COURT ROYAL (*falling to his knees, arms extended as in loving prayer, to a bright light falling on him, racing around the space*) Oh, yes . . . I hear you. And I have waited, for this promise to be fulfilled.

VOICE This is the fulfillment. You must, at this moment, enter into the covenant of guiltless silence. Perform the rite, Court Royal.

COURT ROYAL Oh, yes, yes . . . I want so much to be happy . . . and relaxed.

VOICE Then carry out your destiny . . .

COURT ROYAL Yes, yes . . . I will . . . I will be happy . . . (*He rises, pointing the gun straight up at the young man's face.*) I must be . . . fulfilled . . . I will. (*He fires the weapon into the boy's face. One short sound comes from the boy's mouth.*)

YOUNG VICTIM Papa. (*He falls.*)

COURT ROYAL *stands looking at the dead boy with the gun still up. He is motionless.*

VOICE Case dismissed, Court Royal . . . you are free.

COURT ROYAL (*now suddenly to life, the lights go up full, he has the gun in his hand; he drops, flings it away from him*) My soul is as white as snow. (*He wanders up to the body.*) My soul is as white as snow. (*He starts to wander off the stage.*) White as snow. I'm free. I'm free. My life is a beautiful thing. (*He mopes slowly toward the edge of the stage, then suddenly a brighter mood strikes him. Raising his hand as if calling someone.*) Hey, Louise, have you seen my bowling bag? I'm going down to the alley for a minute. (*He is frozen, the lights dim to BLACK.*)

CITIES IN BEZIQUE

Two One-Act Plays:
THE OWL ANSWERS
A BEAST STORY

by Adrienne Kennedy

Adrienne Kennedy was born in Pittsburgh in 1931 and grew up in Cleveland. She attended Ohio State University but found the social structure so opposed to blacks that she did hardly any academic work. She started writing at twenty, but her writing received no real recognition until she joined Edward Albee's workshop in 1962. She won an Obie award for *Funnyhouse of a Negro,* done off-Broadway in 1964, and received a Guggenheim fellowship. *In His Own Write,* an adaptation of the writings of John Lennon, was presented at the National Theater in London in 1968, and *Cities in Bezique* was produced by Joseph Papp's Public Theater in New York in 1969. Her other plays are *A Lesson in Dead Language* and *Sun.* Most recently she has been working on a movie of *Funnyhouse of a Negro* with Pablo Ferro. She is currently a Teaching Fellow at Yale University and is the recipient of a National Endowment of the Arts fellowship.

THE OWL ANSWERS

CAST OF CHARACTERS

SHE WHO IS CLARA PASSMORE WHO IS THE VIRGIN MARY WHO IS THE BASTARD WHO IS THE OWL.

BASTARD'S BLACK MOTHER WHO IS THE REVEREND'S WIFE WHO IS ANNE BOLEYN.

GODDAM FATHER WHO IS THE RICHEST WHITE MAN IN THE TOWN WHO IS THE DEAD WHITE FATHER WHO IS REVEREND PASSMORE.

THE WHITE BIRD WHO IS REVEREND PASSMORE'S CANARY WHO IS GOD'S DOVE.

THE NEGRO MAN.

SHAKESPEARE, CHAUCER, WILLIAM THE CONQUEROR.

The characters change slowly back and forth into and out of themselves, leaving some garment from their previous selves upon them always to remind us of the nature of SHE WHO IS CLARA PASSMORE WHO IS THE VIRGIN MARY WHO IS THE BASTARD WHO IS THE OWL's world.

The scene is a New York subway is the Tower of London is a Harlem hotel room is St. Peter's. The scene is shaped like a subway car. The sounds are subway sounds and the main props of a subway are visible—poles. Two seats on the scene are like seats on the subway, the seat in which SHE WHO IS *sits and* NEGRO MAN'*s seat.*

Seated is a plain, pallid Negro woman, wearing a cotton summer dress that is too long, a pair of white wedged sandals. She sits staring into space. She is CLARA PASSMORE WHO IS THE VIRGIN MARY WHO IS THE BASTARD WHO IS THE OWL. SHE WHO IS *speaks in a soft voice as a Negro schoolteacher from Savannah would.* SHE *carries white handkerchiefs, carries notebooks that throughout the play like the handkerchiefs fall.* SHE *will pick them up, glance frenziedly at a page from a notebook, be distracted, place the notebooks in a disorderly pile, drop them again, etc. The scene should lurch, lights flash, gates slam. When* THEY *come in and exit they move in the manner of people on a train, too there is the noise of the train, the sound of moving steel on the track. The* WHITE BIRD'*s wings should flutter loudly. The gates, the High Altar, the ceiling, and the Dome are like St. Peter's, the walls are like the Tower of London.*

The music which SHE *hears at the most violent times of her experience should be Haydn's* Concerto for Horn in D (*third movement*).

Objects on the stage (beards, wigs, faces) should be used in the manner that people use everyday objects such as spoons or newspapers. The Tower Gate should be black, yet slam like a subway door. The gates slam. Four people enter from different directions. They are SHAKESPEARE, WILLIAM THE CONQUEROR, CHAUCER, *and* ANNE BOLEYN. *They are dressed in costumes of Shakespeare, William the Conqueror, Chaucer, and Anne Boleyn but too they are strangers entering a subway on a summer night, too they are the guards in the Tower of London. Their lines throughout the play are not spoken specifically by one person but by all or part of them.*

THEY Bastard. (*They start at a distance, eventually crowding her. Their lines are spoken coldly.* SHE *is only a prisoner to them.*)
You are not his ancestor.
Keep her locked there, guard.
Bastard.

SHE You must let me go down to the chapel to see him. He is my father.

THEY Your father? (*Jeering.*)

SHE He is my father.

THEY Keep her locked there, guard.

SHAKESPEARE *crosses to gate and raises his hands. There is a slam as if a great door is being closed.*

SHE We came this morning. We were visiting the place of our ancestors, my father and I. We had a lovely morning, we rose in darkness, took a taxi past Hyde Park through the Marble Arch to Buckingham Palace, we had our morning tea at Lyons then came out to the Tower. We were wandering about the gardens, my father leaning on my arm, speaking of you, William the Conqueror. My father loved you, William . . .

THEY (*interrupting*)
If you are his ancestor why are you a Negro?
Yes, why is it you are a Negro if you are his ancestor?
Keep her locked there.

SHE You must let me go down to the chapel to see him.

Subway stops. Doors open. CHAUCER *exits.* ANNE BOLEYN *and* WILLIAM THE CONQUEROR *remain staring at* SHE. CHAUCER *and*

SHAKESPEARE *return carrying a stiff dead man in a black suit. The most noticeable thing about him is his hair, long, silky, white hair that hangs as they bring him through the gate and place him at her feet.*

THEY Here is your father.

THEY *then all exit through various gate entrances.* SHE *picks up the dead man, drags him to a dark, carved, high-backed chair on the right. At the same time a dark* NEGRO MAN, *with a dark suit and black glasses on, enters from the right gate and sits on the other subway seat. Flashing, movement, slamming the gate. The scene revolves one and one-quarter turns as next action takes place. The* NEGRO MAN *sits up very straight and proceeds to watch* SHE. *Until he speaks to her he watches her constantly with a wild, cold stare. The* DEAD FATHER *appears dead. He is dead. Yet as* SHE *watches, he moves and comes to life. The* DEAD FATHER *removes his hair, takes off his white face, from the chair he takes a white church robe and puts it on. Beneath his white hair is dark Negro hair. He is now* REVEREND PASSMORE. *After he dresses he looks about as if something is missing, subway stops, doors open.* FATHER *exits and returns with a gold bird cage that hangs near the chair and a white, battered Bible. Very matter-of-factly he sits down in the chair, stares for a moment at the cage, then opens the Bible, starting to read.* SHE *watches, highly distracted, until he falls asleep. Scene revolves one turn as* ANNE BOLEYN *throws red rice at* SHE *and the* DEAD FATHER *who is now* REVEREND PASSMORE. *They see her.* SHE *exits and returns with a great black gate and places the gate where the pole is.* SHE *runs to* ANNE BOLEYN.

SHE Anne, Anne Boleyn. (ANNE BOLEYN *throws rice upon* SHE.) Anne, you know so much of love, won't you help me? They took my father away and will not let me see him. They locked me in this tower and I can see them taking his body across to the chapel to be buried and see his white hair hanging down. Let me into the chapel. He is my blood father. I am almost white, am I not? Let me into St. Paul's Chapel. Let me please go down to St. Paul's Chapel. I am his daughter.

ANNE *appears to listen quite attentively but her reply is to turn into the* BASTARD'S BLACK MOTHER. *She takes off part of her own long dress and puts on a rose-colored, cheap lace dress. While she does this there is a terrific screech.* SHE'*s reaction is to run back to her subway seat. She drops her notebooks. The* BASTARD'S BLACK MOTHER *opens her arms to* SHE. SHE *returns to the gate.*

Anne. (*As if trying to bring back* ANNE BOLEYN.)

BBM (BASTARD'S BLACK MOTHER; *laughs and throws a white bridal bouquet at her*) Clara, I am not Anne. I am the Bastard's Black Mother, who cooked for somebody. (*Still holding out her arms, she kneels by the gate, her kinky hair awry. Eyes closed, she stares upward, praying. Suddenly she stops praying and pulls at* SHE *through the gate.*)

The WHITE BIRD, *with very loud fluttering wings, flies down from St. Peter's Dome and goes into the cage.* REVEREND PASSMORE *gets up and closes the cage door.*

SHE Anne, it is I.

BBM Clara, you were conceived by your Goddam Father who was The Richest White Man in the Town and somebody that cooked for him. That's why you're an owl. (*Laughs.*) That's why when I see you, Mary, I cry. I cry when I see Marys, cry for their deaths.

WHITE BIRD *flies.* REVEREND *reads. The* BASTARD'S BLACK MOTHER *stands at the gate, watches, then takes off her rose lace dress and black face (beneath her black face is a more pallid Negro face), pulls down her hair, longer dark hair, and puts on a white dress. From a fold in the dress she takes out a picture of Christ, then kneels and stares upward. She is the* REVEREND'S WIFE. *While she does this the scene revolves one turn.*

REVEREND'S WIFE (*kneeling;* REVEREND *stands and watches her;* REVEREND'S WIFE *takes a vial from her gown and holds it up*) These are the fruits of my maidenhead, owl blood Clara who is the Bastard Clara Passmore to whom we gave our name, see the Owl blood, that is why I cry when I see Marys, cry for their deaths, Owl Mary Passmore.

SHE *gets up, exits from a side gate. Subway stops, gates open, they come in, gates close. Subway starts.* SHE *goes to the* REVEREND *as if to implore him. He then changes into the* DEAD FATHER, *resuming his dirty white hair.* THEY *stand about.*

SHE Dear Father, My Goddam Father who was the Richest White Man in the Town, who is Dead Father—you know that England is the home of dear Chaucer, Dickens, and dearest Shakespeare. Winters we spent here at the Tower, our chambers were in the Queen's House, summers we spent at Stratford with dearest Shakespeare. It was all so lovely. I spoke to Anne Boleyn, Dead Father. She knows so much of love and suffering and I believe she is going to try to help me. (*Takes a sheaf of papers from her notebooks; they fall to the floor.*) Communications, all communications to get you the proper burial, the one you deserve in St. Paul's Chapel, they are letting you rot, my Goddam Father who was the Richest White Man in the Town—they are letting you rot in that town in Georgia. I haven't been able to see the King. I'll speak again to Anne Boleyn. She knows so much of love.

Shows the papers to the DEAD FATHER *who sits with his hair hanging down, dead, at which point scene revolves clockwise one-half turn. There are screeches, and bird flaps wings. The* REVEREND'S WIFE *enters and prays at gate.*

DEAD FATHER If you are my ancestor why are you a Negro, Bastard? What is a Negro doing at the Tower of London, staying at the Queen's House? Clara, I am your Goddam Father who was the Richest White Man in the Town and you are a schoolteacher in Savannah who spends her summers in Teachers College. You are not my ancestor. You are my bastard. Keep her locked there, William.

THEY *stare at her like passengers on a subway, standing, holding the hand straps.*

SHE We were wandering about the garden, you leaning on my arm, speaking of William the Conqueror. We sat on the stone bench to rest, when we stood up you stumbled and fell onto the walk—dead. Dead. I called the guard. Then I called the Warder and told him my father had just died, that we had been visiting London together, the place of our ancestors and all the lovely English, and my father just died. (*She reaches out to touch him.*)

DEAD FATHER You are not my ancestor.

SHE They jeered. They brought me to this tower and locked me up. I can see they're afraid of me. From the tower I saw them drag you across the court . . . your hair hanging down. They have taken off your shoes and you are stiff. You are stiff. (*Touches him.*) My dear father. (*Music: Haydn.*)

DEAD FATHER Daughter of somebody that cooked for me.

Smiles. He then ignores SHE, *changes into the* REVEREND, *takes the Bible and starts to read. The* WHITE BIRD *flies into the cage. Wings flutter. The* REVEREND'S WIFE *prays, lights a candle. The* REVEREND *watches the* BIRD. REVEREND'S WIFE *then puts on her black face, rose dress. Some of the red rice has fallen near her, she says, "Oww," and starts to peck at it like a bird.* SHE *wanders about, then comes to speak to the* BASTARD'S BLACK MOTHER *who remains seated like an owl. End music.*

SHE It was you, the Bastard's Black Mother, who told me. I asked you where did Mr. William Mattheson's family come from and you, my Black Mother, said: I believe his father came from England. England, I said. England is the Brontës' home. Did you know, Black Bastard's Mother, who cooked for somebody, in the Reverend's parlor—there in a glass bookcase are books and England is the home of Chaucer, Dickens, and Shakespeare. Black Mother who cooked for somebody, Mr. William Mattheson died today. I was at the College. The Reverend's Wife called me, Clara who is the Bastard who is the Virgin Mary who is the Owl. Clara, who is the Bastard who is the Virgin Mary who is the Owl, Clara, she said, the Reverend told me to call you and tell you Mr. William Mattheson died today or it was yesterday he died yesterday. It was yesterday. The Reverend told me to tell you it was yesterday he died and it is today they're burying him. Clara who is the Bastard, you mustn't come. Don't do anything foolish like come to the funeral, Mary. You've always been such a fool about that white man, Clara. But I am coming, the Black Bastard's Mother. I am coming, my Goddam Father who was the Richest White Man in Jacksonville, Georgia. When I arrive in London, I'll go out to Buckingham Palace, see the Thames at dusk and Big Ben. I'll go for lovely walks through Hyde Park, and to innumerable little tearooms with great bay windows and white tablecloths on little white tables and order tea. I will go all over and it will be June. Then I'll go out to the Tower to see you, my father.

Subway stops. Doors open. THEY *enter.*

THEY

If you are his ancestor, what are you doing on the subway at night looking for men?

What are you doing looking for men to take to a hotel room in Harlem?

Negro men?

Negro men, Clara Passmore?

Gates close, subway starts, BIRD'*s wings flap.*

SHE (*runs to the* BIRD) My dead father's bird: God's Dove. My father died today.

BIRD (*mocking*) My father died today, God's Dove.

SHE He was the Richest White Man in our town. I was conceived by him and somebody that cooked for him.

BIRD What are you doing in the Tower of London then?

The REVEREND *becomes the* DEAD FATHER *who comes forward, pantomimes catching the* BIRD, *puts him in the cage, shuts the door.*

SHE My father. (*He turns, stares at her, comes toward her and dies. There is a clang.*) What were you saying to William, my father, you loved William so? (*She holds him in her arms. He opens his eyes.*)

DEAD FATHER (*waking*) Mary, at last you are coming to me. (*Music: Haydn.*)

SHE I am not Mary, I am Clara, your daughter, Reverend Passmore—I mean Dead Father.

BIRD *flies in the cage.*

DEAD FATHER Yes, my Mary, you are coming into my world. You are filled with dreams of my world. I sense it all.

Scene revolves counterclockwise one and one-quarter turns. Lights flash. SHE, *trying to escape, runs into* NEGRO MAN.

NEGRO MAN At last you are coming to me. (*Smiles.*)
DEAD FATHER Mary, come in here for eternity. Are you confused? Yes, I can see you are confused.
THEY (*entering*) Are you confused?

One of them, CHAUCER, *is now dressed as the* REVEREND. *He comes, falls down onto the empty high-backed chair, and sits staring into the Bible.*

DEAD FATHER So at last you are coming to me, Bastard.

BASTARD'S BLACK MOTHER *exits from gate, returns, part owl with owl feathers upon her, dragging a great dark bed through the gate.*

BBM Why be confused? The Owl was your beginning, Mary.

There is a great clang. Begins to build with the bed and feathers the High Altar. Feathers fly.

SHE He came to me in the outhouse, he came to me under the porch, in the garden, in the fig tree. He told me you are an owl, ow, oww, I am your beginning, ow. You belong here with us owls in the fig tree, not to somebody that cooks for your Goddam Father, oww, and I ran to the outhouse in the night crying oww. Bastard they say, the people in the town all say Bastard, but I—I belong to God and the owls, ow, and I sat in the fig tree. My Goddam Father is the Richest White Man in the Town, but I belong to the owls, till Reverend Passmore adopted me they all said Bastard . . . then my father was a Reverend. He preached in the Holy Baptist Church on the top of the hill, on the top of the Holy Hill and everybody in the town knew then my name was Mary. My father was the Baptist preacher and I was Mary.

Subway stops, gates open. THEY *enter. Gates close. Subway starts.* SHE *sits next to* NEGRO MAN.

I who am the ancestor of Shakespeare, Chaucer, and William the Conqueror, I went to London—the Queen Elizabeth. London. They all said who ever heard of anybody going to London but I went. I stayed in my cabin the whole crossing, solitary. I was the only Negro there. I read books on subjects like the history of London, the life of Anne Boleyn, Mary Queen of Scots, and sonnets. When I wasn't in the cabin I wrapped myself in a great sweater and sat over the dark desks in the writing room and wrote my father. I wrote him every day of my journey. I met my father once when my mother took me to visit him and we had to go into the back door of his house. I was married once briefly. On my wedding day the Reverend's wife came to me and said when I see Marys I cry for their deaths, when I see brides, Clara, I cry for their deaths. But the past years I've spent teaching alone in Savannah. And alone I'm almost thirty-four, I who am the ancestor of somebody that cooked for somebody and William the Conqueror.

DEAD FATHER *rises, goes to her, then dies again. Great clang.* BASTARD'S BLACK MOTHER *shakes a rattle at* SHE. SHE *screams at the* DEAD FATHER and the MOTHER.

You must know how it is to be filled with yearning.

THEY *laugh.* MOTHER *bangs at the bed.*

NEGRO MAN (*touches her*) And what exactly do you yearn for?
SHE You know.
NEGRO MAN No, what is it?
SHE I want what I think everyone wants.
NEGRO MAN And what is that?
SHE I don't know. Love or something, I guess.
NEGRO MAN Out there Owl?

DEAD FATHER In St. Paul's Chapel, Owl?
THEY Keep her locked there, guard.

Great clang.

BBM Is this love to come from out there?
SHE I don't know what you mean.
DEAD FATHER I know you don't.
THEY We know you don't.
SHE Call me Mary.
NEGRO MAN Mary?
THEY Keep her locked there.
DEAD FATHER If you are Mary what are you doing in the Tower of London?
NEGRO MAN Mary?

The REVEREND *gets up, goes to the chair, puts on a robe, sits. The* BASTARD'S BLACK MOTHER *reappears on the other side of the gate, owl feathers about her, bearing a vial, still wearing the long black hair of the* REVEREND'S WIFE.

BBM When I see sweet Marys I cry for their deaths, Clara. The Reverend took my maidenhead and I am not a Virgin anymore and that is why you must be Mary, always be Mary, Clara.
SHE Mama.

BASTARD'S BLACK MOTHER *rises. Steps in costume of* ANNE BOLEYN.

Mama. (*Watches her change to* ANNE BOLEYN. THEY *watch.*)
BBM What are you doing on the subway if you are his ancestor?

ANNE *makes circular cross around stage until she is back in same position she started at.*

SHE I am Clara Passmore. I am not His ancestor. I ride, look for men to take to a Harlem hotel room, to love, dress them as my father, beg to take me.
THEY Take you?
SHE Yes, take me, Clara Passmore.

THEY Take you, Bastard?

SHE There is a bed there.

The WHITE BIRD *laughs like the mother.*

WILLIAM THE CONQUEROR And do they take you?

SHE No, William.

WILLIAM THE CONQUEROR No?

SHE Something happens.

WILLIAM THE CONQUEROR Happens?

CHAUCER Happens?

SHE Something strange always happens, Chaucer.

CHAUCER Where?

SHE In the hotel room. It's how I've passed my summer in New York, nights I come to the subway, look for men. It's how I've passed my summer. If they would only take me! But something strange happens.

ANNE Take you, Mary. Why, Mary? (ANNE *has now reached gate.*)

BASTARD'S BLACK MOTHER *steps out of costume, crosses to bed.* SHE *talks to* ANNE *as if she were there.*

SHE Anne, you must help me. They, my Black Mother and my Goddam Father and the Reverend and his wife, they and the teachers at the school where I teach, and Professor Johnson, the principal to whom I'm engaged, they all say, "London, who in hell ever heard of anybody going to London?" Of course I shouldn't go. They said I had lost my mind, read so much, buried myself in my books. They said I should stay and teach summer school to the kids up from Oglethorpe. But I went. All the way from Piccadilly Circus out there in the black taxi, my cold hands were colder than ever. Then it happened. No sooner than I left the taxi and passed down a gray walk through a dark gate and into a garden where there were black ravens on the grass when I broke down. I broke down and started to cry, oh the Tower, winters in Queen's House, right in front of everybody. People came and stared. I was the only Negro there. The guard came and stared, the ravens flew and finally a man with a black hat on helped me out through the gate into the street. I am never going back, Anne. Anne, I am never going back. I will not go.

Subway stops, gates open.

THEY Keep her locked there, guard.

Light comes through gates as if opened. SHE *makes a crown of paper, and places on the* NEGRO MAN'S *head.*

SHE God, do you see it? Do you see? They are opening the cell door to let me go.

NEGRO MAN See it, Mary?

SHE They are opening the cell door to let me go down to St. Paul's Chapel where I am yearning to go. Do you see it?

NEGRO MAN Love? Love Mary?

SHE Love?

NEGRO MAN Love in St. Paul's Chapel? (*He tries to grab at her.*)

SHE No, no, the love that exists between you and me. Do you see it?

NEGRO MAN Love Mary? (*He takes her hand, with his other hand, he tries to undress her.*)

SHE Love God.

NEGRO MAN Love Mary?

SHE Love God.

THEY (*simultaneously*) Bastard, you are not His ancestor, you are not God's ancestor.

There is a screech as THEY *bring the* DEAD FATHER *and leave him at her feet.*

NEGRO MAN Love Mary?

SHE Love God. Yes.

BBM (*calls*) Clara. Clara.

The REVEREND *watching.*

THEY Open the door. Let her go, let her go, guards. Open the cell door. (THEY *exit, leaving the gates open.*)

NEGRO MAN *will not release* SHE.

SHE Go away. Go away.

The NEGRO MAN *will not release her. The* REVEREND'S WIFE *goes on building the High Altar with owl feathers, prays, builds, prays, stops, holds out her hand to* SHE, *puts up candles, puts up owl feathers, laughs, puts more candles on the High Altar.*

REVEREND'S WIFE (*calls*) Owl, come sit by me. (*The* REVEREND'S WIFE *does not look at* SHE, *but rather stares feverishly upward, her gestures possessing the fervent quality of Biblical images. Sitting on the High Altar, she holds one of her hands over her shoulder as though she drew near the fingers of a deity. Suddenly her hand reaches inside her gown and she pulls up a butcher knife.*) Clara. (*Staring upward, holding the knife.*)

SHE Yes, the Reverend's Wife who came to me on my wedding day and said I cry for the death of brides. Yes?

REVEREND'S WIFE I told the Reverend if he ever came near me again . . . (*She turns the butcher knife around.*) Does he not know I am Mary, Christ's bride? What does he think? Does he think I am like your black mother who was the biggest whore in town? He must know I'm Mary. Only Mary would marry the Reverend Passmore of the church on the top of the Holy Hill. (*Turns the knife around, staring at it.* SHE is leaving with NEGRO MAN. REVEREND'S WIFE *is pulling her.*) We adopted you, took you from your bastard birth, Owl.

SHE *and* NEGRO MAN *exit. Gates close. Subway starts.* REVEREND'S WIFE *drags bed on to center stage.* SHE *enters with* NEGRO MAN *down center.*

SHE Home, God, we're home. Did you know we came from England, God? It's the Brontës' home too. Winters we spent here at the Tower. Our chambers were in the Queen's House. Summers we spent at Stratford. It was so lovely. God, do you remember the loveliness?

Lights flash. Scene revolves clockwise one and one-quarter turns. BIRD *flaps wings. Light comes up on him.*

BIRD If you are the Virgin, what are you doing with this Negro in a Harlem hotel room, Mary?

SHE My name is Clara Passmore.

BIRD Mary. (*Laughs like the* MOTHER. *The* REVEREND'S WIFE *lights candles.*)

NEGRO MAN (*going to her*) What is it?

SHE Call me Mary, God.

NEGRO MAN Mary?

SHE God, do you remember the loveliness?

REVEREND'S WIFE (*lights more candles and moves closer with the butcher knife, calling*) Clara.

The BIRD *flies wildly, the* REVEREND *sits in the chair reading the white tattered Bible.*

NEGRO MAN What is it? What is it? What is wrong? (*He tries to undress her. Underneath her body is black. He throws off the crown* SHE *has placed on him.* SHE *is wildly trying to get away from him.*) What is it?

The WHITE BIRD *flies toward them and about the green room.*

Are you sick?

SHE (*smiles*) No, God. (SHE *is in a trance.*) No, I am not sick. I only have a dream of love. A dream. Open the cell door and let me go down to St. Paul's Chapel. (*The blue crepe shawl is half about her.* SHE *shows the* NEGRO MAN *her notebooks, from which a mass of papers fall.* SHE *crazily tries to gather them up. During this* SHE *walks around bed. He follows her.*) Communications, God, communications, letters to my father. I am making it into my thesis. I write my father every day of the year.

God, I who am the Bastard who is the Virgin Mary who is the Owl, I came here this morning with my father. We were visiting England, the place of our ancestors, my father and I who am the Bastard who is the Virgin Mary who is the Owl. We had a lovely morning. We rose in darkness, took a taxi past Hyde Park, through the Marble Arch to Buckingham Palace. We had our morning tea at Lyons and then we came out to the Tower.

And I started to cry and a man with a black hat on helped me out of the gate to the street. I was the only Negro there.

They took him away and would not let me see him. They who are my Black Mother and my Goddam Father locked me in the fig tree and took his body away and his white hair hung down.

Now they, my Black Mother and my Goddam Father who pretend to be Chaucer, Shakespeare, and Eliot and all my beloved English, come to my cell and stare and I can see they despise me and I despise them.

They are dragging his body across the green his white hair hanging down. They are taking off his shoes and he is stiff. I must get into the chapel to see him. I must. He is my blood father. God, let me in to his burial. (*He grabs her down center.* SHE, *kneeling.*) I call God and the Owl answers. (*Softer.*) It haunts my Tower calling, its feathers are blowing against the cell wall, speckled in the garden on the fig tree, it comes, feathered, great hollow-eyed with yellow skin and yellow eyes, the flying bastard. From my Tower I keep calling and the only answer is the Owl, God. (*Pause. Stands.*) I am only yearning for our kingdom, God.

The WHITE BIRD *flies back into the cage, the* REVEREND *reads smiling, the* DEAD FATHER *lies on the cell floor. The* MOTHER, *now part the black mother and part the* REVEREND'S WIFE *in a white dress, wild kinky hair, part feathered, comes closer to* SHE.

MOTHER Owl in the fig tree, owl under the house, owl in outhouse. (*Calling cheerfully the way one would call a child, kissing* SHE.) There is a way from owldom. (*Kissing her again.*) Clara who is the Bastard who is the Virgin who is the Owl.

SHE (*goes to* MOTHER) My Black Mother who cooked for somebody who is the Reverend's Wife. Where is Anne Boleyn?

MOTHER Owl in the fig tree, do you know it? Do you? Do you know the way to St. Paul's Chapel, Clara? (*Takes her hand.*) I do. Kneel, Mary, by the gate and pray with me who is your Black Mother who is Christ's bride. (*She holds up the butcher knife.*) Kneel by the High Altar and pray with me. (*They kneel;*

she smiles.) Do you know it, Clara, do you, Clara Bastard? (*Kisses her.*) Clara, I know the way to St. Paul's Chapel. I know the way to St. Paul's Chapel, Clara.

MOTHER *lifts knife. She stabs herself. At this moment,* BIRD *flaps his wings, scene removes counterclockwise one turn. There is a screech of a subway. Then the Haydn plays. When revolve stops,* NEGRO MAN *tries to kiss* SHE *and pin her down on the bed.* SHE *is fighting him off. The* WHITE BIRD *descends steps.*

SHE God, say, "You know I love you, Mary, yes, I love you. That love is the oldest, purest testament in my heart." Say, "Mary, it was a testament imprinted on my soul long before the world began. I pray to you, Mary." God, say, "Mary, I pray to you. Darling, come to my kingdom. Mary, leave owldom—come to my kingdom. I am awaiting you."

The NEGRO MAN *tries again to kiss her. The* WHITE BIRD *picks up the* DEAD MOTHER *and takes her to the top of St. Peter's Dome. They remain there, watching down. The* REVEREND *reads the Bible, smiling.*

NEGRO MAN What is wrong?

SHE Wrong, God?

NEGRO MAN God?

SHE Wrong, God?

NEGRO MAN God?

They are upon the burning High Altar. He tries to force her down, yet at the same time he is frightened by her. The DEAD FATHER *who has been holding the candles, smiles.*

SHE Negro! (*Music ends.*) Keep her locked there, guard. (*They struggle.*) I cry for the death of Marys. (*They struggle.* SHE *screeches.*) Negro! (SHE *tries to get out of the room, but he will not let her go.*) Let me go to St. Paul's Chapel. Let me go down to see my Goddam Father who was the Richest White Man in the Town. (*They struggle, he is frightened now.*) God, God, call me, Mary. (SHE *screeches louder.*) God! ! *Suddenly she breaks away, withdraws the butcher knife, still with blood and feathers upon it, and very quickly tries to attack him, holds the knife up, aiming it at him, but then dropping it just as suddenly in a gesture of wild weariness. He backs further. She falls down onto the side of the burning bed. The* NEGRO MAN *backs further out through the gate.* SHE, *fallen at the side of the Altar burning, her head bowed, both hands conceal her face, feathers fly, green lights are strong, Altar burning,* WHITE BIRD *laughs from the Dome.* SHE WHO IS CLARA WHO IS THE BASTARD WHO IS THE VIRGIN MARY *suddenly looks like an owl and lifts her bowed head, stares into space and speaks.*) Ow . . . oww. (DEAD FATHER *rises and slowly blows out candles on bed.*)

CURTAIN

PROPERTY PLOT

Subway bench with notebooks, paper crown inside books, shawl over back of bench; subway bench; great chair with white robe, bible; subway doors; gate—L.:

On gate: Bouquet, votive candle; bird cage with door open: on edge of platform, R.

DEAD FATHER—Leaning against ladder, U. C.

ANNE BOLEYN—R. wings; confetti—in pocket of ANNE BOLEYN

WILLIAM THE CONQUEROR—R. wings; 3 books of matches; vial of blood; statue of virgin with string; newspaper; sunglasses

Personal Prop: White hankie (SHE)

PRE-SET OF ALTAR/BED

Permanent Pieces: Skull—on knob of headboard; doll—leaning on foot of bed, C.; shoes, dress and white beads—draped around bottom post of foot of bed

In piles—going from head to foot of bed: First item named is bottom of each pile—straw and rope, picture frame, purple robe, net with fan

Large candle, helmet and straw, clip candle, leopard, doll with tin cup

Rattle, knife, feathered orange pillow, candle in box

Flower picture and red cushion, mirror with green net, large cushion with cloths, black velvet and rope, paisley cloth

Tambourine, largest candle, clip candle, St. Paul

Chain of cloth with hat on end and shoes in middle, 2 picture frames, plastic bag

On top of pile—at head of bed: Shopping bag with candle

COSTUME PLOT

SHE: beige tweed skirt, bone-colored blouse, beige sweater, blue madonna stole, white shoes (wedged sandals)

BASTARD'S BLACK MOTHER: hot pink lace dress with black mask

REVEREND'S WIFE: The pink dress and the white dress are one. It should be made so it can be changed on stage in front of the audience.

ANNE BOLEYN: authentic period costume sculpture with mask and headdress attached. (This costume is stepped into, moved about in and left where it is stepped out of.) Afro wig with attached straight fall.

GODDAM (DEAD) FATHER: Black suit, white mask with long white hair, white shirt, black tie, black shoes

REVEREND: Same as above plus white academic clerical robe

WHITE DOVE: feathered wings attached to arms, feathered spotted briefs, rhethmic sandals

NEGRO MAN: brown suit, beige shirt, brown tie, brown boots

SHAKESPEARE: authentic period costume—black velvet, portrait mask with attached wig, white hose, slippers

CHAUCER: olive green with black trim, floor-length robe, portrait mask, truncated lirie pipe, boots

WILLIAM THE CONQUEROR: a costume sculpture battle dress, chainmail and helmet (all in one unit), black turtleneck and tights underneath, black boots

SCENE DESIGN

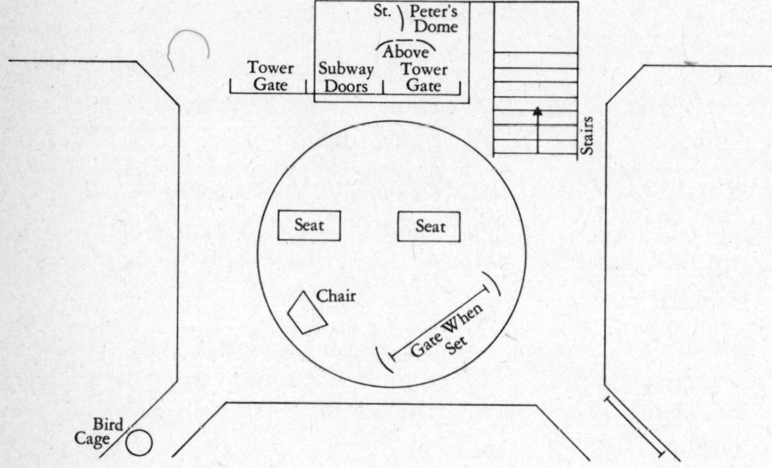

A BEAST STORY

CAST OF CHARACTERS

BEAST GIRL

BEAST WOMAN

BEAST MAN

DEAD HUMAN, *a dark young man*

The beasts are real people, a black family. At times their speech can be slightly unreal or at times their physical movements can suggest a bestiality, but they are real people. Ideally they should all resemble each other. They perhaps could have an artificial pallor or perhaps artificially pale eyes, but it should be subtle.

Floating images should ideally float through space above them.

THE ROOMS

The action takes place in the rooms simultaneously.

BEAST MAN'S ROOM—a great dark chair, hymnals.

BEAST GIRL'S ROOM—mahogany bed; above it a picture of Jesus.

BEAST WOMAN'S ROOM—a great dark dresser, perfume, wine bottles.

ATTIC—an ax hanging on the wall.

HALL—candles.

All the rooms are dim. (Suggested by yellowed wallpaper, etc.) In reality it is the gloomy house of a minister in a drab section of a midwestern city.

Sound of discordant organ music throughout. Images remain still.

BEAST GIRL's *room, in shadow. She sits on a bed.* BEAST MAN *comes toward her from the doorway, smiling, saying something she does not comprehend.* BEAST MAN *catches* BEAST GIRL's *hand, pressing it to his face. Discordant organ music.*

BEAST WOMAN *wanders aimlessly through the downstairs hall and slowly up to her room. She then sits before the dresser, pulling from the drawer undefined objects, moving them from side to side of the dresser. Suddenly she rouses herself, staring at the room, then falling onto the dresser, burying her head.*

Floating dead
the image of the dead human
Dead blue crow dead toad

BEAST WOMAN *comes from her room, stares up at the floating images from her doorway, floating images bright. Image of* BEAST GIRL *and* BEAST MAN *remain.*

BEAST WOMAN The sky above this house is painted a flat shallow blue. All might be warm and sunlit.

BEAST MAN (*staring into his daughter's face*) My daughter sits in shadow. I come toward her smiling, saying something she does not comprehend. Through the house floats the image of the boy she loved and the dead blue crow and the dead toad that hops on her bedpost.

BEAST WOMAN I keep thc ax. I keep the ax to maintain her innocence. She lay down in that field beyond the house with him. I begged her at the wedding to maintain her innocence. I said each evening he will come to you, his face in twilight.

BEAST GIRL My father preached our wedding service and a black sun floated over the altar. A crow flew through an open window while my mother played the organ and the black sun floated. (*Her father still standing before her.*) He had to stop singing, he had to stop singing, the room was silent. He tried to kiss me. It was morning when I awakened, a red sunrise morning, the first day of my marriage. At last I knew who I was . . . no shadow of myself, I was revealed . . . to myself . . . Now I rock the dead baby. I remember when we walked in the field.

BEAST MAN *stares at* BEAST GIRL. BEAST WOMAN *still stares at the floating images. A bright light comes into* BEAST MAN*'s room. A light comes up in the attic, revealing the* DEAD HUMAN.

DEAD HUMAN She kept the ax. She kept the ax to maintain her innocence. The beasts came to the clearing. They remember when we were not here. Now they watch from the trees, beckoning. She fled to the hallway. I tried to kiss her hand.

BEAST GIRL I have killed as she killed. He followed me into the hall and tried to kiss my hand.

DEAD HUMAN It was raining. Beast noises were in the house.

BEAST GIRL I looked down at him sleeping naked, covers thrown from him. I covered him with the sheet, but before I did I looked at him naked. Suddenly he awakened, raising himself smiling, holding out his hand to mine. How cold his fingers were!

DEAD HUMAN You lay down in that field with me. I wanted you to go with me but you couldn't. Your hair grew as you looked into their ravaged faces. The jackals, the toad, and the mice are glad.

BEAST GIRL I slipped my hand from his. He fell back into a strong deep sleep naked again, having tossed the covers from himself.

DEAD HUMAN Your hair grown, eyes turned beast yellow, the toad knew, the toad has always known. The first night of our marriage you fled from our bed. I found you, face ravaged, sitting in your father's room, staring at the candles. Afterwards they made you kill my baby with quinine and whiskey.

BEAST WOMAN *wanders through the hall, picks up an ax from the hall, slowly carries it to the attic, hangs it high and speaks. She does all this without seeing or acknowledging the* DEAD HUMAN.

BEAST WOMAN The jackals are glad.
BEAST GIRL The toad and the jackals knew.
DEAD HUMAN They are glad.

BEAST MAN *wanders through his house and to his room and stares from a window.*

Beast voices. He was the beast that sent you from me. Your father said things I did not comprehend and the sky turned black.

BEAST GIRL The first boy I loved trapped in our forest weeping. Could I have been human?

BEAST MAN I had expected to find love in our married life . . . I sensed a loss of control. Footsteps, I could hear her humming.

BEAST GIRL And that dawn.

BEAST MAN That dawn your life began.

DEAD HUMAN The beasts that came to the window each night knew.

Sound of footsteps, floating images. BEAST GIRL *runs to the hall, staring at the* DEAD HUMAN *who has come down into the hallway and stands before her. They remain staring at each other.* BEAST MAN *remains at the window.* BEAST WOMAN *is at her vanity, head fallen on the table asleep. She awakens, cries out. Organ music.*

BEAST WOMAN Each evening my husband kneels at my bedside, his face in twilight. I've begged him to wipe the blood from my bed, pleaded with him to lift me from those sheets of blood where I cut the throat of a pigeon poult to keep myself untouched. He is spending all his days grieving.

BEAST GIRL *and the* DEAD HUMAN *stand before each other.*

My daughter was born in September. I went into labor at my dead sister's funeral. Twenty hours later she was born. It was a girl.

BEAST MAN (*at the window*) The collar of my suit hung about my neck. The collar. She had snatched my collar. I walked to my table, sat down and opened the Bible. I had raped my wife.

BEAST WOMAN I came close to death in that birth. When I tried to hold the baby I became hysterical and broke into weeping.

BEAST GIRL *goes to her room.* DEAD HUMAN *follows her. He tries to rape her. They struggle. She falls back on the bed. He lifts his face from her. Her body jerks queerly. The room is silent. He tries to rouse her, caressing her. She looks up at him as he disappears into a darkened hall.*

BEAST GIRL My father comes to the door of my room, smiles, stopping in the hallway. He rests his head against the wall. My mother sits staring at a blank wall, brushing her beast hair. Dust fills the room. Our supper bones are on the floor, noises in the forest. Rain blew the trees. He stared at the floor in a peculiar manner, a half smile on his lips. Unbelievable, he said. He began to pray. He went on praying in the soft voice those lips mysterious. I looked at them in the dim living room, in the yellowed church and in their separate rooms. My father took on the appearance of an animal in his black preacher's suit.

BEAST WOMAN *is humming harshly a lullaby.* BEAST GIRL *lies back, appears to sleep.* BEAST WOMAN *walks up and down the stairs.* BEAST GIRL *rises and stares down the hallway at the stairs. The* DEAD HUMAN *enters from the darkness. She speaks to him.*

A toad jumps about. My mother holds out her arms to me. I run to her, dropping my bridal bouquet. When I come close to her I realize she is sitting on the bed in our room, the curtains drawn, the bed sheets crumpled. On the wall hangs the doleful picture of the Virgin and Child. She is kneeling by the window, her hair awry, her pale eyes closed. She does not look at me but stares fixedly toward the ceiling, praying.

BEAST MAN *calls her. She descends the stairway slowly.* BEAST WOMAN *walking in the hallway bursts into a sob.*

BEAST WOMAN Our ravaged beast faces . . . the jackals, the toad, and the mice are glad. The toad remembers when we were southern Negroes who came to the city.

BEAST MAN *beckons.*

BEAST GIRL What is it?

BEAST MAN It was a woman she wanted to be. I said what has beguiled you? I drew her upon the sofa. Was it death, she said. Death? You spoke of death at our wedding. I did not answer. Was I speaking of death or was it God? I smiled at her.

BEAST GIRL He will stop singing. (*Floating black sun.*) I sit on the bed. He tries to take me. I want him to. Yet we struggle on the bed. The room is silent and animals wander through our house. Now in the attic the boy I loved rocks our dead baby in his arms, sliding in lifeless steps. I cry out, calling him, but he does not answer. Outside the sun withdraws.

BEAST WOMAN How sad it makes me that you love him. I must go and pray.

BEAST MAN Outside wolves and bears. I sit in my room calling someone. A golden light comes into the room, a mysterious peace.

In the attic the DEAD HUMAN *rocks the dead baby,* BEAST WOMAN *hums harshly. The* DEAD HUMAN *hums his lullaby.*

He must stop singing.

BEAST GIRL My father built a crib. (*Staring at her father.*) How he loved me, saw me in the crib, circled by the golden aureole. My mother. Black shadows were etched under those pale eyes, for she hardly slept at night and suffered endless wakeful fits. She was constantly tired, giving the feeling of someone in continual child labor. Above the bed hung a doleful picture of the Virgin and Child. Beneath the picture was a print of a downcast Christ. Now the moon is out. A bird perches on my bedpost, a great toad runs through the house. I killed his baby with quinine and whiskey. Now he never leaves the attic.

DEAD HUMAN *slides from side to side rocking the dead baby.* BEAST GIRL *calling to him.*

You must stop singing the lullaby. (DEAD HUMAN *stops. She calls again.*) You must stop singing. (*He listens, then goes on. He goes on rocking the baby, humming. Appearance of the floating dead.*)

Darkness

BEAST WOMAN (*from her room*) Now I wander through the rooms, gaze at the dead. The flat sunlight bright. The jackals and I are glad. (*She goes to the door, locks it, sitting before the dresser, drinks wine and bursts into loud crying. The lights in all the rooms are dim and golden. Organ music.*)

BEAST GIRL (*before* BEAST MAN'*s doorway*) I dream, dead man. Dead blue crow, dead toad. My mother comes from her room, stands and stares at the dead. Beasts stare into the windows. Inside, my father's room is bright, full of the image of the dead boy I loved. Dead blue crow and a dead toad all bright.

BEAST MAN *smiles, leaves the room. Sound of footsteps.* BEAST GIRL *runs to the hall. The* DEAD HUMAN *appears from the hall. They stand before each other and stare.* BEAST WOMAN *awakens as from a bizarre dream, cries out.* DEAD HUMAN *and* BEAST GIRL *stand before each other.*

DEAD HUMAN Your hair grown, eyes turned beast yellow, the toad knew the first night of our marriage you fled from our bed. I took you on our bed. We struggled. I was stronger. When I lifted my face from you the room was silent. You said I had raped you like your father had raped your mother the night you were conceived. You fled from our bed.

Darkness

Organ music. BEAST GIRL *enters the hall outside* BEAST MAN'*s room. A yellow velvet cover drapes his shoulder. She remains outside. He beckons her. All is dark except* BEAST MAN'*s room. Candles burn. He pulls the velvet cover about his shoulder. She hangs outside the room. He beckons. She enters, sits on a pile of dark green books.* BEAST WOMAN *starts up the stairway to the attic.*

BEAST GIRL (*staring at him*) My father comes toward me, saying something I do not comprehend. His face exudes a yellow light. The sky turns black. He catches my hand. He begins to sing, no particular melody yet the tone is unwavering and free. No words are distinct. Silence. He goes to the window, looks out, continues to sing. He sings a beast song. Our hair grown, our eyes turned yellow. We are trapped in this beast house singing beast songs.

BEAST MAN *starts to move as if to strike* BEAST GIRL *in the face. His arm swings up, he drops his arm. He looks as if he is going to fall down, his big body swaying, then puts his hand to his eyes as if the lights suddenly blind him. He darts to the left side and then to the right still looking as though he might fall to the floor.*

Darkness

Flat moon bright. Sky very black, BEAST WOMAN *hums harshly. Her voice trails off.*

BEAST GIRL'*s room. A flat sunlight appears through her window. She is asleep.*

BEAST MAN'*s room. He is sitting in his room, calling someone unseen. A golden light comes into the room, seeming to fire him. He lifts himself from the chair, seizes his head.*

Darkness

BEAST WOMAN *falls across a tumbled bed, breathing heavily.* BEAST MAN *comes to the door. She sits up.*

DEAD HUMAN Now in the attic I weep over our dead baby. I am trapped in this beast house.

BEAST MAN, *listening, comes to the hall. He darts to the left and to the right, then suddenly sits on the stairs.*

BEAST GIRL'*s room. She awakens.* BEAST WOMAN *comes in, carrying the ax, going straight to* BEAST GIRL, *falling upon her, clasping her neck.*

BEAST WOMAN How sad it makes me that you love this boy.

Darkness

BEAST MAN'*s room.* BEAST GIRL *is staring at the candles in her father's room, sitting in his chair.*

BEAST GIRL All might be warm and sunlit. My father comes toward me, saying something I do not comprehend and the sky turns black. Why does he smile when he leaves my room?

Darkness

Floating dead images. BEAST WOMAN *sits in* BEAST GIRL'*s room, staring from the window.* BEAST MAN *suddenly stands on the stairs and starts to sing, no particular melody, and continues to sing looking up the stairs.*

BEAST MAN He has to stop singing. It was morning when I awakened the first day of my daughter's marriage. At last I knew who I was . . . no shadow of myself . . . I was revealed to myself.

BEAST WOMAN *goes on staring from the window.* BEAST MAN *goes on singing. A great light comes onto* BEAST GIRL. *She is wearing a satin wedding gown, sitting in her father's room staring at the candles.* BEAST MAN *looks up the stairs.*

I am more than your father. I am the accomplice to your fate. I believe in the connection too of dreams of dark winter nights. I believe in the joining of nightmares and visions.

Darkness

DEAD HUMAN *enters the house, stands at* BEAST GIRL'*s door. He goes to the bed, lies down.* BEAST GIRL *enters, wearing wedding gown, face ravaged, wedding gown torn, buttons fall from bodice. She takes a pillow, bends down, never taking her eyes from him, smothers him with all her strength. He moves fiercely as though he will spring up but instead totters backward, eyes open, tongue out. He holds out his hand, trying to reach her.* BEAST WOMAN *watches from her place at the window.*

BEAST WOMAN My daughter takes a pillow, never taking her eyes from him, smothers him with all her strength. He moves fiercely as though he will spring up but instead totters backward. He holds out his hand, trying to reach her.

Floating dead images bright. A strange flat sunlight comes out. BEAST WOMAN *watches.* BEAST MAN *stands on the steps, staring toward his daughter's room.* BEAST GIRL *flees to the hallway through it and into the attic, pulls down the ax. He has followed her into the hall. They meet. She swings the ax upon him. He tries to kiss her then falls dead in his blood. A blue crow behind her, she turns and instantly kills it with the ex. A giant toad hops to the room, croaking. She sees it and wildly axes it to pieces. Beast noises. She swings the ax, wildly screaming. Noises louder. She drops the ax, falls down weeping.*

Silence

BEAST MAN *and* BEAST WOMAN Our daughter fled to the hallway and into the attic. She pulled down the ax. She swung the ax upon him. He tried to kiss her but fell dead in his blood. Now the sky above our house is blue, three robins with red chests appear on the horizon. All is warm and sunlit.

Silence. Strange bright sunlight, then darkness.

COSTUME PLOT

BEAST GIRL—white organdy dress

BEAST WOMAN—nightgown

BEAST MAN—black preacher suit

DEAD HUMAN—very plain shirt and trousers

SCENE DESIGN

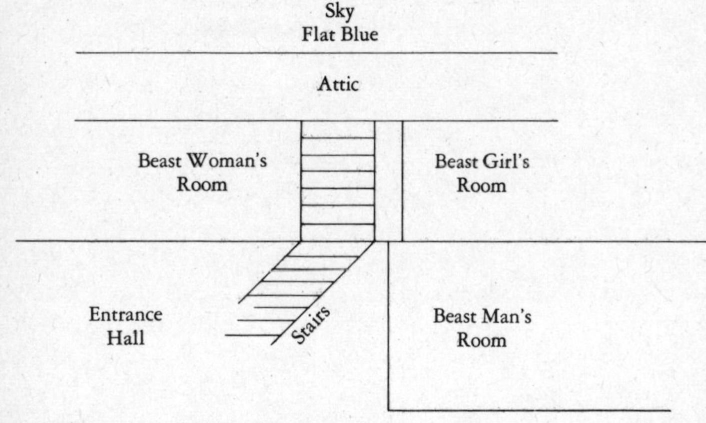

DEVIL MAS'

A Play in Three Acts

by Lennox Brown

Lennox Brown is from Trinidad and is currently living in Toronto. His plays have been published and produced on stage, television, and radio in the West Indies, the U.S., Canada, and in translation in Holland. Holder of B.A. and M.A. degrees in English and West Indian literature, he has already won seven prizes and has been a runner-up twice in national playwriting competitions in North America. In the U.S., he has been a winner in the Eugene O'Neill National Playwriting Conference in 1972, and runner-up in the annual Shubert Fellowship Contest in 1970. In Canada, he is the only playwright to have won the annual National One-Act Playwriting Competition four times in a row, 1965–69. In 1970 he won the Canada Council Arts Bursary. Recent productions in the U.S. include the widely-acclaimed *A Ballet Behind the Bridge* in 1972 off-Broadway by the Negro Ensemble Company. He is currently writing two separate cycles of plays dealing with the mythological black consciousness. *Behind the Bridge* is a cycle set in a

CAST OF CHARACTERS

NARRATOR *a little white girl about 12*

MANO DRAYTON *a black mechanic about 20*

JOSEPH DRAYTON *his younger brother, about 12*

MRS. DRAYTON *their mother, early 40's*

JEAN MANO'*s fiancée, a university student, 19*

PRIEST *white English or Irishman, about 50*

BORBON *black street-sweeper, about 50*

LALSINGH *East Indian bottle-vendor, about 50*

ACHONG *Chinese, owner of small grocery, about 50*

SPIRITS *Heroes of the Dead*

multi-racial ghetto in Trinidad. *West Indian Winter* is a cycle of plays set in urban areas of North America and Europe.

NOTE TO DIRECTOR

The spirit of Trinidad's Carnival is at the background of this play. It is only incidental to the plot, one vital aspect of the plot: and even so only its spirit or essence is suggested.

At the points in the play where such references are made, the author does *not* want a literal transplanting of the carnival spirit, aurally or visually to the stage, this being both unnecessary and impossible.

It is rather the essence and spirit of the reference that are desired. Another small point: the author feels that the Narrator of the play *must* be played by a little white girl, reading in the fairy-tale manner, for the successful working of this drama.

—*Lennox Brown*

ACT I

SCENE 1

TIME *The present.*

PLACE *A semi-rural district called St. Babb's on the outskirts of Port-of-Spain, Trinidad.*

A little girl, about 12, the NARRATOR, *enters a bare stage. She carries a stool and a book. She sits under a spotlight and reads in fairy-tale manner.*

NARRATOR

Dawn breaks on Sunday before Carnival
and the Season of Lent.
Night-Moon lies down to Bed in blue silk.
Earth rolls over.
Day-Sun, in yellow, climbs
the ancient Hill of Laventille
to float over soft Dawn.

Lights—this happens at back wall as she reads.

The early-morning noise of Animal, Man and Nature intermarry in primitive sounds to awake the World.

Sound—as she describes them.

Night turning into Day:
the turning of the first Leaf
in the Genesis of this Island's Bible.

Screech parrot. Crow rooster, and
flap your wings.
Bark and howl hungry dogs without a home.
Trees: rustle your leaves in the Wind like
soft brushes against the white skins
of Jazz Drums.

Sound—gradually increases in volume.

The Bells of St. Mart's are ringing
the early morning Mass.
Hear the Holy Christian Bells, unknowingly,
add a Pagan beat to our Melody.
Tyrrell is tuning his big Congo Drum,
occasionally, unconsciously,
beating it in time to the Music of the Cosmos.
Tomorrow is Carnival Monday.
Many jungles echo here in this Dawn
with our archetypal Music.
Our earliest cry of Creation.

Sound—grows loudly and fades slowly to be heard occasionally, spasmodically, not only from the stage, but around the whole auditorium, surrounding the audience. NARRATOR *exits, taking stool with her. Pale yellow light of Dawn. Multiple staging. At down right, a neatly-made bed with sheet gleaming white to suggest a bedroom.* MRS. DRAYTON *stands somberly looking at the bed. She is deeply troubled. Enter* JOSEPH, *with a small boy's sense of excitement, but suppressing it, because of his mother's somberness. Let his mother's mood dominate the stage.*

MRS. DRAYTON (*quietly*) He didn't sleep home again last night. Almost every night now . . . for months

JOSEPH Mother, I saw him.

MRS. DRAYTON When?

JOSEPH This morning. I know where he is this morning.

MRS. DRAYTON You know?

JOSEPH Over the hills. In a little shack make of rotten wood and dry bush. It hiding behind the tall mango vert trees.

MRS. DRAYTON He sleeping there?

JOSEPH And working. Making something . . .

MRS. DRAYTON His Carnival costume.

JOSEPH It must be. He have it so that even if you can find the shack, you can't see inside, what he doing.

MRS. DRAYTON But what it is he have to hide from us? All these months?

JOSEPH Don't tell him on me. I spied and crawled like a snake to find out where he always going. He will be vex with me.

MRS. DRAYTON I have to see the priest.

JOSEPH The priest in this?

MRS. DRAYTON I know something wrong. In my bones I could feel it like ice.

JOSEPH But is Carnival tomorrow. Nothing could go wrong.

MRS. DRAYTON I having lunch for the priest here today. I going to have a talk with him.

Sound—"nature" sounds. Fade up and hold. Enter MANO. *Tall. Strong. Serious. A tired, almost imperceptible air of tragedy hovers around his face.*

MANO Morning.

MRS. DRAYTON Morning.

A silence ensues that forbids questions. Slow blackout.

SCENE 2

TIME *A little later the same day. Stronger shade of yellow Sun.*

PLACE *The same.*

Multiple staging. Almost bare stage except for a table and three chairs at which are seated the PRIEST, MRS. DRAYTON, *and* JOSEPH *at lunch. This suggests a dining room. Sound—"nature" sounds, but dawn has receded, and because tomorrow is Carnival there are snatches of music, steelband and other kinds.*

JOSEPH Finish Mother. My plate clean like the Sky. I could go now?

PRIEST But surely you'll die from too much Carnival excitement.

JOSEPH Tomorrow! Tomorrow morning! Just hours from now! Sailors, wild Indians, midnight cowboys, robbers, dragons, ju-ju warriors, and kings and queens and all the big bands in Frederick Street and the Savannah. And things to eat—channa, ice-cream, and rhoti . . .

PRIEST Can you sleep tonight for excitement?

Sound—snatches of Desperadoes Steel Band practicing lower down the Hill.

JOSEPH They practicing the road-march again! O God! They practicing it again! Mother, I could go? I could go?

MRS. DRAYTON (*preoccupied*) Don't stay too long, you hear?

JOSEPH *has already vanished in a burst of speed. Pause.*

PRIEST Where is he now?

MRS. DRAYTON Sleeping, Father . . .

PRIEST Jimmy. Don't call me Father. The old days are gone for good.

MRS. DRAYTON A lot more rice and curry beef still here, you know. Don't waste food. I make it too hot for you?

PRIEST A cook-up too hot for me? After ten years in Trinidad?

Pause.

MRS. DRAYTON This morning Joseph find out where he was going all the time—hiding and working alone in secret in a old shack.

PRIEST Carnival costume?

MRS. DRAYTON Must be. Joseph couldn't see inside.

PRIEST Has he said yet what mask . . . ?

MRS. DRAYTON Not a word to a single human being.

PRIEST Must be a surprise he's planning for the whole island . . . and all the tourists from New York, Toronto, and London . . . his African Prince costume . . .

MRS. DRAYTON No. Is something different this time. Something wrong. The hiding. Not talking. Not sleeping under his own roof. Everything a secret.

PRIEST What about his helpers . . . Borbon, Lalsingh, Achong . . .

MRS. DRAYTON No. He become like an enemy to them. His best friends.

PRIEST But why? It's strange . . .

MRS. DRAYTON Every year Mano telling everybody what kind of African prince he is playing. And every year he winning the first prize for the whole island in front of thousands of people from here and from away. This year only silence and secrecy come from his mouth.

PRIEST It must be just a passing mood . . .

MRS. DRAYTON No. Is more than that. No laughter. No smiles. Eyes hard and looking into the Earth as if to read things buried deep under the ground. Face drawn tight. Serious. No joy. Something have to be wrong.

PRIEST He's keeping it a secret for some special reason . . .

MRS. DRAYTON It was the same with his father . . .

PRIEST No. No. No. You mustn't even think that.

MRS. DRAYTON I tell you the same thing is happening. His father was happy for Carnival every year. Then that year he was a changed man. A strong and healthy man with a broad back . . . spreading like a range of mountains. Arms like the trunks of twin trees. And all his teeth white with the soundness of fresh milk. Then suddenly that year, just before Carnival, he start to behave like Mano now . . .

Pause. Sound—"nature" music. Fade up, then out.

PRIEST It was an accident. The doctors examined him right away.

MRS. DRAYTON The doctors didn't know what to say. They said it was a mystery. And the papers and the magistrate at the inquest said the same thing. Is not a lie I telling.

PRIEST I know . . . they couldn't explain in medical terms . . .

MRS. DRAYTON You do God's work. You didn't know. He died on his feet, while living . . .

PRIEST I'll talk to Mano when he wakes up. I'll ask him what mask he's going to play.

MRS. DRAYTON Dead cold like ice his father was. So sudden . . .

Slow blackout.

SCENE 3

TIME *Same day. Few hours later. Sun's deep yellow.*

PLACE *Same multiple staging. This time it's* MANO*'s secret shack.*

The shack is suggested at down left. The preceding scene took place at right to facilitate and expedite the change. An elemental and primordial quality is suggested by the shack with its old boards, sheets of galvanized iron and bushes. A feeling of paganism is evoked. There are contrasting colors here and there, but these should not be brilliant. Color has to be built to a peak gradually in later scenes. Dried animal skins and furs hang from the walls. Dried skulls and animal bones have been "mounted" in an improvised manner. There are knives, spears, swords—all actually wood painted silver—and chains. There is no consistent pattern to suggest what MANO *is making.* JEAN *enters. She hasn't been here before and reacts accordingly.*

JEAN (*trying to hide her apprehension*) Nice place you have here—the Jungle Hilton. Going modern, eh?

MANO You bring it?

JEAN So this is where you've been hiding. I got lost completely, four times, just trying to find the tall mango vert trees. Now I know how Columbus felt—like a complete ass.

MANO You remember to bring it?

She hugs him from behind and kisses his neck as he works. Then she takes a book from her bag.

JEAN This is the right one?

MANO (*quietly*) Yes.

JEAN I stole it from the library. It's a rare book. The only copy they've got. I could get expelled for that.

MANO They should have more than one copy. Mechanics could read too. Not only university students.

JEAN Is something for Carnival, Mano?

MANO Yes. (*He's been leafing through the book.*)

JEAN Can I help?

MANO No.

JEAN Finding what you looking for?

MANO Some.

JEAN (*suddenly changed mood, serious, even angry*) Why you wouldn't let me help you? I love you. You big beautiful black man. Mano! Mano! ! !

MANO (*absorbed in the book*) What?

JEAN Something's gone wrong. What is it?

MANO (*quietly*) Nothing.

Pause.

JEAN Sorry. I always shout when I get vex.

MANO Is alright.

JEAN When two people love each other, they share their lives, secrets, plans. We'll have to do that when we get married.

MANO We will.

JEAN Why can't you tell me what you're going to play?

MANO Tomorrow is Carnival. You'll know.

JEAN You won't tell me—even now.

MANO No.

Pause.

JEAN I love you, Mano.

Slow blackout.

SCENE 4

TIME *Same day. A little later. Yellow Sun beginning to put on patches of red silk.*

PLACE *The same shack.*

Sound—"nature" music as before with occasional snatches of steelband. MANO *is still working alone.* JOSEPH *enters stealthily, lies on his belly, spying.*

MANO (*without looking around*) You see enough?

JOSEPH (*so startled, he leaps up like a jack-in-the-box*) Oy!

MANO Come inside, Mr. Snake.

JOSEPH I sorry, Mano. I didn't get on like a real big man. How you teach me to.

MANO Is alright. Man best friend does stab him in the back. I see you spying on me this morning too.

JOSEPH You see me this morning? How?

MANO You ain't know I have two secret eyes in the back of my head? Bring that book over there.

JOSEPH Is a library book from the university.

MANO Thanks for telling me. I woulda never know. You could read them pages I mark off?

JOSEPH Yes! Yes! Yes! I could read anything for you . . .

MANO Not now. Tomorrow morning.

Pause. JOSEPH *can't believe his ears.*

JOSEPH Tomorrow morning? Carnival morning?

MANO No. Christmas. What else?

JOSEPH Where?

MANO On stage in the Savannah.

JOSEPH You mean . . . I going to play mas' with you? You the champion?

MANO Yes.

Pause.

JOSEPH This is the best, biggest, most important, happiest day in my whole life—even happier than when school close for holidays.

MANO Good.

JOSEPH But what *I* could do?

MANO Just read them pages loud from the stage.

JOSEPH Mano . . . what mas' . . . ?

MANO Don't ask me no question. Just sit down there and practice reading them pages.

JOSEPH Yes boss.

MANO Don't tell nobody about this. I ain't joking. I serious like a dead man. Don't tell *nobody.*

JOSEPH Mano, if I tell anybody, I hope God smash up this whole Earth like a egg-shell. Then kill me afterwards.

MANO Just practice reading. You have to be perfect to win anything in life.

JOSEPH Yes boss.

MANO Joseph, I mean it. You can't tell nobody. Not a single person.

JOSEPH Not even myself.

JOSEPH *crosses himself. Blackout.*

SCENE 5

TIME *Same day. A little later. More streaks of red afternoon silk in Sun-Sky*

PLACE *Multiple staging. Bare stage this time. Only a rocking chair to suggest a living room.*

Sound—snatches of Carnival music more insistent. "Nature" sounds. At center, MRS. DRAYTON *rocks with a slow deliberation, the inevitability of doom in each sway of the rocker. A somber mask of tragedy has etched itself more deeply on her face.* JOSEPH *is at her feet talking excitedly.*

JOSEPH He have goat skin, cattle skin, rabbit fur, snake skin, and the skull of a pig, and the skulls of three manicou hanging . . .

MRS. DRAYTON You ask him what mas' he going to play tomorrow?

Pause.

JOSEPH Yes, but he wouldn't tell me nothing, Mother.

Pause.

MRS. DRAYTON Try to remember good, Joseph. Take your mind back right inside the shack. You notice a big wooden fork?

Pause.

JOSEPH Yes . . . with prongs . . . a ancient-looking fork . . .

MRS. DRAYTON *rises slowly, tension in every bone and muscle.*

I didn't remember, Mother . . . how you know . . . ?

MRS. DRAYTON It belonged to your father.

JOSEPH Father? You told me he died . . . all of a sudden one Carnival day . . .

Slow blackout. Music and "nature" sounds are more insistent.

SCENE 6

TIME *Afternoon the same day. Specks of a dying yellow streak a blood-red sky.*

PLACE *The same. Multiple staging.*

Almost bare stage. At back center, the vague outline of an altar to suggest the inside of a Roman Catholic church. At down center are the PRIEST, MRS. DRAYTON, *and* JEAN. *They are all taut like drums tensed for beating.*

PRIEST Just having the same fork doesn't mean anything . . .

MRS. DRAYTON Is the only sure sign. And we know it.

PRIEST (*to* JEAN) And the book was on history?

JEAN But I know that book. It has no connection at all.

PRIEST He won't talk to me about it.

JEAN It's no proof. Everything will be alright. We'll be married. Everything *must* be alright . . .

MRS. DRAYTON Secrets. Sadness on his face. Hiding away in a little shack deep in the bush. No talking. No joy.

PRIEST No. I don't think he's going to do it.

JEAN Even if he does do it . . . the same thing doesn't have to happen.

PRIEST That's right. That was five years ago.

JEAN What happens in life before doesn't have to happen once more. Like the Sun rising and the Moon waxin every day.

MRS. DRAYTON (*rising*) Five years ago after a happy life, my husband suddenly decide to play Devil Mas'. He never play it before. He was strong like a horse and jumped and pranced full of life. Carnival Monday morning he put on the Evil costume with the skins of animals and their dead skulls. He danced with the big band to the Savannah. He lead them on stage. He raised his fork. "I call the Devil from Hell," he shouted. (*Pause.*) The strength flowed from his limbs suddenly. I saw him look up to God's Sky for help. But it was no use. (*Pause.*) Now some awful Power on Earth, some Unknown Spirit, some Mysterious Evil is gripping my oldest. Mano is going to play Devil Mas' just like his father. In his warm green youth, something is forcing him to walk into the Cold House of Death tomorrow morning. To be crushed from the Earth.

Lights begin to fade. From JEAN'*s throat comes a single painful, muffled, sobbing cry. This must not be overdone. It must be skilfully played—a piece of human agony in the face of sudden but inevitable terror.*

JEAN No . . . not Mano.

Blackout. In the dark, Afro-Caribbean music, snatches of steel-band and the "nature" sounds mixed together.

SCENE 7

TIME *The same day. Sun grows sleepy. Sky wears her wine-dark gown of Evening.*

PLACE *The same multiple staging. Bare stage to suggest an open-air, outdoor scene, perhaps a suggestion of a tree in the background.*

Sound—Small snatches of more Carnival-like music, but the "nature" sounds are growing different because it is evening and Night approaches. Male voices are heard singing—raggedly—off stage. Raucous, tipsy, but not drunk (yet). Enter BORBON, LALSINGH, *and* ACHONG. *They more or less dance on in a moderate Carnival shuffle. This "dance" is very brief and underplayed. One of them has a bottle of rum. Each of them is carrying, not wearing, last year's Carnival costume. The color on stage is now growing. We're getting an idea of the Color that is Carnival—but only an idea. The stage isn't brilliant yet. The peak of Color is still to come. Nevertheless we now have vivid splashes of it in the costumes they are carrying. We catch a bit of the wild spirit in their brief dance. As they come on, we get quick dazzling flashes of silk and velvet: reds, blues, greens, and yellows—"strong" colors.*

BORBON Dance if you dancing
Jump if you jumping . . .
LALSINGH Mas' in me ass
Mas' bursting up me ass . . .

ACHONG O God! Lemme break away
Make room
Play mas' . . .

They sit down with their bottle of rum, folding the costumes and putting them away so the audience has to imagine and anticipate what lies ahead tomorrow. The PRIEST *enters.*

BORBON Aha! *You* tell we. Why Carnival does send we so mad in Trinidad? I ain't know myself.

LALSINGH If a man mad already, how he could know he mad or why he mad?

ACHONG If he did know, he wouldn't be mad in the first place, or else he wouldna know he was going mad.

LALSINGH So in that case, he wouldn't be mad at all.

The bottle makes the round.

BORBON That is what I like about rum-talk. It so sensical. I asking Jimmy here to tell me, personally, why on Carnival Day in my case, the blood does go pelting like a hurricane through the veins in my body. Like . . . like . . . it ain't have no "like" word to put beside that feeling.

ACHONG Words fail him.

LALSINGH No. *He* fail words. He didn't go too far in school.

BORBON *You* could go to hell right now.

ACHONG No thanks. I ain't want no personal invitation to visit your home.

PRIEST It's not only *your* blood that sings and screams on Carnival Day, Borbon. Carnival is as old as Mankind.

LALSINGH Even older than Borbon?

PRIEST (*smiling*) Yes.

LALSINGH That is really old, boy.

PRIEST But it has a special meaning for Borbon and his ancestors.

BORBON I didn't tell you so? I ain't have to boast. Only Lalsingh. Just because the other day he enter a singing competition with a frog—he come second.

PRIEST Carnival is Universal. All over Roman Catholic Europe.

ACHONG In Brazil too.

LALSINGH And in New Orleans.

PRIEST It's Man taking Joy to withstand Suffering. Pleasure to ease Pain. Good/Evil. Darkness/Light. The Union of Opposites. The Rhythms of the Universe . . .

LALSINGH Put it this way—is a hell of a good fete.

BORBON And nowhere in the Universe it is like in Trinidad. Is not so much the Ending. Is the Beginning that does make me mad . . .

PRIEST See? The Union of Opposites: Beginning/Ending.

BORBON Tomorrow, Jouvert Morning, when I hear them deep bass drums from Desperadoes, and I see the bush waving like trees, and I hear the feet sweeping sweet like surf, my Heart does melt in with the Whole Sight and Sound. I does become One. With Everything. I does feel Holy like God. But is only the bass drums, and the bush and the Dawn and Desperadoes that can cast that kind of magic.

LALSINGH Up here we have the best steel band.

ACHONG And the best Prince . . . you forgetting Mano?

BORBON Is funny how we have them best things, yet strange things does happen up here in St. Babb's.

PRIEST Strange things happen all over the Universe.

BORBON But especially up here in St. Babb's. Like Mano father dying so sudden on stage that Carnival Day. They say it was because he call the Devil from Hell.

LALSINGH Or the time they find that little girl hanging from the Silk Cotton tree. They was searching for her with lanterns all night. They say it was suicide. Like it have a curse on St. Babb's.

BORBON Or what cause all them goats to jump off the Quarry and kill themselves all together that night a few years ago?

ACHONG Something like that happen in the Bible, not so?

PRIEST Yes. That was Beelzebub.

Enter MANO *carrying wrapped packages and sheets of paper—like manuscripts.*

BORBON Look the champion Carnival Prince.

LALSINGH What you calling yourself this year?

ACHONG When you going to stop winning all them prizes, eh?

MANO I want some help.

BORBON You know you don't have to ask for it. That is what we here for. Years now we leading you on stage like a true Prince.

MANO Is different this time. Is like a play. I want you to wear these (*hands out the scripts*) and to do this . . . tomorrow morning.

Pause as they read. The stage suddenly becomes very serious.

BORBON This different in truth . . .

LALSINGH I ain't understand why . . .

ACHONG Me too. You never do this before.

Enter MRS. DRAYTON, JEAN, *and* JOSEPH *from different directions. They converge on the scene beautifully in a ballet-like grouping.* MANO *gives* JEAN *and* JOSEPH *papers and costumes too.*

BORBON You ain't playing African Prince this year?

Pause.

MANO No. This year I playing Devil Mas'. With the ancient fork my father did use.

Beautiful tableau of the whole group. The NARRATOR *enters with her stool and sits down center dominating the tableau.*

NARRATOR

Yellow Day-Sun was trailing red silk all day
across the Sky.
To Blood-Red he changed this afternoon.
But now he's getting sleepy,
and Sky wears her wine-dark Gown of Evening.

Lighting—The change she is describing takes place.

Dying Day-Sun has sunk and disappeared
beneath the Horizon.
But climbing the same ancient Hill of Laventille
is Night-Moon,

Swaying her hips in her blue silk dress.
Soft ripening female coming to life.
The Creatures of Night creep out
to sing their primal song.

Sound—tropical night sounds as she describes them.

Crickets whispering their bush secrets,
owls hooting. Frogs and crapauds hoarse from
croaking about Carnival tomorrow.
Jumbie-birds whistling bad news and evil messages
of Death.
Sandflies and Moths dancing in wild circles to the
buzzing of Mosquitoes filled with Blood.
Black beetles and Bats flapping wings.
Fire-flies flashing on and off in the glowing dark
like traffic-lights.
Creatures of the Night—celebrate!
Moon, now full and riper than Mango Rose,
Replace Sun. The exact opposite
of thc Celestial lighting
the Universe switched on this morning.

NARRATOR *exits. Pause.*

MANO Tomorrow morning. Jouvert. I going to call the Devil from Hell.

Lights begin to fade, leaving the soft silvery Moon floating serenely above the Dark Earth—and the tableau of human beings standing on it.

CURTAIN

ACT II
SCENE 1

TIME *About five o'clock the following morning—Monday Jouvert.*

PLACE *The same multiple staging. This time a bare stage.*

NARRATOR *enters with stool, reads from book as before.*

NARRATOR

Night, turning over and over,
was too restless with excitement to sleep.
So hours later, Dawn breaks open
like the Universe of an Egg.
It is Jouvert Monday Morning.
Turn the second leaf in the Bible of our
tropical Genesis.
Day-Sun is waking up again, opening and rubbing
his eyes, but his yellow house-robe,
he has not yet draped over his shoulders.
It is Lady Night Moon, soft and silvery,
floating serenely above the Dark Earth,
who will descend the ancient Hill of Laventille
to bed below.

Lighting—the Moon at back center wall is slowly descending. A bluish light fills the stage. This will continue to change to yellow throughout Act II until the sun has fully arisen.

Animal, Man and Nature tremble in every nerve this morning with the excitement of the Cosmic Music waking up the world. Each heart is a drum going mad. Our special World today of Carnival.

Sound—"nature" sounds mixed with the music of the steelband and brass orchestras. NARRATOR *exits, taking stool with her. The music grows, especially the drums. Dancing figures will appear, singly, at various spots in the auditorium. This is to suggest to the audience that they are surrounded by the wild abandon of Jouvert. The operative word here is "suggest." There must be no crowd scenes dancing. Individual dancers appear. We suddenly hear a warrior-like scream at the back of the auditorium at left. A spotlight picks out a masked figure of a half-man, half-animal. His costume motif reminds one of the rich imagination behind traditional African sculpture. The music pulsates, and standing in one place, he writhes, gyrates, twists and turns: he's really doing an interpretation or suggestion of the Spirit of Carnival. There is another weird animal-like call from the auditorium. The spotlight shoots across to the front of the auditorium, on the right this time. There is another dancer, with the same costume motif, but different colors and a different animal suggested. The costumes are a mixture of furs, animal skins, raffia cloth, straw, shells, bush, fiber, bits of glass and clay, painted wood and stone, copper, wire, brass, and flowers, and of course, every color of the rainbow is there. These materials suggest elemental Nature. Some of the figures are disguised as part alligator, part bird, part squirrel, goat, monkey, manicou, etc. The head masks, which completely cover the faces, look unreal and weird, as if these are strange disembodied Spirits. The spotlight picks out more figures in different parts of the auditorium—depending on the amenities of the theater—individual dancers should appear on stage, in the aisles, at exits, on balconies, even hanging from the rafters like bats. Everywhere and anywhere, as if the world has gone mad: which is correct because the God of Disorder, Chaos, rules over Cosmos-Order.*

Sudden silence.

MANO *appears on stage at down center. The rest of the stage is dark. He is dressed as the Devil, more outstandingly and colorfully than the others. He slowly, almost ritualistically, puts on his head mask, so that we can recognize him when he's wearing it. He takes up the Fork which his father had used on that fateful Carnival Day. Lights fade slowly on* MANO. *Sound—raise volume of music to a high peak, fade and hold softly. Blackout. But keep pulsating music going in the dark.*

SCENE 2

TIME *A little later the same day.*

PLACE *Same multiple staging. Specific scene to be described by* NARRATOR.

Enter NARRATOR *with stool. Reads from down center of darkened stage, except for her spotlight.*

NARRATOR

The Eyes of the World are on Us today.
Tourists from the United States, and Canada,
and Europe.
Our stage is set for the main show in the Savannah.
Our audience awaits this massive spectacle.
Many huge bands, the color of the Sea and the Sun,
the Moon and the Sky have come and gone.
And now we are waiting for the champion Mano.
The Eyes of the World are on us today,
but even more important,
Our own Eyes are on Us.
Our own Eyes are on Us.

Exits quickly with stool. General lighting comes up. The stage has not really been used between Acts I and II, and hardly at all during the first scene of this Act. This has been done deliberately to give time to get on a special prop at back center. It is a huge towering statue of a papier-maché man, ten feet tall. There is a huge cavity in his stomach, somewhat like a pouch. He is dressed in a patchwork suit, a crazy-quilt pattern made up of the flags of Canada, the United States, and of as many European countries as possible. He looks harmless, yet sinister with that air of fantasy and reality that Carnival floats have about them. This huge statue holds in his hands many leashes. These extend downwards and fit around the necks (like pet dogs) of the following masquerade characters:

1. *A white* FOREIGN INVESTOR, *cigar-smoking, black pin-stripe suit, carries new shiny briefcase.*

2. *A* WHITE TRINIDAD BUSINESSMAN, *well-dressed, but not as well as the foreign investor. Has a battered briefcase.*

3. *A Trinidadian* CHINESE BUSINESSMAN, *middle-class, incongruously an old-fashioned shop-counter weighing scale.* (ACHONG)

4. *A Trinidadian* BROWN-SKINNED MULATTO *of the professional class.*

5. *An* EAST INDIAN TRINIDADIAN, *small-proprietor type. He carries incongruously a length of sugar-cane and a cutlass, although he has already risen several economic and social rungs above this.*

6. *A black* CIVIL SERVANT, *Trinidadian. Half of his face is painted white. He carries a book of Civil Service regulations.* (BORBON)

7. *A black* SOCIAL CLIMBER, *Trinidadian. A woman in a formal evening gown. She wears false breasts and a false bottom, padded deliberately, hugely, to farcical proportions. Holds elegantly in her hand, a Martini, in a huge glass: a parody of a real Martini.*

8. *A black* SHANGO WOMAN, *Trinidadian. In her white dress and white head-tie, she looks like a mad prophetess. Has a bell and lighted candle.*

9. *A black* POLICEMAN, *Trinidadian, in uniform. He holds at arm's length the figure of a male dummy dressed in rags, a black dummy. From its face we can tell it's the policeman's "double." Mounted on top of the* POLICEMAN'*s head is a white mask with European features.*

These are grouped imaginatively. They're not quite a tableau, but each holds a different pose and faces a different direction. They appear to be in different worlds, but they're all connected by the action that is to follow, and by the leashes from the huge towering statue which dominates the stage, and everyone on it.

SHANGO WOMAN (*rings bell*)

Together we conspire
Each other to deceive
Together we conspire
Each other to deceive.

CIVIL SERVANT (*reads, savoring the sound of each word*) ". . . in view of the exigencies of the Service . . . on the advice of the appropriate authorities . . . on secondment from another department . . . responsible public opinion . . . substantial elements of the society . . ."

He and EAST INDIAN *put friendly arms around each other's shoulders.* EAST INDIAN *"stabs" him in the back with cutlass.* CIVIL SERVANT *falls and "dies."* EAST INDIAN *takes huge roll of bills from* CIVIL SERVANT'*s pocket.*

SOCIAL CLIMBER

I sincerely regret
there was no etiquette
when I went to the African ballet
Shall I forget
the son-of-a-bitch who stole my wallet?

BROWN-SKINNED MULATTO *snatches some of the money from* EAST INDIAN. *As he starts counting,* CHINESE BUSINESSMAN *snatches some from him.*

FOREIGN INVESTOR Our foreign policy? We respect the territorial integrity of every foreign state. We will not interfere in the internal affairs . . .

POLICEMAN *continuously circles the group, as if on patrol. All the time he senselessly, viciously beats the dummy with his night stick.* WHITE TRINIDAD BUSINESSMAN *takes some of the money from* CHINESE BUSINESSMAN. FOREIGN INVESTOR *takes some from the* WHITE TRINIDAD BUSINESSMAN.

SHANGO WOMAN (*rings bell*)

Together we conspire
Each other to deceive.

FOREIGN INVESTOR *puts roll of money bills into the huge cavity in the statue's stomach.* CIVIL SERVANT *gets up from being "dead." He smiles and embraces his Indian brother.* EAST INDIAN *stares at audience in utter mock disbelief.* CIVIL SERVANT *"shoots" him with wooden gun.* EAST INDIAN *falls and "dies." This falling and dying act is deliberately over-acted, the way bad American actors die in Westerns. Sound—Music more loudly, then sudden silence. Suddenly, as if appearing from thin air,* MANO, *fully-dressed as the Devil, leaps into the middle of the group. His wild colorful costume contrasts sharply with theirs. Blackout.*

SCENE 3

TIME *The same.*

PLACE *The same.*

Sound—snatches of Carnival music. MANO, *armed with his ancient fork, walks among the group, examining them as if he has just landed from a strange planet. They stand in tableau, and although they speak, they do not break their poses. As he passes them, each, except* SHANGO WOMAN, *places a collar attached to a chain around* MANO'*s neck, chest, etc., but he is still free to walk. The situation is that they are being held on leash and are in turn holding him in leash.*

SOCIAL CLIMBER Who invite *him?*

BROWN-SKINNED MULATTO Is he blue-black, black, black-brown . . . ?

CIVIL SERVANT Dark-brown, chocolate-dark, red-skin, brown-skin . . . ? Light-brown, fair, light colored?

EAST INDIAN Don't trust him.

MANO *does a slow, sinuous, writhing kind of dance using arms, head, shoulders, feet, but standing in one place—all part of his attempt to throw off the chains.*

CHINESE What kind of hair he have?

SOCIAL CLIMBER Bad? Tacky-tacky? Curly? Goodish?

BROWN-SKINNED MULATTO Where he went to school? Where he living? What class-person he is?

CIVIL SERVANT Low? Lower? Lowest? Lower-middle? Middle? Middle-middle? Upper-middle? Or . . . high? How much money he have?

WHITE TRINIDAD BUSINESSMAN Call the police for him.

FOREIGN INVESTOR Hold him tight. Be careful never to let him go. Never.

MANO, *with guttural, jungle-like grunts keeps gesturing to the ground with his fork as if he's trying to tell them about something under the stage.*

WHITE TRINIDAD BUSINESSMAN What he trying to do?

BROWN-SKINNED MULATTO Trying to tell us something?

EAST INDIAN About the ground? The floor? What under there?

FOREIGN INVESTOR No! Stop him! Stop him! Not that! Keep him away from there!

MANO *is now at down center. Looking down on the ground and gesturing towards it with his fork. In order to restrain him the better, all of them, in a beautifully choreographed movement, start walking backwards forming a circle on the perimeter of the stage, the center of which is* MANO, *from whom chains radiate.* SHANGO WOMAN, *with her bell and candle, stands near him, as if she wants to help him do whatever he's trying to accomplish. As he dances he throws off the chain collars one by one.*

FOREIGN INVESTOR I told you to hold him tight! Now you'll see! I warned you!

MANO *opens a trap door, and slowly descends, disappearing under the stage. The circle of people on stage exit in a ballet-like movement, walking backwards, as in slow-motion film.* JEAN *and* JOSEPH *enter at down right and down left respectively. They are carrying lecterns and what look like long roll-call sheets. They're dressed simply in a pastel shade—brown maybe, but both must be wearing the same color. They stand looking at the roll-call sheets on the lecterns. Lights begin to fade. Spotlight lingers on the black hole left by the open trap door. It looks ominous. Blackout. Music pulsates with soft drums in the dark.*

SCENE 4

TIME *The same.*

PLACE *The same.*

The huge statue is gone. JEAN *and* JOSEPH *are standing in the same positions.* NARRATOR *enters with a stool, places it just behind the ominous-looking black hole. She reads under spotlight.*

NARRATOR

A Black Hole opens in the Face of the Earth,
Night-Moon in her blue silk dress
slowly lies down to Bed,
as Day-Sun climbs the whitening Sky.

Lighting—this takes place along the back wall.

The blue-eyed Sea is shiny
with the whitest of ships,
Locked Below.
The Brown Earth waves with the golden green
of rows of cane fields.
Millions came to this Carnival of Cane and Sugar.
Millions came.

Lighting—Grows and reveals a backdrop on which are painted the sea with a fleet of white ships, and on land, fields of cane.

From the fields of sweet cane and red blood
drums beat, torches flame and Conch shells blow.

Sound—as she describes them, ominously martial.

And the stage is set,
And the stage is set.

Exits quickly with stool.

JEAN (*reading in a neutral level voice, and looking at the audience*) You are a thing. You are not a human being. You are owned. You have no name. You are not allowed to wear shoes. You are forbidden to marry, or to go to church. You are forbidden to learn to read or write.

JOSEPH (*reading in same way*) You are strictly forbidden to start the slightest business enterprise. You must not show any economic endeavor, regardless of how small. You are forbidden to sell even the cane, coffee, sugar or cotton you yourselves make. It is against the Law for you to go into business.

JEAN If you run away and you are caught, the judges are free to order you burned alive. The first time your nose will be slit, the second time it will be cut right off. Your leader will be pinched three times with a red-hot iron, then hanged. And each of you will have a leg chopped off.

JOSEPH If you are pardoned, your ear will be cut off and you will receive 150 lashes. If you know anyone planning to run away and you don't inform on him, you will be burned on the forehead and given 100 lashes.

JEAN If you raise your hand against a white, or even a child of his, *your* hand will be cut off, or you will be hanged.

JOSEPH And if you rebel or even try to rebel, you will be flogged. You will be torn to pieces alive. And your arms, legs, head, and hands will be left hanging in different public parks and places.

Pause.

JEAN What are you going to do?

Blackout. Conch shells blowing and drums beating in the dark.

SCENE 5

TIME *The same.*

PLACE *The same.*

JEAN *and* JOSEPH *in same positions. Lighting the same.*

JOSEPH Hundreds of thousands of human beings became angry.

JEAN In the very Beginning, they fought back. They rebelled. On land and sea.

JOSEPH St. Kitts—1639; Barbados—1649; Haiti—1679; Jamaica—1690 . . .

JEAN Cuba—1729; St. Thomas, St. John—1733; Antigua—1736; Guadeloupe—1737 . . .

JOSEPH Martinique—1752; Nevis—1761; Surinam—1763 . . .

JEAN St. Vincent—1769; Tobago—1769 . . .

JOSEPH St. Lucia—1795; Grenada—1795; Trinidad—1805; Guyana—1808.

Pause.

JEAN But who were their leaders? Who were these men who remained human? What were they like? How did they know in the very marrow of their bones Universal Right from Universal

Wrong? Were their souls larger than average souls? Their intelligence genius? Their hearts bigger? Who were these men born on this very soil we stand on?

Lights fade on JEAN *and* JOSEPH. *The Black Hole remains lighted, but the coloring of the lighting has been changed into something especially poetic. A new kind of light also grows at back, left, and right.* JEAN *and* JOSEPH *intone the following names. The Heroes of the Dead ascend from the black hole as if returning to Life. In a beautiful and imaginative piece of choreography and grouping, the Heroes of the Dead form two crescents on either side of the black hole. This is the play's peak of color. These Heroes, even the ones dressed in blood-stained rags, must suggest the artistic brilliance and vividness that underlies the psychology of Carnival.*

JEAN The Jamaican Maroons: Accompong, Quao, Cudjoe, Cuffee. Trinidad: Thisbe (a woman), Congo King, Captain Simon.

They enter as their names are called. Serious expressions.

JOSEPH Chief Tackey and Boukman—Jamaica.

JEAN Basterre Peter and Jingo—St. Kitts.

JOSEPH King Court, Tomboy, and Hercules—Antigua.

JEAN Toussaint L'Ouverture, Henri Christophe, and Dessalines—Haiti.

JOSEPH Captain Adoe—Surinam.

JEAN Paul Bogle, George William Gordon, and Marcus Garvey—Jamaica.

JOSEPH Maceo—Cuba.

JEAN Chief Daaga, Captain Samson, Old Michel, Marie—Trinidad.

Pause. Shimmering poetic tableau. Lights fade slowly. Blackout. Silence.

SCENE 6

TIME *The same.*

PLACE *The same.*

Lights up. Only the Heroes of the Dead are on stage now. They watch the audience seriously, silently, then one by one, alternating from each side of the two crescents, they descend back into the Black Hole of the Past. After they have disappeared, MANO *emerges from the Hole. He closes the trap door.* PRIEST *appears. They exchange a silent stare. Blackout. Curtain.*

ACT III
SCENE 1

TIME *The next day. Carnival Tuesday Evening.*

PLACE *The same multiple staging.*

Solitary spotlight on dark stage. NARRATOR *enters with stool and reads.*

NARRATOR

Carnival Monday born and dead in joy.
Carnival Tuesday happy, but dying.
The big bands wrapped in rainbow costumes
already have thundered through the streets,
Lightning music flashing from
horn, drum, and pan.

Sound—Faintly in the background, street-sounds of Carnival as she describes them.

Hundreds of thousands of feet, surfing
sweet waves rolling on rhythm shores.
And Mano, who called the Devil from Hell,
leaping and dancing wild, and bending
like a tree in a September Hurricane.
Carnival Judges, sitting high in their Judgment sky
like, Gods,
soon will hand down prizes to the best on Earth.
Who will win? Devils or Gods?

Exits with stool. General lighting comes up. Immediately the joyful sounds of Carnival are faded right out. Table and chairs are at down left to suggest dining room. A bed at down right to suggest bedroom. In tableau are MRS. DRAYTON, JEAN, JOSEPH, *and* PRIEST. *They cast a tense, sad mood on stage. An air of tragedy hovers. They are looking at left where* MANO *will enter. He comes in. He has already taken off most of the Devil costume. He is wearing a Roman-type tunic and African kilt. He carries something wrapped in velvet. He appears extremely tired in every limb. Pause.*

MANO Why nobody ain't come to see the Judgment?

Pause.

MRS. DRAYTON Was different this year . . .
JEAN You looking so tired . . . why . . . ?
MANO What wrong?
MRS. DRAYTON Yes . . . so tired . . .
MANO Nobody ain't want to know if I win or lose?
JEAN Yes. But . . . you must sit down first . . .

He sits down, actually collapses with fatigue in a chair. Even his voice is slowing down.

MANO What . . . everybody so . . . sad . . . about?
JOSEPH You win or lose?
MANO Look . . . look at this . . .

He unwraps the package. It is a Monstrance, almost blindingly beautiful. He places it exactly at center stage, as if the stage were an altar.

JOSEPH What is that?
MANO First prize . . .

Pause.

PRIEST Congratulations.
MANO (*voice growing weaker*) Nobody ain't saying anything else? But what wrong?
JEAN It's beautiful . . .
MANO Why you going to cry? What wrong . . . ?

JEAN Nothing. I'm not going to cry . . .

MANO You too, Mother. Your eyes brimming with tears . . . why?

MRS. DRAYTON You hungry? I cook a special Supper. We could eat now . . .

They sit at the table. Everyone is tense as they begin to eat.

JEAN You can't eat?

MANO Is strange. I feeling so tired . . . I can't even lift the spoon . . . maybe I should lie down . . . for a rest . . . for a little bit . . . (*He tries to get up, but can't. They help him.*) But what wrong with me at all? I never feel so . . . tired . . . before. In my whole life . . .

The women can't restrain their tears anymore. Tears roll down their faces as MANO *is helped to bed.* BORBON, LALSINGH, *and* ACHONG *enter slowly, like ballet-dancers from left, right, and back. They form an outer tableau—adding another dimension of some Inevitability to the feeling and mood of this scene.*

MRS. DRAYTON You feeling comfortable?

MANO Yes . . . but so tired . . . in every limb . . .

MRS. DRAYTON You want anything?

MANO Just some light. So dark in here . . .

JOSEPH But the lights already turn on . . .

Pause.

MANO Why everything so dark then? My eyes . . . I can't see . . .

PRIEST *starts to pray and to give* MANO *extreme unction.*

JOSEPH My prize . . . let me see it . . .

JOSEPH *holds up the Monstrance for him to see it.*

MRS. DRAYTON (*very quietly*) Mano . . . ? Mano . . . ?

Lights start fading slowly. In the dark, the soft, stifled sobbing of the women—all of this is extremely underplayed as MANO *dies. A spotlight lingers on the Monstrance. Blackout.*

SCENE 2

TIME *The next day. Ash Wednesday, the beginning of Lent. It is dusk.*

PLACE *The same. Multiple staging. This time the inside of St. Mart's Church at St. Babb's is suggested.*

Sound—Off-stage, softly the Church choir is singing a Miserere, a beautiful Renaissance-Reformation choral hymn. It continues throughout this scene. Lights up. At back center, the altar, with lighted candles is suggested. The Virgin and Child look down. JOSEPH *is just leaving the altar, presumably after praying, when the* PRIEST *enters and calls him back.*

PRIEST I know how you feel. It's hard . . .

JOSEPH First my father. Then my brother . . .

PRIEST Try not to think about it.

JOSEPH Nothing wrong with playing Devil Mas'! Nothing! Everybody does play it! Nothing ever happen to them! Why my family have to die? Why?

PRIEST They just shouldn't play it.

JOSEPH But why?

PRIEST They shouldn't.

JOSEPH I hate whatever or whoever it is that kill my father and brother!

PRIEST I know you do. I understand.

JOSEPH I hate it so bad, I . . . I . . . (*Pause.*) Father?

PRIEST Call me Jimmy.

JOSEPH I going to play Devil Mas' next year.

PRIEST No. Not you . . .

JOSEPH I not afraid! I have a right! It ain't fair!

PRIEST Don't do it. You'll die if you play it.

JOSEPH Me too?

PRIEST You'll call the Devil from Hell.

JOSEPH I going to do it! I ain't afraid!

PRIEST (*quietly with sincere regret*) And I'll have to kill you too.

Long pause.

JOSEPH You?

PRIEST Yes.

JOSEPH You? The Devil? You is the Devil . . .

PRIEST Yes.

JOSEPH But a priest stand for God . . .

PRIEST And the Devil.

JOSEPH God is the Devil?

PRIEST Yes.

JOSEPH But you can't be . . . it can't . . . it don't make no sense . . .

PRIEST You're too young to know. Good is Evil. Evil is Good.

JOSEPH You killed my father . . . and Mano . . . ?

PRIEST . . . and the little girl hanging from the Silk Cotton tree all night, and the goats with the broken necks.

JOSEPH Why?

PRIEST You won't understand it now. The Universe isn't simple. It's the union of opposites. Nothing is ever simple. It's . . . O, what's the use?

JOSEPH I going to tell everybody. You is the curse on St. Babb's. We will kill you . . . tear you to pieces.

PRIEST (*patiently*) No. You won't have a chance to. I'll have you dead before you take two steps out of here. Before you can form the words . . . You'll have to do what I say. No more Devil Mas'. Play a clown or something harmless.

JOSEPH You mean we have to obey? Like slaves?

PRIEST You have the free will to choose what to do. Like Mano.

JOSEPH So Mano knew all about this?

PRIEST He made his choice on his own.

As they talk, the Heroes of the Dead have begun entering in a quietly marching phalanx. They line up at back behind a trans-

parent gauze curtain. This gives them a spirit-like appearance. They stand looking at JOSEPH. PRIEST *does not see them.*

JOSEPH But I want to live.
PRIEST (*quietly*) Then do what I say.
JOSEPH Obey like a slave or die?
PRIEST I'm sorry, Joseph. Truly sorry. I suffer too.

JOSEPH *is gripped by a conflict beyond his comprehension, but the Heroes of the Dead are looking at him. He sees them for the first time. They are obviously trying to tell him something by the expressions on their faces. Lights fade slowly. In the dark, the beautiful Miserere continues softly. Blackout.*

SCENE 3

TIME *Same day. Minutes later.*

PLACE *The same multiple staging.*

The dining room is suggested by the chairs and table. MRS. DRAYTON *and* JEAN, *two tragic figures wearing black, are standing silently staring into space.* JOSEPH *enters carrying parts of* MANO'*s costume. Pause.*

JOSEPH (*fighting back tears*) Mother, I getting to be a big man now. I going to be thirteen next year. I going to play Devil Mas' next year Carnival.

Long pause. An excruciatingly painful decision wrenches from the very bottom of her soul.

MRS. DRAYTON Yes! Yes! Play it!

BORBON, LALSINGH, ACHONG, *and the* PRIEST *have converged on stage from left, right, and back in a ballet-like movement. They form an outer tableau. General lighting fades, except for a single spotlight.* NARRATOR *enters with her stool and sits under spotlight. She reads in a stronger fairy-tale manner.*

NARRATOR

As in the Beginning,
like turning the first Leaf
in the Genesis of this Tropical Bible,
Yellow Day-Sun is expiring. Blood-Red,
the color of Death, he is now.
Sinking and disappearing.

Lighting—This is happening on the back wall.

But climbing the same Hill is Night-Moon
swinging her hips in her blue silk dress,
coming to life, soft female ripening.
The Creatures of Night creep out
to sing their primal song.

Sound—tropical night sounds as she describes them.

Crickets whispering their bush secrets,
Owls hooting. Frogs and crapauds hoarse
from croaking about the Carnival to which
Millions came.
Jumbie birds whistling bad news and evil messages.
Sandflies and moths dancing in mad circles.
Black beetles and bats—flap your wings!
Fireflies—wink like traffic lights.
Creatures of Night—Celebrate!
Moon, floating in silver over the Dark Earth,
Replace Day-Sun. Spread celestial light over
this Dark Universe. Ascend, descend the
ancient Hill of Laventille,
today, tomorrow, every other day,
forever.

NARRATOR *exits. Night-Moon hovers beautifully mysteriously over Dark Earth. Sound—Archetypal jungle sounds of tropical nature.*

CURTAIN

MARS

Monument to the Last Black Eunuch

(title from a sculpture by Ed Love)

by Clay Goss

Clay Goss is a young poet/playwright who developed his dramaturgical style while serving as playwright-in-residence at Howard University. He later joined the faculty at Howard in 1970. His play, *Homecookin',* was produced by the Negro Ensemble Company and will soon be published by Howard University Press. Goss' *Of Being Hit* and *Oursides* opened the Billie Holiday Players premiere season, 1973–74, at the Billie Holiday Theater in Brooklyn. His other works, including *Andrew,* have been seen on both coasts, largely on university campuses. *Mars* was first performed at Howard University.

CAST OF CHARACTERS

BLACK MAN, *middle-aged, laborer*

WIFE, *who the* BLACK MAN *calls baby.* WIFE *has only one line at the end of the play. Throughout the play she never speaks, but does movement with her body. Her body should reflect thought patterns.* WIFE *should be played by a strong actress who can demand power and stage presence through her body.*

CHORUS, *five to eight people who play other roles throughout the play. One of the female members must be able to sing extremely well (extremely well as an Aretha or Nina or even Nancy Wilson). The scat-singing part should be done very creatively and effectively. Nothing is worse than having a so-called good actress with a bad voice. Preferably a singer should have the role. Also the* CHORUS *should have body movements that are exaggerated; after all, this is a monumental play. And all the characters are monumental.*

SETTING A very large (gigantic) sliding board with a large swing connected underneath the middle of the board between the ladder and the sliding part. The WIFE sits on the swing. The CHORUS should have rhythm (as in rhythm and blues).

COSTUMES CHORUS females wear long robes which are bed sheets that have been tie-dyed (African tie-dyed). CHORUS males are dressed similar to the mud men of Australia. Gray-beige mud on their bare chests and legs. They wear shorts and they look like false faces. Their heads are shaven.

ACT I

BLACK MAN *is down at apron of stage left shaping a piece of scrap material into a work of art. While he is constructing a voice is singing in the background. When he finishes he exits.* CHORUS *assembles onstage wearing white working uniforms walking like robots making mechanical-type movements. They put the set together which turns into a children's playground. They disrobe and take various positions on the playground. Lights come on.* CHORUS *becomes children playing games, jumping rope, etc.* BLACK MAN *and his* WIFE *enter.* WIFE *goes and sits down on swing.* BLACK MAN *begins rapping.*

BLACK MAN Maybe it's because we're married, baby. Maybe it's because we've been married so long . . . you know . . . like the whole routine and shit that it's kinda become a standard . . . like "Moon River" . . . with us. Between us. "Moon River" between us . . . "Moon River" between us. Noise between the scratched-up grooves with Jerry Butler groanin' over and over again "Moon River . . . Moon River." 'Cause I almost expect to hear the disc jockey say: "One more time." And I really don't know if I can take it again! . . . Really, I guess it's hard . . . kinda hard for you to understand . . . you bein' in the church and all but damn . . . I mean . . . a man has got to *see* if he can *SEE* for real, once. Really see if he can *SEE* . . . If he can feel if he can stand on the boardwalk naked, maybe except for a make-shift loin cloth. Ha ha. Except for one jock strap and see . . . see and feel . . . if the moon can pull a psyche on his body just like it psychs those stupid waves day in, day out . . . In . . . Out . . . High Tide . . . Cow-Tide . . . Ebb Tide . . .

Wed . . . Thurs . . . Tues . . . Sunday . . . For Christ's sakes Sunday too with that old minstrel Uncle Ben's peddlin' his stupid instant rice to Sapphire over the supermarket behind the King Fish's back. You know he died broke . . . The King Fish . . . the cat who played the King Fish died . . . *D I E D* . . . died broke, busted, robbed, lynched . . . the whole western world bit. But I laughed at him baby, me and Fred and Briggs and Jackie and a lot of people saw the cat if just for once and we laughed at him. Even Andy laughed at the cat 'cause King Fish was always tryin' to US and move uptown to the high rent district. I remember roaches standin' proudly right out in the middle of the living room floor . . . And they was singing, baby. Singing the Lord's Prayer better than the Wings Over Jordan Choir. I was so weak that I just stood there proud they had chose my house. They didn't even notice me and then suddenly . . . real fast like . . . this thought came to my head and I said out loud . . . real loud . . . (*loudly*) I AM THE ROACH. He that can withstand DDT. The Meat. The wieny. Faster than a flying bullet. More powerful than an enraged elephant . . . ROACH-MAN. And the roaches they like to died they was so happy they was scampering about so. While one by one got his ass crushed by the soles of my shoes and I ain't sorry about a damn thing, baby. Shit. No! Not when I was God. Not when I was the roach. Maker of *all* life some*where.* If just somewhere and someplace. Somebody's home place. Home land. Goddamnit where am I from? Who are my great grand relatives? Who is related to me? Am I, am we? Am we? We, baby. Two by threes. Rotten bark fallin' off of trees. The circus in town with a horse act in the center ring that's dying. A clown smiled at me. I caught his wink and he ain't funny, see. See, baby. See and feel yourself . . . Me. We ain't . . .

TOGETHER Free . . . yet . . . yet . . . or is there really a word called yet or just a feeling yet felt. Like I ain't rich yet or I ain't free yet or I ain't gonna ever yet . . . yet. I ain't gon' never yet . . . yet . . . yet . . . yet . . . yet . . . yet! yetyetyetyetyetyetyetyet . . . It was never ever nothin that you done to me. How can I explain it? I can't it yet! 'Cause cellophane flowers don't need to be watered. They always the same and Christ comin again is still to come. *Yet* to come. Yet to come. And that's who you need, baby, Christ. You and Christ for you to come. For you to yet. For you to experience feel yet. Orgasm yet. Climax yet. Gut scream. Bust your rocks yet. He gotta come around you for you to come around with me.

BLACK MAN And I just can't wait, baby, see . . . I just can't wait, baby, see. I just can't be cool and hang around any longer for the blond-eyed, blue-haired Christ to sound the word for you to come 'cause everyday I'm gettin' closer to Yet without ever Get. Do you understand? Without ever Get . . . Yet. (*Sadly; change of thought.*) The other morning I was goin' to work on the bus and . . .

The CHORUS *become people on an overcrowded bus. They begin acting out their lines.* CHORUS MEMBER *becomes bus driver, kid, cripple, drunk, old talkative woman.*

CHORUS (*jazzy chant*) Oooh——aaah. Oooh——aaaah. Ooooh. Ooooh. Ah. Ah. Ooh-ah. Ooh-ah. Ooh-ah. Ooh-ooh-ah. Ooh-ah. Ooh-ah. Ooh-ah. Ooh-ooh-ah. (*Repeat; different* CHORUS MEMBERS *say the following lines.*)

On this bus
some dirt-face kid spat
on this cripple woman's leg
Bus so crowded
until the spit wouldn't
reach the floor
so it landed on her muscle part
and
slid on down.
Cripple woman didn't say nothing.
She was too old to feel it.
Other people didn't say nothing.
They acted like they didn't see it.
Bus driver didn't say nothing.
He was smoking.

He couldn't fight that drunken man's arms.
So that's comfort in taking the transit bus
and leaving the driving to them and all that.
And incidentally the fare had gone up—15 cents.

BLACK MAN And on the bus this old colored lady, she must've been a domestic worker, was talkin' the ear out of this bus driver.

TALKATIVE WOMAN *makes huge, exaggerated physical gestures with her arms, hands, head, eyes, etc. Her voice gives out sighs and releases do's and da's and sobs and wa's, etc. throughout* BLACK MAN'*s talk.*

I think he was Italian or something or other but this old lady was talkin' the shit out of the bus driver. And you know what, baby. I got to feeling sorry for that bus driver sonofabitch. Yea, feeling sorry for the cat 'cause in a way that is what is what he deserved. Pity. (*Louder.*) Pity . . . Pity 'cause in a sense he was the cause for it. The cause for that old black woman talkin' his ears off. Makin' her think he was *even* God or Jesus or Rock Hudson even, I could choke. Hell, the old bitch was trying to get her Yets. Yet (*laughs*) trying to be an intergral . . . In-te-gral part of that bus . . . That world . . . That Heaven . . . With Jesus Christ driving the T6 to Takoma Park . . . (*Sadly.*) . . . Yet she got off like she was cool. But I could see. I could see the hurt in her eyes. While all the while the bus driver was cracking up inside thinking she was some ol' silly bitch. Some silly ol' black bitch like them past-present-roaches who met their yets under my shoes.

CHORUS *scrambles away like roaches.* BLACK MAN *stops one of the* CHORUS *who becomes* SALESMAN.

Uh Salesman, would you hold up for a second, I've been waiting here to talk to you about— (SALESMAN *turns to walk away.*) Look here! (*Fiery.*) Don't walk away from me when I'm talking to you! I said I been waitin' here to tell you about that mattress and box spring you sold me six weeks ago and was never delivered. Why you didn't tell me the factory didn't have that set. Did a goddamn commission mean that much to you? . . .

SALESMAN I don't lie.

BLACK MAN What? You don't lie!

SALESMAN I never lie.

BLACK MAN You never lie?

SALESMAN I don't lie. (*Shows him sales slip.*)

BLACK MAN Bullshit, if you don't lie and don't get me no sales slip 'cause there ain't no nevermind between a written and a said word, you understand?

SALESMAN I never lie. (*Walks away.*)

BLACK MAN I hope you vomit in your sleep and strangle to death . . . Dream-maker . . . Myth-maker . . . Money makin' hip-shaker, ha-ha. Punk. Yet. Ha-ha-Yet. (*New mood.*) Yet I read the papers, the *Times,* and I listen to the news on the radio and the only thing gettin' better is the commercials, it's been such a long time since 1954. Commercials the only thing that done got better and they ain't nothin' to brag over . . . Yet my son . . . (CHORUS MEMBER *becomes* SON.) I kinda caught my son combing his natural hairstyle the other morning and Jesus Christ the kid looked almost grown and he ain't but 15.

SON (*speaking his father's lines, imitating him*) I said to myself: Man, it's about over really if you think about it and even if you don't you know . . . (*Pause; fast.*) Across the street the people's dogs were barking like fire engines speeding to get paid Fridays. My radio played also in the background like next week's coming attraction down at the "Republic" kids was outside and below practicin' the "Popcorn Mother" without music. With just two fingers and a soul . . . groovin' as my son, my beautiful black man/son would say to me at the breakfast table. When he speaks? I don't prompt him none . . . When he *does* speak . . . to me . . . (*Blackout on* SON.)

BLACK MAN My hair just won't grow long anymore. It seems like all the breezes seem colder, chillier more colder. Pavement seem harder, shoulders sloping 45% farther down. It takes even longer to park the car or get some lovin'. Bright lights scare me. So do my dreams. So do my dreams make me kinda feel mad in the mornin'. My magic is going.

CHORUS There's life! There's life! There's life on Mars and Venus.

MUSLIM (*a* CHORUS MEMBER; *selling papers*) Hey brother, there's life on Mars and Venus. Especially Mars where there is True Life. The Truc Life. Can you beat that? Can you, brother, huh? The True Life on Mars millions of miles from here. (*Laughs.*) Listen, you know all them UFOs people been reportin' about? They are really them folks from Mars checkin us out. And check this out, brother, them little green men from Mars ain't really green at all but black. Yeah. Can you beat that, black. (*Laughs.*)

BLACK MAN I bought the paper, baby. I bought the paper cause for once I believed them Muslims. Don't ask me why. Don't laugh at me 'cause ain't nothin' funny.

CHORUS *laughs hysterically.*

BLACK MAN Yet. For once I believed that cat, that ha-ha brother selling them papers on the corners. It was something about his eyes when he said it. I believe it. Mars. Uh-huh. Mars. Black people on Mars leading the True Life. Free from, free from yets. And that night I prayed to Mars and I said (*Praying—female* CHORUS *voice hums blues tune during prayer.*) Dear Mars . . . dear black brothers on Mars please help us out down here in hell. Down here where we lead the Lie Life, and not the True Life. The Credit Life. Pay next week, until you die. Then die, nigger, die. Die, simpleton, die from heat exhaustion. Die from your own heated-up smell. Your own heated-up mind wondering what? Or who? Or how? Wonderin'.

CHORUS Wonderin'.

BLACK MAN Who to believe.

CHORUS Who to believe.

BLACK MAN What to believe.

CHORUS What to believe.

BLACK MAN Wonderin'. Wonderin'.

CHORUS Wonderin'.

BLACK MAN Wonderin'.

CHORUS Wonderin'.

BLACK MAN Who to believe.

CHORUS Who.

BLACK MAN What to believe.

CHORUS What.

BLACK MAN Wonderin'.

CHORUS Wonderin'.

BLACK MAN Yet. Yet. I believe.

CHORUS I believe.

BLACK MAN I believe our yet is in Mars.

CHORUS Our yet is in Mars!

BLACK MAN Our yet is in Mars. (*End of prayer.*) On Mars gettin' ready to explode in our brains. And mind. Yea brains and mind they ain't the same. One for destruction and one's for construction. Our yet is on Mars. Our yet is yet to come but our yet is to come it's related to Mars and Venus too. The breeze is on our side. Animals too. Grass. Clouds. Sound. Liver. Beats. Thoughts. Hope. Faith. Charity. Nature. Time. Time. Everything. 'Cause the man done messed with everything and now he's up in outer space tryin' to mess with our brothers. Our allies. Natural allies in outer space and that cat on the corner ain't even worried 'cause he believes Yet is to come. To come without some Jesus playin' rock music and high on speed. Baby, a man got to follow his feelings, sometime. At least onc time. At least one time. That's why I bought them dashiki shirts and them beads. 'Cause Junior's got a point though I ain't sure he knows why. Though that ain't the point. He just does that all 'cause he got faith in hisself. Faith in hisself. For once faith in oneself. Hell, I ain't never been in trouble. We make out o.k. Never been sick. My min's all right. You trust my decisions. . . .

INTERMISSION

ACT II

BAND *is playing. Dance sequence. The* CHORUS *assembles onstage dancing. During their dialogue a* FEMALE CHORUS VOICE *scats—Do-be-dobe-da-de-da de-da, etc.*

CHORUS MEMBER 1 The true life's on Mars and Mars is on our hearts called rhythm anytime we hear the music. Space is the place. Black folks is the space race. The cosmic people who make up the space pace.

CHORUS MEMBER 2 The sun reflects our true names and enters our bodies called color. We can talk with our hands making congo drums scream with laughter or shudder with sorrow.

CHORUS MEMBER 3 Santa Claus is unkissed Sunkist compared to our shine. Shine, shine you looked so fine. (*Sticks out behind.*) Miss one stroke and your tail is mine. Ha.

CHORUS MEMBER 4 John Coltrane, the train—the lo-co-motive man. Choo-choo-chooooo. Blow de horn and breathe awhile. Lady Day singing "Blue Holidays." Duke of Ellington—one time man giging at one night stands creating his own cola across the land . . . Wasn't nothin' ever fin-ah then Dinah . . . ah Washington . . . that is. (*Dance sequence ends.*)

BLACK MAN Ever heard the water drop from a cool clean clear ice cycle or was it a popsicle . . . Yea . . . Yeaaaaaah! Rhythm! Rhythm! Rhythm!

BAND *plays "I Can't Get No Satisfaction" slowly.*

I used to hear Junior talking about this guy, Otis Redding. You know, baby, like how good the guy is and all. Well, I remember this one day I read in the papers that this Otis guy dies in a plane crash. I don't know why . . . maybe 'cause of Junior or maybe 'cause I felt here was some kind of connection, some kind of bridge between me and the man, but I started listenin' to all his records. Soon I was *buying* the guy's records they were so mean. I couldn't get enough of him and I kinda got to thinking to myself of all the niggers who never really got no recognition until they was dead. Like if me and all my friends would have listened to the man. Really listened to the man. Really listened to this Redding cat. Really sat down and listened to the cat singing "Try a Little Tenderness" maybe we might have tried a little soft touch. Maybe we might have laughed and slapped each other on the backs and gotten closer with each of our "Juniors." Maybe by now we could of all been great. Or *felt* great. Or *thought* we was great. Or *Junior* would have *thought* we was *great.* 'Cause, 'cause, 'cause, 'cause the O— the big O ain't . . . yet no Otis ain't yet with rhythm . . . rhythm spirit . . . His spirit is here and even Christ can't hang with that. All he can do is sit on "The Dock of the Bay" gettin' "No Satisfaction." And yet . . . (*He cries and laughs.*) And yet . . . (WIFE *is dozing.* BLACK MAN *looks at her curiously then disgustingly.*) And yet I see my wife over there (*sound of drums* BLACK MAN *chants his lament*) gone to sleep with a headache in her dreams and the world outside blizzing on by.

And I know I'm mad
And I know I'm glad
And I know I'm sad
And mad and sad and
GLAD/MAD/SAD—All together

Blue lights shine from the sky and I don't know what to do. The curtain hangs, the garbage smells, the ants and roaches dance on the floor as my foot is numb and can't stump them out I see *Ebony* statues given to me last Christmas laying on the floor dead one arm broken and the white wood shinning from within I see the cellophane flowers blooming in the spring the bugs the fleas and ticks ignoring them, I see clock radio vaguely behind the time and I wonder who am I and who was I and who am I will be who am

I and who was I and who am I will be the morning comes . . . The stars are shinning and I know the morning comes . . . A tongue is in my mouth and I look at myself and scratch my balls and wonder is Peter Pan for real? . . . Do I have to grow up and feel the hate of 300 years upon my back? . . .

CHORUS MEMBER (*horn—rhythm*) I see broom in the corner yellow broom straw, straw yellow broom, Fire ablaze . . . 14th Street ablaze . . . Neon signs on the ground, little black children reshaping their echo tubes to form freedom NOW.

Speech repeated overlapping other CHORUS MEMBERS—*has own rhythm.*

CHORUS MEMBER (*bass—rhythm*) I see floors, floors. I see floors and florist and flowers being sent to mothers long lost and forgotten . . . to celebrate . . . long lost and long forgotten Mother's Day . . . I see fathers smiling patting their forlorn sons on the back for bringing about the dream.

CHORUS MEMBER (*congas—rhythm*) I see apartment buildings . . . silent at night with hope flowing out the window thinking about the 8 o'clock in the morning when the man shows his presence which he rules by day, leaves by night.

CHORUS MEMBER (*bass—rhythm*) I see green yellow, red flag of Africa waving in my eyes and I say to myself I believe I believe.

All sounds halt.

BLACK MAN (*rising like a fiery black preacher—sermon*) I *believe* that YOU (*points to black audience members*) and ME maybe God in Disguise. YOU and ME *might* be GOD! in de skies (*points to sky*) rising every morning like the sunshine on my mother—my beautiful black mother nature . . . creating another black life motion from the motion ocean motion in the ocean—leading to you and me brothers, you and me and you and you-me-WE US . . . Brothers and sisters, You and Me might—be *God* in de skies, yellow and om-mitting ray-zuns in the sun shrivelled UP small with the mind of a black ton, a ton a black nation, ton 2,000 strong and can't be wrong. Rampaging and raving up the biggest street in the north side of town and coming downtown to tell down stories to the mean man, fiend man, the mean fiend man who sit downtown laughing at niggers uptown well it's all over because YOU and ME just might be God, be God-eating fried chicken on the moon . . . (*Laughs.*) Hear that, baby, "eating fried chicken in disguise on the moon." Going around in costumes demanding trick or treat. Singing white Christmas songs or collecting trading stamps for all your life. For all your goddamn life without ever hearing any applause. Just for once I'd like to hear a loud voice coming from anywhere saying "Man, I saw you" or "Man, I felt you like, Man, I felt and saw you." Felt and saw you. You. You. You. For real you actually I ain't jiving—as a you know.

CHORUS *becomes workers in post office sorting out mail.* BLACK MAN *sits beside workers in post office, begins sorting.*

The other night, I got to thinkin' 'bout you and Junior, baby. Then I started thinkin' 'bout Momma and Dad and my brother, Willie . . . my God, when was the last time I've talked to Willie . . . and everybody in the apartment house and on the street and . . . and . . . (*He freezes on his stool, reminiscing, forgetting about mail.*)

CHORUS *continues sorting.* CHORUS MEMBER *becomes supervisor.*

SUPERVISOR Hey you, sort that mail. (BLACK MAN *does not respond.*) Sort that mail, remember that scheme? The scheme. Remember, that scheme.

CHORUS Ooooooooooooooh. Aaaaaaaaaaah. Oooooooooh AAAAAAAH.

SUPERVISOR Remember that scheme, sort that mail. (*Yells.*) What is the matter you are you ill or something?

BLACK MAN (*shaken*) Am I ill or something? I have been working at this P.O. sorting out mail for 19 ill-ass years, six thousand, seven hundred and 55 days, one hundred and twenty-four hours, that by dividing that tremendous total into 8-hour days with annual leave and sick leave I can't stop and THINK for one moment. Not a second but a moment. Not one moment but a moment. There's a difference . . . Yea just like in brain and mind . . .

SUPERVISOR (*interrupting him*) Pick up your check.

BLACK MAN (*continuing on not paying the* SUPERVISOR *any attention*) . . . One moment is a second in time while a moment is a moment of MINE. A moment of my TIME. Not yours. Not the P.O.'s time but my TIME. My Time.

SUPERVISOR Pick up your check, I said.

BLACK MAN Boo. Booooooooooooooo! (SUPERVISOR *leaves;* BLACK MAN *continues with his moment.*) My time. My moment. My moment to sit back, a moment proudly and say to myself Roy Campanella is in the HALL OF FAME. Can't you hear the crowd applauding? (CHORUS *begins to applaud and build as he does.*) James Brown's band is the best in the world. Can't you hear the crowd applauding?

CHORUS Can't you hear the crowd applauding?

BLACK MAN My son made all-city in his year in high school.

CHORUS Can't you hear the crowd applauding?

BLACK MAN Save up my money and got my wife a color TV.

CHORUS Can't you hear the crowd applauding? (*Louder, wilder.*)

BLACK MAN Applauding . . . Applauding . . . yea, yea, yea, yea. Received telegram and roses congratulating me for makin' it so long.

CHORUS Can't you hear the crowd applauding?

BLACK MAN For . . . for being . . . appearing alive.

CHORUS I wanna hear, I wanna hear, I wanna hear the crowd applauding.

CHORUS Can't you hear the crowd applauding?

BLACK MAN You colored brothers on Mars come on down here and help us. You hear me now. Why don't yawl come on down here and help your brothers out. We need you, things ain't gettin' no better. I know you hear me talkin' to you. Prayin' to you. Wishin' to you. Treating you almost like some God and all. Don't pretend you don't know nobody, yawl! Why don't you . . . I say, why don't you hand out a big gold collection plate in the sky. Right over my apartment roof. I'll be out there. I'll see you. Got change too, plenty of silver. Ain't been to church in years, been savin' up for you 'cause I can't be cool forever with my face out there is space. I know it's just a matter of time. A matter of a few more moments. A few more a moments. My moments. Applaud.

(CHORUS *becomes active again.*) Our moments. Applaud. His, our, moments. Applaud . . . together . . . applaud . . . together . . . yet the true life is on Mars, baby, you woke? Yet is on the planet Mars.

VOICE (*off stage*) Junior? Junior, it's time to come in.

BLACK MAN (*as a small boy*) Aaaaaaaaaaaaaaaaaaaaaaaaaaaaaah shucks, Ma.

VOICE (*off stage*) Tell them you'll see them later.

BLACK MAN We were just gettin' ready to go to Mars.

VOICE (*offstage*) You can go to Mars tomorrow.

WIFE (*as a small girl*) I wanna play playhouse tomorrow, don't like this game. (*Exits.*)

BLACK MAN See yall, tomorrow.

END

THE GREAT MACDADDY

by Paul Carter Harrison

Paul Carter Harrison, playwright, director, and teacher, is the author of *The Modern Drama Footnote* and *A Rebel's Dialogue* published by De Bezige Bij in Holland and *The Drama of Nommo* published by Grove Press. A number of his earlier plays have been published and performed in the United States. *The Great MacDaddy* is his most recent full-length play. He also conceived the play *Ain't Supposed to Die a Natural Death* based on the poems of Melvin Van Peebles, which enjoyed a great success on Broadway. He is Professor of Theater Arts and Afro-American Studies at the University of Massachusetts and is also a Resident Fellow of the Institute of Pan-African Culture at that institution. In addition, he was Literary Advisor to the Lincoln Center Repertory Company in 1972–73. *The Great MacDaddy* was produced in New York in 1974 by the Negro Ensemble Company.

CAST OF CHARACTERS

Primal Rhythm

MACDADDY
DEACON JONES
SCAG PHOTOGRAPHER
CHORUS/COMMUNITY
WINE

Beat One

SHINE
OLD GRANDAD (WINE)
MOMMA
SCAG
SOLDIER (WINE)

Beat Two

FAST-LIFE CHORUS
LEIONAH
SKULL (SCAG)
SKULETONS
CAR DEALER
PAWN BROKER
STREET HUSTLER
ALLEY RAT
OUTRAGED COMMUNITY
SIGNIFYIN' BABY
MICKEY MOUSE ORDERLY
SONG
DANCE
DRUM

Beat Three

FOUR JACKALS
WHITE TRACK MAN

Beat Four

SHERIFF (SCAG)
BARTENDER
COWBOY
NIGGERTOE
BEASTS OF PREY

Beat Five

SCARECROW (SCAG)
MR. MIDDLESEX
MRS. MIDDLESEX
EAGLE
SPIRIT OF WOE

Beat Six

MOTHER FAITH
STAGOLEE/SCAGOLEE
POPPA (WINE)
COMMUNITY AT REST

Beat Seven

RED WOMAN/TREE
BLOOD LEADER/TREE (WINE)
BLOOD SON
BLOOD FOLK
BENNY
RED
HUMDRUM (SCAG)
SONG
DANCE
DRUM

Terminal Rhythm

No new characters

AUTHOR'S NOTE

The Great MacDaddy is a ritualized African/American event inspired by the African story-telling technique advanced by Amos Tutuola in his world famous novel, *The Palm Wine Drinkard.* While the event is developed in such a way as to parallel the continuity of the story, no attempt has been made to seek a representative identification with its content. Rather, the content of the event might be considered a translation of African mythic and cosmic references as they appear in the African/American modes of experience which receives cosmic focus from the Black Church, and gives expressive weight to such mythic heroes as The Great MacDaddy, Stagolee, Shine, John Henry, and The Signifyin' Monkey. The intention of the ritual, then, is to identify, rather than simulate African sensibilities as perceived in the context of African/Americans.

The ritual is rhythmically developed in a force-field. All the forces in the event are recognizable aspects of African/American existence, with SCAG being a force that appears in several inimical manifestations; and Song, Dance and Drum appearing as the civilizing forces. MACDADDY experiences the forces as personified realities: they are not to be considered aspects of his fantasy or subconscious life, thus, should not be construed as cartoons. Nor is he bound by the strict definition of linear Time, since his progress forward is *backward:* wherever he might be located during any Beat of the ritual is a result of his contextual relationship to Time, since Time, as conceived here, is never static, and merely serves the transitional Beats of the event.

Stylistically, the ritual is conceived as rhythmical pulses, rather than scenes: Primal Rhythm, Beats, Transitional Beats, and Terminal Rhythm all contribute to lock the ritual, compositionally, into the changes of the musical mode. Song and Dance are used to heighten the mode, as any dramatic device should, rather than as specialty numbers, as described by American musical forms. The set should have enough plasticity to be orchestrated within the rhythmical pulses, allowing for quick-magical-changes of the environment which is never static. And while the music may be described by the American Twenties—secular and sacred—its underlying designation is rhythmically African.

The environment is total: at no times must the audience/participator feel separated physically/emotionally from the event. When plausible, and without strained efforts at improvisation, certain texts may be delivered directly to the audience/participators, inviting their response. And while the ritual may seem composed of innumerable characters, it may be adequately executed with 12–15 players and a five-piece band. All aspects of the ritual must be in harmonious relationship to the rhythmic pulse so as to assure—spiritually—revelation of the event.

PRIMAL RHYTHM

Los Angeles, California. No curtain. The room is covered with a pliable plastic material, including exits, to create a total environment. Upstage, raised level, MUSICIANS *are vaguely seen behind material. They are playing a Twenties jazz riff as audience/participators enter the house.*

The Time is the Twenties, during Prohibition; the space is a funeral parlor speakeasy: upstage right is a door; left of the door, two candelabra stands; further left, an empty coffin. Downstage left is a large wine cask and an ornamental gold tray with long-stemmed glasses upon a small table. Down right, an old-fashioned box-camera on tripod. Plastic flowers laden around the area.

With house lights still on, MACDADDY *enters through the door upstage-right, signals for the others to follow as he ambles over to the wine cask to pour a glass of wine. A gathering of black people* (CHORUS/COMMUNITY), *stylishly dressed, enter as if having returned from a burial; they speak to a few people among the audience/participators about the passing of Big Mac as the* SCAG PHOTOGRAPHER, *who has entered downstage right, dressed in duster and cap, his face painted like a skull—a white-faced death mask—adjusts the lens of the camera.*

House lights begin to fade out, as well as the music: lights up in a sepia tone on the CHORUS/COMMUNITY *who are now posed in a gay still-life photographic attitude; the* SCAG PHOTOGRAPHER'*s head under the camera's black cloth as he raises a powder-flash instrument.* MACDADDY *is the only one animated, sipping from a glass as he observes the scene.*

SCAG PHOTOGRAPHER's *flash instrument flashes sending up a cloud of smoke, breaking the frozen attitude—lights changing and music playing instantaneously—as the* CHORUS/COMMUNITY *commences to dance a vigorous Charleston, the steps, however, indicating an African influence. A party is in progress: the occasion is a wake for Big MacDaddy, who has just been buried, leaving his fortunes to his son who is now the Great MacDaddy, great lover, great patriarch, great hustler.*

The SCAG PHOTOGRAPHER *moves unobtrusively through the dancing group, exiting with a smile of contentment. The flamboyant, young* MACDADDY *looks on with an air of confidence owing to the social prestige attendant to his recent acquisition of power. He is offered condolences and congratulations from his friends, both in the same breath, for inheriting his father's business status. The tone of the festivities indicates a greater concern for the party than the recent burial of Big MacDaddy. Everybody seems to be enjoying a certain vicarious sense of pride through having an association with the Great MacDaddy's money/power. Women smother* MACDADDY *with affection, though his charm is merely superficial, his worldliness not yet tested. He is generally indolent, never having worked for a living, having always been dependent upon his father or others. He is not, however, naive: he understands that the gathering's loyalty is directly proportionate to his money/power.*

DEACON JONES (*after dance ends*) Sure hated to see Big Mac go.

MACDADDY (*patting flirtatious* YOUNG WOMAN *on her bottom*) I know.

DEACON JONES He sho' was a good man!

MACDADDY (*casually*) I know that too, Deacon.

DEACON JONES (*attempting to inject humor*) But he didn't go 'way mad, did he, young Mac?

MACDADDY (*correcting* DEACON JONES) Great . . . MacDaddy!

DEACON JONES Yes suh, yes suh! I guess that's what you bees now. The Great MacDaddy, son of the Big MacDaddy who is dead, making you the greatest Daddy of all the MacDaddies who can do anything in this world.

MACDADDY Every day that God send, Deacon!

DEACON JONES Naw, Big Mac didn't go 'way mad. He done left you the world, MacDaddy. Ain't many of us gon' get our hands on the world like you got it. Yup, you sho' nuff got it made!

MACDADDY (*pouring a glass of wine*) As long as the wine flows, the barrels will roll, and my dough will glow in the eyes of the world. Got plans, Deacon. Grand plans. Gonna start movin' my wine across country. Lotta niggas in Chicago and New York that ain't never had their lips on my Palm Wine.

DEACON JONES (*anxiously*) You mean, you movin' outta Los Angeles?

MACDADDY And give up all this sun? You talk like a fool, Deacon. I'm just movin' my wine. Spreadin' out a lil taste. So don't worry, Deacon, I'll be around to scratch your plate on Sundays.

YOUNG WOMAN (*sassy*) C'mon, let's dance, Junior Mac!

MACDADDY (*emphatically*) Great . . . MacDaddy!

YOUNG WOMAN (*compliantly*) Sure . . . sure, honey. The greatest MacDaddy of 'em all. C'mon, let's dance, nigga!

MACDADDY (*patting her bottom*) Not now, sugar. You just run along now and keep the mustard hot 'til MacDaddy finishes talkin' business. Go on, now! (*Observes* DEACON'S *worried expression.*) Hey, Deacon, I know you loved Big Mac, but you ain't got to be lookin' down in yo' mouth. Everything's gon' to be everything. Just like it always been, only greater. Go on and have some more wine.

DEACON JONES MacDaddy, you might be great, but maybe you better give this movin' out . . . or movin' in . . . a bit more thought. After all, I don't know if your movin' around gon' sit right with The Man.

MACDADDY The Man? What Man? You lookin' at The Man . . . who can do anything in this world he pleases. And if I'm The Man, can't be no other Man runnin' my game.

DEACON JONES Now, MacDaddy, you know as well as I know, the ways of The Man. He don't like ugly. And as long as you don't make a wave there won't be no ugliness. It's the law of the land. And on his land, the fruits of the land must pass through his hands.

MACDADDY (*unconcerned*) Uh-uh!

DEACON JONES (*sermonizing*) Ain't never been a man, on this land, who didn't have to come by The Man, at least once. Who didn't have to pay by hook or crook, for his benevolence. And he that don't know 'bout sacrifice, I say sacrifice, I mean sacrifice, can only know the back-hand of The Man's patience.

MACDADDY Well, we'll save the bones for Deacon Jones! How's that?

YOUNG MAN (*exuberantly*) Hey yawl, I'm makin' a toast to my man MacDaddy, my main man, my ace boon coon, my horse if he never wins a race, my nigga if he never gets bigger . . .

YOUNG WOMAN (*interjects*) The jelly in my roll, honey!

YOUNG MAN (*to the gathering's delight*) . . . MacDaddy with pimps as caddies, blame all the young 'hoes for his new game . . . Big Bear hugger, Momma plugger . . . the maker of crumb snatchers, the smasher of crummy crackers . . . carved the world out of a wooden nickel and called it The Bucket of Blood . . . my main stem under a lady's hem and a gangster's brim, MacDaddy!

Everyone drinks to the toast: the festive moment is interrupted by an urgent rhythmical rapping at the door. An anxious hush comes over the room. MACDADDY *suggest everyone be cool as he approaches the door and a* WOMAN *collects all the glasses and returns tray to table.* MACDADDY *taps a rhythmical signal on the door; there is a feeble response. He repeats the gesture; again, the response. Cautiously, he opens the door: in sprawls* WINE, *the keeper of the illegal still and the possessor of the precious Palm Wine formula that has produced* MACDADDY'*s greatness.* WINE *appears to be badly beaten and delirious as he collapses in the arms of* MACDADDY *and a few* MEN.

WINE Turn me loose . . . turn me loose.

MACDADDY (*befuddled; embarrassed*) Bring him down here! Hurry! Make room for him!

YOUNG WOMAN (*as other guests stare anxiously*) Who's that old dude?

YOUNG MAN That's Wine! He runs the still. It don't look too good.

WINE Turn me loose . . .

MACDADDY (*bending over* WINE *and holding up his head*) It's alright, Wine, it's just me.

WINE (*practically prostrate*) Yeah . . . yeah . . . young Mac . . .

MACDADDY Great Mac! . . . What happened?

WINE The Man . . . he done come down on Wine . . .

MACDADDY What man?

WINE Thee Man . . . you know? . . . like man-in-the-moonshine? . . . Thee Man. And I'm a dead man, Mac.

MACDADDY Don't worry 'bout a thing, Wine. You gonna be awright. But what about the still?

WINE He . . . he just swoop down on me . . . you know how he do . . . he just swoop down on me when I wasn't lookin' . . .

MACDADDY Sure . . . sure . . . but who's lookin' after the still?

WINE . . . I ain't give him no cause to do that! I ain't botherin' nobody back there in the bush . . . back there in the bush where the spirit come to me . . . where the spirit come to me and fix my hand on the tree . . . fix my hand on the palm leaf . . . fix my soul on the palm leaf juice . . .

MACDADDY Yeah. Sure, Wine. Nobody should be botherin' you. But who's watchin' the operation?

WINE I'm a dead man now, MacDaddy. The Man done gone too far with Wine. He done fix Wine so that he a dead man now. Wine ain't got no time. He done swoop down on me and dragged me away from the tree . . . dragged me away from the tree that fix my soul . . . the soul that fixed my mind . . . he done taken advantage of Wine . . .

MACDADDY (*annoyed, grabs* WINE *roughly*) On yo' feet, Wine, you goin' back to the bush!

WINE (*resisting as other guests reproach* MACDADDY, *exhorting him to leave* WINE *alone*) Turn me loose! I'm a dead man now.

MACDADDY (*complies momentarily to his guests' demand; unable to cope with the situation, he grabs* WINE *once more*) Get up, nigga, get up! You ain't gettin' paid to lay on yo' ass!

WINE (*gagging, as guests reproach* MACDADDY *once more*) Wine ain't got no time. He gon', MacDaddy . . . he gon' 'way from here!

MACDADDY (*complies once more to guests' irritation: suspecting that* WINE *is actually upon his last breath, he tries desperately to extract the formula from him*) You can't go, Wine. You hear me?

WINE I'm gone! And by-the-by, The Man will come to you in curious ways and you'll see why Wine is a dead man.

MACDADDY (*shaking* WINE) The formula, Wine. What about the formula? C'mon, quick, write it down. (*He fixes a pencil in* WINE'*s hand and urges him to write, but is unsuccessful.*) C'mon, I'll help you. Write it down, nigga, before I get mad. Okay. Okay, whisper it to me . . . Whisper in my ear. Louder . . . louder!

WINE *struggles to whisper something into* MACDADDY'*s ear, but collapses dead.*

Wine? Wine, are you still there? Wine! (*He releases* WINE *and postures as if he has at least secured the formula: adjusting his composure, he commands a few of the men to place* WINE *into the casket.*) A couple of you dudes make Wine comfortable over there. (*He begins to light the candelabra.*) I think it's time to pay our respects to Wine. Deacon, you preside, if you will, over the remains of this wasted brutha.

Transitional Beat: MUSICIANS *play a hymn as* DEACON JONES *moves in between the candelabra to face the gathering downstage for his eulogy;* MACDADDY *resting his elbow on the casket appearing to be in deep thought; lights change.*

DEACON JONES Wine was good. Wine was great. Wine was everybody's mistake! Though Wine was a gift of God. Wine is of the Blood . . . and the Father . . . and the Weary Spirit . . . but Wine was abused. It's a mistake to abuse the gift of God. It's a mistake to let Blood bleed blind when wine is plentiful and adversary deep. Wine, in a good time, would never bleed Blood blind. But these are bad times, brethren, these are not the times of wine. I say, these are not the times of wine, those earthly times when Wine was host to the ancestral spirit, those good times when Blood would catch fire and the Body would rock with Dance, and the heart would burst with Song, and the ground would rumble under our stomp like Drum, those real times, those vital times that soothed our minds with revelation, those revelations that revealed the mystery of Hell on Earth, I say reveal the mystery of Hell on Earth . . . (*He becomes progressively more incantative, causing the* COMMUNITY/CHORUS *to respond with shouts, sighs, and jerking motions.*) I say, those revelations that come down from the wisdom of wine, the Blood River rolling over its banks, rolling over the Dikes of Time, rolling over Creation, movin' with the magic of Wine, out of Time but movin' down the line anyhow, like the ancestors say, Wine is good, Wine is great, Wine is everybody's mistake. I say, it's a mistake to abuse the gift of God. Right here in Los Angeles, from the tastiest palm trees in the West, Wine brought the gift of God . . . put his life on the line in the name of the Father, the Blood and the Weary Spirit, brought joy to the wasteland and peace to the mind in these sad and merciless times. And now Wine done passed. I say, now that Wine done passed, what has this scorched land in store for us now? Lawd, what on earth is in store for us now, since it was a mistake to abuse po' Wine, a gift of God. Lawd . . . Lawd . . . Lawd . . . how we gonna miss our Wine!

MUSICIANS *continue playing as sanctified atmosphere settles;* MACDADDY *looks up from his disengaged posture. Lights normal.*

MACDADDY (*perfunctorily opens casket*) At this time, I would like to invite everybody to review the remains of Wine.

As the COMMUNITY/CHORUS *lines up and slowly approaches the casket,* MACDADDY *goes over to* DEACON JONES *to shake his hand and eases some money into his palm: the first* WOMAN *to approach the casket screams with great consternation etched upon her face.*

What's wrong with you, woman?

WOMAN (*greatly agitated*) Nothin' remains of the *remains!*

MACDADDY (*anxiously runs over to the casket, and with great agitation and bewilderment, searches interior and exterior*) Where did he go? Where'd he go? (*To perplexed* COMMUNITY/CHORUS.) What happened to Wine?

Silent astonishment is the response.

Well, he ain't here, where in Hell is he?

OLD WOMAN (*nodding head sagaciously*) Gone back!

MACDADDY (*eyes searching audience*) Back where?

OLD WOMAN (*to bewildered* COMMUNITY/CHORUS) Back to the source! He done gone back to the source. Just like Wine to do a thing like that. Always knew he had the power. Poof! Evaporate in thin air. Just like a spirit. He done left here and gone back to the source, chile!

MACDADDY (*irritated; searching audience*) Uh-huh! Like Hell he did! Not with my formula.

COMMUNITY/CHORUS *respond with amazement.*

If he ain't in this casket, he's out here somewhere. And when I find the low-life sucker with my formula, I'm takin' it out his ass.

YOUNG MAN (*pursuing* MACDADDY) Wait-wait-wait, hold on, MacDaddy. You mean . . . he didn't tell you nothin' before he split? . . . I mean, he got away . . . and you ain't got no wine?

MACDADDY (*boastfully*) There's plenty wine, dude! Just keep drinkin' while I get it together.

YOUNG MAN (*pursuing* MACDADDY) Wait-wait-wait, hold on, ain't got no formula, you ain't got no wine. And if you ain't got no wine . . .

YOUNG WOMAN You ain't got shit!

MACDADDY (*reaches for* YOUNG WOMAN) Let me tell you somethin', lil momma . . .

YOUNG WOMAN Uh-uh! Don't be puttin' your fumblin' hands on me. Don't you ever do that! And the next time you put your hands on my back-side, just be lookin' out for a heel upside your jaw. In fact, I jes' left!

As YOUNG WOMAN *exits, she takes off a bunch of plastic flowers, thereby prompting the rest of the* COMMUNITY/CHORUS *to leave, each removing some aspect of the room; flowers, rolling off casket and wine cask, and finally, one man removes the door in one motion as he exits.*

MACDADDY (*as everyone is leaving*) Where yawl goin'? Yawl ain't got to leave. I said I'd find him. Wine can't be too far. Just wait awhile. I'll bring him back. Just stick around one minute!

The room is empty. Abandoned, MACDADDY *stands in the middle of the stage adjusting his clothes while the stage darkens and* MUSICIANS *play calamitously: sounds of wild beasts, screams, hoots, and hollers, suggesting a perilous mood.* MACDADDY *tightens up his appearance/attitude, adjusting hat on his head to the "perfect" degree of angularity: a light downstage focuses on a heavy wooden cane, bedecked like a fetish and shaped like an elephant's head at the top. It has the appearance of a carved tree branch. The object is a cane inherited from his father:* MACDADDY'S *juju stick. He moves down to hold up the juju-cane for inspection of its power. Confident, his attitude locked into place, he now looks out into the audience as if frontally confronting the dangers in the world lurking behind their eyes.*

BEAT ONE

Nevada desert. MACDADDY *moves upstage right, returns downstage left to discover a young-blood on the desert with a bell around his neck sitting by a shoe-shine box. He is surprised to find someone on the desert giving shoeshines, but places his foot up on the stand and issues a command.*

MACDADDY Shine!

SHINE (*popping rag rhythmically*) On the job, suh!

MACDADDY What's a young blood like you doin' out here on the desert shinin' shoes?

SHINE Workin' my way 'cross country, suh.

MACDADDY Now, Blood, that's sho' 'nuff simple-minded. Ain't nobody gettin' no shine on the desert.

SHINE You gettin' one right now, suh.

MACDADDY Well . . . that's different!

SHINE Don't make me no difference. Any shoe will do . . . right along through here.

MACDADDY Well, you'll never make it, June. Ain't that many shoes out here to carry you 'cross country.

SHINE Guess I'll jes' work up a sweat 'til I get there.

MACDADDY What you 'spect to find 'cross country?

SHINE A better job!

MACDADDY Don't see what you got to be worryin' 'bout workin' so hard for . . . as young as you are. Shit, when I was your age, party-time occupied my mind . . . and I sho did party!

SHINE Well, I'm growin' fast. By the time I get across country, I'll probably be a man.

MACDADDY What you figure on doin' by the time you become a man?

SHINE (*popping rag*) Well, I'm pretty good with my hands. And I hear they layin' train track back East. So I figure they gon' need some pretty strong men to shape that steel . . . and I got a callin' that means me!

MACDADDY Shit, you gotta be plenty cock-strong to be thinkin' 'bout bendin' steel.

SHINE Oh, I'm plenty strong. Used to work in a mill back home in Milltown. Could tote quite a load for a young nigga. That's what the mill captain used to say.

MACDADDY Hell, you oughta be glad you gave up that job.

SHINE Oh, I didn't give it up. Mill caught fire and I ran for my life. Had to keep gettin' up, though, 'cause the captain and his daughter got burned to death and you know how 'em white folks get 't pointin' the blame.

MACDADDY You got that right, every day that God sends. A nigga's story ain't worth two cents when a cracker judge strokes his chin.

SHINE

Yeah, I knew they wouldn't hear it
  though I was littler then;
how I look talkin' 'bout sniffin' 'round for smoke
  when the fire broke in.

SHINE *leaps to his feet and begins detailing the story demonstratively.*

I run to the captain shoutin',
  "there's a fire all about!"
He say, "nothin' to it, Shine,
  the automatic sprinklers will put it out."

The fire raged and the sprinklers pumped,
  filled the room with smoke and a whole lot of funk.
I say, "Captain, captain, those sprinklers ain't worth a damn."
  He say, "You talk like a fool, Shine, they were made by Uncle
    Sam."

But that fire told me captain's talk was some jive,
I leaped outta the window without any alibis.
I say, "There was a time your word might've been true,
but this is one Goddamn time your word won't do!"
I hit that window so unbelievably fast
I passed right through without ever breakin' the glass.

Then I hear captain shoutin', "Shine, Shine, please save poor me.
I'll give you more money than any black boy ever did see."
I say, "You ain't got enough money to get me for hire,
not if I've got to get back in that fire!
If money ain't on land, I'll find it at sea,
so you'd better get out here and boogie like me!"

Then captain's daughter start to shoutin',
drawers in her hand, brassiere 'round her neck;
she gon' put me to the test
by steppin' out her dress.
She say, "Shine, Shine, save poor me,
I'll give you more bootie than any black man ever did see."
I say, "Hoe . . . you know my color, you know my race.
you'd better get out here and give these rats a chase.
'Cause bootie ain't nothin' but meat on a bone;
you can kiss, fuck it, or leave it alone."

I even ran up on captain's dog, you know,
one of 'em German shepherds whose teeth snap logs.
I say, "You may be man's best friend,
catcher of squirrels, even smart as him;
but before I let you sink your green teeth in my knee,
you gonna have to be a runnin' sombitch to outrun me."

And that's how I lived to tell the story that wasn't told!

MACDADDY You must be a pretty mean young dude, Shine. I guess that's why you wear that bell 'round your neck, you know, just to let people know you comin'.

SHINE (*resuming shoe shine*) Aw, shoot, that ain't nothin'.

MACDADDY (*inspecting bell*) Where'd you get it?

SHINE I made it. I told you, I'm pretty good with my hands.

MACDADDY Let me see that. (*Closer inspection.*) Could you make another one?

SHINE Sure, anytime. Ain't nothin' to it really.

MACDADDY Look, I'll give you the price of two shines if you let me have it.

SHINE Two shines don't add up to one, mistah. But you can have it just the same. Like I said, I can make another bell. But you can only get one shine. Anyhow, it was nice talkin' to somebody for a change. It do get lonely out here.

MACDADDY (*takes bell; pays for shine*) You know, you're a good lil' nigga, Shine. You'll make it! By the way, what's your real name?

SHINE Well, my friends call me Shine, but my real name is John Henry!

MUSICIANS *play.* MACDADDY *stares at* SHINE *curiously as he departs upstage. Transitional Beat:* MACDADDY *comes upon* OLD GRANDAD *and* MOMMA *sitting around a fire in the evening chill. Curiously, he approaches them.*

MACDADDY Hey now! How you folks doin'? (*No response.*) See you got your fire. (*No response.*) Been warm out here on the desert, but I guess yawl know somethin' 'bout night I don't know. (*No response.*) Yeah, I guess it do be chilly! (*No response.*) I said, yeah, it do get chilly on the desert. (*No response.*) Dry too! (*No response.*) Yawl been here long? (*No response.*) Hey, what's wrong with yawl? It don't get that cold that you can't warm up to a cousin. Look here, I'm lookin' for somebody, so why don't you give cuz a hand? I gotta find Wine.

OLD GRANDAD *chuckles.*

You seen Wine?

OLD GRANDAD (*a manifestation/personification of* WINE) On the desert?

MOMMA Ain't nothin' out c'here but Old Grandad and me, son.

OLD GRANDAD Don't tell the ig'nant oil rough-tail nothin'!

MACDADDY What's your problem, Grandad, what you got against me?

OLD GRANDAD Nothin'!

MOMMA But you ain't no cousin, and you don't look like our kind. He bees a pretty lil' nigga, Grandad, but his shoes ain't shined.

MACDADDY Hey now, Momma, all I'm tryin' to do is find Wine. Can't help it if I kick up a bit of dust. But we ain't got to fuss about it, do we?

MOMMA Don't rain every time the pig squeal, do it?

OLD GRANDAD But it sho' 'nuff look like stormy weather comin' 'round.

MACDADDY Look here, what you people doin' out here anyhow?

OLD GRANDAD Livin'!

MACDADDY (*slapping at flies*) On the desert?

OLD GRANDAD Only way I know to get my nuts outta the sand is to get as close to the sand as I can.

MOMMA We done give up on 'em crackers with wheat on their land, and come out here to make somethin' out the sand. 'Course, I'd rather be a nigga than a poor white man!

MACDADDY Well, yawl jes' keep right on gettin' up!

OLD GRANDAD Got to! Nigger got to keep movin' the way these grasshoppers be eatin' up everything. Move or die.

MOMMA Back there in Backwater, the grasshoppers be eatin' up your britches and spittin' up yo' shirts. And got an appetite that's growin' mo' bigger. So we packed up and hit the dirt before they starts in on the nigga.

MACDADDY (*slapping at flies*) Hell, yawl sure can't come to much out here on the desert. Plenty of flies out here. White flies! They sting and stick to yuh too. You can slap at 'em all day, but they get to yuh. Ain't nothin' nastier than a fly, and there bees plenty sand-flies out here. Can't stand flies myself.

OLD GRANDAD Don't blame you, son. But like I was gonna say, soon as I get my nuts outta the sand, we pushin' on for Diddy-Wah-Diddy.

MACDADDY Where that bees?

OLD GRANDAD (*with self-titillation*) Way off somewhere, but I'll find it. 'Spose to be a place where you ain't got to work or worry 'bout man nor beast . . . a restful place where every curbstone is like an easy chair. And when you gets hungry, all you gots to do is sit on that curb and wait. Pretty soon you hear something hollerin', "Eat me! Eat me!" and is bees a big baked chicken come struttin' along with knife, fork, and bread too. After you done eat all you want, there's still plenty left over for neighbor. And before you know it, a great big, deep, sweet potato pie comes shoving itself in front of you with a knife stuck up the middle so you can cut the size that fits your mouth. Can't nobody ever eat it all up, though. The mo' you eats, the bigger it gets! (*Laughs with* MOMMA *joyously.*)

MACDADDY C'mon, Old Grandad, you sure you ain't been dippin' in your bottle?

OLD GRANDAD Now, I ain't got to lie to you. Not out here on the desert.

MOMMA 'Sides, a nigga don't sing much when plowin' on a hillside!

MACDADDY Come off it, Momma. Yawl don't even know the way. So I guess ain't nobody gonna live there today.

OLD GRANDAD It is said that everybody would live in Diddy-Wah-Diddy if it wasn't so hard to find and so hard to get to, even after you know the way.

MACDADDY In the meantime, cousin, since yawl ain't goin' nowhere, maybe you can point out the direction of Wine.

OLD GRANDAD I ain't seen no Wine in many a day.

MACDADDY But you must have seen him, cousin. I'm sure he passed this way.

MOMMA Old Grandad ain't got nothin' to do with Wine. And stop gettin' familiar, 'cause you ain't no cousin of mine.

MACDADDY Damn! Talkin' to you old folks is like gettin' blood out of a stone.

OLD GRANDAD Watch your mouth, son. Don't like no talk like that 'round Momma.

MACDADDY Listen, I'll walk, talk . . . bark anyway I want to!

OLD GRANDAD Not around here you won't!

MACDADDY You must not know who I am.

OLD GRANDAD I ain't gon' lie! Naw, and don't care much if I do!

MACDADDY Well, get hip, Old Grandad. I am the Great MacDaddy, son of the Big MacDaddy who is dead, making me the greatest Daddy of all the MacDaddies who can do anything in this world.

OLD GRANDAD (*unimpressed*) So?

MACDADDY So I wanna know about Wine!

OLD GRANDAD Well, I don't know now. You be the greatest of the great, don't see what Old Grandad can do for you, though few have ever gotten past Old Grandad without calling his name. All I can tell you is go-for-yuh-self, mistah . . . er . . . how you call yo' name . . . ?

MACDADDY MacDaddy!

OLD GRANDAD (*he and* MOMMA *tickled*) Uhm-hmm . . . !

MACDADDY (*threateningly*) . . . and I'm gettin' tired of foolin' with yuh!

MOMMA Mole ain't 'fraid of the moonshine, now!

MACDADDY You'd better tell yo' ole lady somethin'!

OLD GRANDAD Naw, I'm gonna tell you somethin'!

MACDADDY You can't tell me nothin'!

OLD GRANDAD Uh-huh, that's jes what I thought. I guess Wine will be mellow without yo' company anyhow.

MACDADDY C'mon, Old Grandad, I ain't got no time to lose. Can you turn me onto Wine or can't you?

OLD GRANDAD I guess I could.

MACDADDY Then give him up!

OLD GRANDAD What have you done for me lately?

MACDADDY What . . .?

MOMMA Folks on the rich bottom stop braggin' when the river rise.

MACDADDY (*hesitantly*) Okay. Okay, how much dough you want?

OLD GRANDAD What kinda dough do I be needin' on the desert? Now, that's sho' 'nuff dumb. And if you that dumb, I don't see what you can do for me.

MACDADDY What do you want? Just tell me, what is it?

OLD GRANDAD That bell!

MOMMA Can you deal with that?

MACDADDY I can deal with anything! But, uh-uh, that ain't gonna get it, ole lady. If Old Grandad wants this bell so bad, he gonna have to run down Wine right here and now. Okay, you want this bell, let me see you foam at the mouth. Go on!

OLD GRANDAD Look here, son, I'm tired. I ain't gonna argue with yuh. You see, I know why I need that bell and you don't. Ever since I saw the red clay breakin' 'foe a pale face moon, I knew I had to have that bell. And the moon is plenty pale this night. Now, Old Grandad through talkin' to yuh. You jes do what you wanna do!

MACDADDY (*reluctantly gives up bell;* OLD GRANDAD *snatches it anxiously*) Okay. Now you give up Wine!

OLD GRANDAD (*gleefully ties bell around neck*) Well, now, you see, it ain't as easy as all that. Wine is hard to find in stormy weather. Maybe you'd better come with us to Diddy-Wah-Diddy, son.

MACDADDY What you puttin' down, Grandad? Don't bring that jive to me.

OLD GRANDAD I ain't jivin'! In Diddy-Wah-Diddy there bees a powerful man, the most powerful man in the land. He bees the Moon Regulator. He can make the moon do what he wants it to do. And I just got to thinkin', since the moon do be kinda pale around 'bout now, maybe he been sick lately. Ain't easy to find nothin' in pale moon.

MACDADDY Hold it right there, Grandad. You ain't slick! I don't wanna know nothin' 'bout Ditty-Witty, 'less it's mommas with fat titties. Ou-blah-dah and ou-blah-dee don't mean nothin' to me, 'cause I ain't goin' there. Just turn me onto Wine and we can forget we ever met. (*He draws back his juju-cane threateningly.*) Now break it down for me!

OLD GRANDAD (*withdrawing*) Ain't no need in all that, young fella . . .

MACDADDY MacDaddy . . . the Great MacDaddy.

OLD GRANDAD Uhm-hmm, I know a fella greater than you. He bees on the other side of the moon. That's why we gettin' stormy weather for sure. But I didn't want you to get mixed up with that fella . . . 'cause he be bad . . . mean as left over Death! But he knows how to get around in stormy weather.

MACDADDY Ease up, Old Grandad. You ain't crackin' no ice with me.

OLD GRANDAD I mean what I say. It's the only way we gonna find Wine in this weather. But then, if you ain't that bad . . .

MACDADDY If I ain't, Skippy is a faggot! Who's the dude? Spoke up!

MOMMA Needun be walkin' 'round c'here with yo nose all snotty. When you don't know, jes ask somebody!

OLD GRANDAD Scaggarag! Ain't never met him, but I hear'd 'bout him. But I can't blame you for not wantin' to deal with Scaggarag. He's mean!

MACDADDY Where bees the dude?

OLD GRANDAD Out there somewhere with the other desert rats, I guess.

MACDADDY Awright, Old Grandad, this is the only time I'm gonna go for this shit. When I get back, you'd better have some facts.

MOMMA (*as* MACDADDY *leaves*) The distance to the next mile post depends on the mud in the road.

Transitional Beat: MUSICIANS *play traveling music as* MACDADDY *peers through the audience and calls "Scaggarag" three times. He then supports himself on his juju-cane as if napping.* SCAG *appears—in death mask as earlier—and dances adroitly around the napping* MACDADDY.

SCAG (*curiously inspects*) Uhm-hmmmm . . . Uhm-hmmmm . . . Uhm-hmmmm! Could this man still be alive or dead?

MACDADDY (*quickly spins and fronts* SCAG; *brandishing his juju-cane*) I'm very much alive . . . and ain't thinkin' 'bout dyin'! (MACDADDY *enters dance rhythm of* SCAG.)

SCAG Yeaaaaah, you look pretty live to me. Maybe you can tell me, just who you be?

MACDADDY I'm the Great MacDaddy, son of the Big MacDaddy who is dead, making me the greatest Daddy of all the MacDaddies who can do anything in this world!

SCAG Oh yeaaaah? That's good enough for me!

MACDADDY Then run it on back, Jack, before I jump into the third degree.

SCAG (*making intricate dance movement*) Uh-uh, that won't be necessary, Cherry! (*Negotiates another intricate movement.*) Scag! I'm the one . . . I'm the one . . . I'm the one . . . (*Repeated rhythmically.*)

MACDADDY (*interpolating each of the last phrases and maintaining a simple dance movement*) Yeah, you the one!

SCAG Where you from?

MACDADDY Where they scrapple-at-the-apple not far from your place.

SCAG And what did you come to do?

MACDADDY Been hearin' 'bout you on the drum . . . the talk of the town . . . thought I best get to know you personally!

SCAG Well, here I bees . . . Let's do-the-do . . . do-the-do . . . do-the-do . . .

MACDADDY (*interpolating between each phrase of "do-the-do"*) Doo-aaaaaah! Doo-aaaaaah! Doo-aaaaaah!

SCAG (*begins song/monologue about himself while engaging* MACDADDY *in a dance designed to capture him within* SCAG'*s influence. While* SCAG'*s dance is quite supple, yet intricate,* MACDADDY'*s dance is rudimentary, but intense, with a few improvisations on the basic step as he dances furiously, using his juju-cane as a support, to off-set* SCAG'*s challenge*)

You're talkin' to one of the meanest Sidewinders
 in Babylon.
They call me Scag, but my real name is
 Heroin;
 a cousin to the Caesars,
 a nephew of Napoleon,
 got a Spartan pedigree.

I came to these borders in a cellophane bag!
 mess with me a taste, if you wanna waste;
 I'll make your liver quiver,
 your body sag like a rag.

But I'm a thrill, you see
 yeah, thrill you to death;

as you ride into the lower depths,
that adventure into unreturnable Seas.

I can put a hex on your sex;
put your mind under arrest;
make a young girl sell her body,
for failin' the acid test.

Reality!
Reality is called Miss Jones.
When the Jones come down strong
she can make you
shake, rattle,
and throw up your bones.

You may sigh until your nose bleeds,
but there ain't much you can do
with her stew,
'cept CRY my misery blues.

You be hooked!
Hooked on me,
and ridin' a race through Hell.
We ridin' together,
at break-neck speed;
til that day you fall off the pace
and you SCREAM your death knell!

"Scream" is repeated three times with response from MUSICIANS. *At the end of song/monologue,* SCAG *and* MACDADDY *dance furiously until* SCAG *is overtaken by the intensity of* MACDADDY'S *determination to win. He raises his juju-cane triumphantly and a net falls from above which is used to cover the fallen* SCAG. *Transitional Beat:* OLD GRANDAD *and* MOMMA *approach the net trepidly yet curiously.*

OLD GRANDAD Back so soon, son?

MACDADDY (*downstage tightening up his appearance with his back on net which is upstage*) What do it look like to you?

OLD GRANDAD Looks like you been pushed outta shape a little bit. (*Curiously.*) What you got in that net?

MACDADDY Just what you asked for. Scag!

OLD GRANDAD (*he and* MOMMA *are alarmed*) No. You didn't! How could you do a thing like that? (*Fearfully, he begins to shake the bell furiously toward the audience as if sending out an alarm signal, while* MOMMA *withdraws from net.*)

MACDADDY What's wrong with you, Grandad? Stop actin' simple! (*He grabs* OLD GRANDAD *on collar desperately.*) You hear me, nigga? What in the world are you tryin' to do?

OLD GRANDAD (*as* MOMMA *tries to separate* MACDADDY'*s grip from* OLD GRANDAD) You done brought Scag among the livin', son. That ain't right! Ain't even wrong. That's Death!

As MACDADDY *deals with* OLD GRANDAD, SCAG *stealthily escapes the net and creeps away from the scene smiling.*

MOMMA (*prayerful attitude*) Only a blind mule ain't 'fraid of darkness. Lawd, oh Righteous Father!

MACDADDY (*furious*) You asked for him, now you got him.

OLD GRANDAD Naw we ain't. You ain't even got him no more. Look, see there, the net's empty!

MACDADDY (*views empty net with astonishment*) But I had him!

OLD GRANDAD (*picks up net and backs away with* MOMMA) And you let him go! It's yo' fault! All yo' fault! You done taken Scag outta Hell and turned him loose to roam with decent people.

MACDADDY Where you goin'?

OLD GRANDAD Naw, don't come near us. Stay back! We leavin' here.

MACDADDY (*as they prepare to exit*) We had a deal!

OLD GRANDAD Find Wine on your own time. We gon'!

They exit briskly.

MACDADDY (*bitterly; shouting after them*) Nigguhs . . . and flies . . . I do despise. The more I see nigguhs, the more I like flies!

MUSICIANS *respond.* MACDADDY *appears annoyed with himself for having made such a harsh indictment, compensating for the self-hate by tightening up his appearance/attitude, then moving on. Transitional Beat:* MACDADDY *comes upon a weary looking First World War veteran—another manifestation/personification of* WINE*—togged in remnants of "battle" dress. He is drinking from a canteen.*

Hey! Soldier! How far is the next town?

SOLDIER (*sitting on an old suitcase*) Next town? Hmm, far as you wanna go, and even farther than that as far as I'm concerned.

MACDADDY Well, how far is that?

SOLDIER On the otherside of Far, in the land of Zar. Ever been to Zar? Naw, I guess you too young to have been that far.

MACDADDY Look, can you jes get me to the next town?

SOLDIER Who, me? I can get you farther than that. I been to West Hell and back. 'Course, you know 'bout West Hell, don't yuh? Where the soul bounces 'round like a rubber ball cause the Devil ain't gon' carry you through, you know what I mean?

MACDADDY (*prepares to leave*) I'm sorry I asked. So, if you don't mind, I'll just get off your trip and make my own way, thank you!

SOLDIER Hold on there, sonny . . .

MACDADDY MacDaddy . . . the Great MacDaddy!

SOLDIER Yeah, sure, but before you start trippin', you'd better have a sip outta my canteen . . . 'cause what you got before you is a trip and a half which might not even be worth the trip!

MACDADDY *accepts the offer: turns up canteen, sips, tastes, drinks gluttonously.*

Ever been to war? Now there's a trip that tripped me half way 'round the world to trip on some hellified trippers who weren't just trippin', but stompin'! And after nearly gettin' stomped, I didn't realize what a trip that was until I got back on this trip and got my butt kicked by the dudes I was trippin' for. Now, ain't that a blip!

MACDADDY (*removing canteen from mouth; face expresses astonishment*) Wine!

SOLDIER 'Nuff to last me the rest of my trip, though it's one trip I hate to make.

MACDADDY (*anxiously*) Where'd you get this wine, Soldier?

SOLDIER Over in the next town.

MACDADDY Well, where is the next town?

SOLDIER Oh, it's a trip and a half, son.

MACDADDY That's what you said before!

SOLDIER And that's what it still is!

MACDADDY Okay, then show me, I'll follow.
(*Sipping wine.*)

SOLDIER No suh-ree-suh! I ain't ready for the trip. I'm tired. So I'm gonna sit here with this wine 'til I'm ready to get back in the world. Got enough problems. And I got that wine from a man who didn't have a care in the world.

MACDADDY Was he 'bout your height . . . your color . . . with a scruffy beard . . . kinda walk, you know, like you . . . even talks like you?

SOLDIER Sho 'nuff sound like him!

MACDADDY (*raises juju-cane threateningly*) Get steppin', Soldier!

SOLDIER (*unimpressed*) Now, hold on just a minute. (*Snatches canteen from* MACDADDY.) And give me back my canteen! I done told you I ain't ready to go into the world, and I ain't got no intentions of goin'. Ain't nothin' in the world I ain't seen, so you don't scare me. I done lived too long with fear, and there ain't nothin' more fearful in the world than fear. So as long as we gon' be in the world, why don't we sit down here and have a drink in the world, so we can ease up on the world quietly together.

MACDADDY Fuck the world! You talkin' to the Great MacDaddy, son of the Big MacDaddy who is dead, making me the greatest Daddy of all the MacDaddies who can do anything!

SOLDIER Is that right? Is that the God's truth or are you trippin'?

MACDADDY I done told you, didn't ah?

SOLDIER Well, looka here, God-son, you may be the answer to my worldly problem.

MACDADDY You got a problem for real if you don't get steppin'!

SOLDIER That ain't no problem. When I'm ready to step . . . (*Self-mockery.*) . . . I be marking the cadence of time. But I do have a little girl in the world who givin' me a big problem. My daughter done let herself get swallowed up in the jaws of some evil dude in the world. And since I'm tired and you can do anything, maybe you can go into the world and bring her outta that world so she can get hooked up with some nigga in the world who is sittin' on the world. That should be like stuff for you, God-son.

MACDADDY No good, cousin. I can do anything, but I ain't goin' for that! So, start markin' time!

SOLDIER I ain't ready yet! So you might as well put that weapon away. Hell, I guess you ain't as interested in this wine as I thought.

MACDADDY (*lowering juju-cane to ground*) That wine probably done gone to yo' head anyway. You don't know nothin'. Later!

SOLDIER (*as* MACDADDY *starts to leave*) MacDaddy . . . Great MacDaddy!

MACDADDY *stops.*

Just listen to my story. Have a little sip of wine so I can tell you 'bout the world. You got time for that, ain't cha?

MACDADDY (*takes canteen*) Where's the place?

SOLDIER Las Vegas!

BEAT TWO

Las Vegas. Dramatization of SOLDIER'*s tale about daughter.* MUSICIANS *play Fast Life music: downstage, several men stand around in formal attire outside gaming room craps-table which has been moved onto stage on a wagon from upstage behind plastic; several* FAST-LIFE WOMEN *carouse around table. Impressionable* LEIONAH *appears, doing her best to make a worldly appearance among the "fast" men outside the gaming room who flirtatiously pursue her.*

FAST-LIFE CHORUS:

Hey now, gurlie,
wha'cha doin' foolin' 'round
  here so early
you sho' look bright and dandy
  in the noon day sun;
you a long way from yo' mammy
  but we playin' for fun.

Yeah,
  you sho' look good gurlie
  feathery as my rooster;
  if I could wear you in my hat
  you'd give my soul a booster.

Gurlie,
  it's early

didn't you know?
If you dance to the music
you gotta pay to the piper.
Yo' mammy must have told you so!

And
if you lookin' for a daddy,
you ain't got far to go.
Cause here I am lil momma,
to show you everything I know.

Yeah,
you sho' look bright and dandy
in the noon day sun;
you're a long way from yo' mammy
but we playin' for fun.

So,
what you gonna do
when the sun goes down,
gurlie?

Repeat three times as they head for gaming-table, leaving LEIONAH *to ponder the question as she trepidly advances toward the gaming-room to join the men with the* FAST-LIFE WOMEN. *As she approaches the area,* LEIONAH *encounters the resplendent* SKULL*—another manifestation/personification of* SCAG*—who has entered from upstage right, dressed in white-on-white ensemble: awe-struck, she gazes at him, though* SKULL *merely glances at her and continues onto the game-room platform to join the others at the craps-table; he is greeted enthusiastically by the gathering as he takes over the dice.* LEIONAH *enters the gaming-room, attracted by* SKULL'*s magnificence; he is impeccably dressed, fingers laden with jewelry, and owns a smooth, cold, countenance as he observes his ladies' handling of the men around the table, hustling them into betting, while generating applause for each pass made with the dice.* LEIONAH *tries to make her* *presence felt, but is ignored by* SKULL *and pushed aside by the* FAST-LIFE WOMEN. *After his last pass,* SKULL *signals for the women to leave with the men. As he collects and counts his winnings,* LEIONAH *searches for a cigarette from her purse, then follows him outside the gaming-room which is rolled away.*

LEIONAH (*affected deep voice*) You got a match, mistah?

SKULL *looks off his shoulder, then coldly turns away to continue counting money downstage;* LEIONAH *approaches awkwardly.*

I said, do you have a match, mistah?

SKULL *repeats gesture/attitude and walks down a bit further stage-left;* LEIONAH *makes another attempt, somewhat aggressive, but coquettish.*

A girl's feet could get tired lookin' for a match!

SKULL (*harshly*) Piss off home, kid! You ain't ready for the pace!

He gestures as if opening a car door, enters, and postures himself in a frozen attitude as if leaning at the wheel. LEIONAH *backs off, but doesn't leave, hovering in the shadows as if spying upon* SKULL. MUSICIANS *playing. A* CAR DEALER *in white mask appears.* SKULL *steps out of the "car" and counts off some bills while the man inspects the "car." Satisfied, the* CAR DEALER *takes the bills, climbs into the "car" and stylistically "drives" off.* SKULL *walks across to down-right,* LEIONAH *close behind without his knowledge, where he comes upon a white-masked* PAWN BROKER *with three gold-balls suspended above his head from a rack attached to his shoulders.* SKULL *takes off the lovely white suit, returning it to* PAWN BROKER, *now exposing his shabby garments underneath as well as a reduced body size. After paying off the* PAWN BROKER, SKULL *moves up-stage,* LEIONAH *following, where he comes upon a shaddy* STREET HUSTLER *to whom he returns all the jewelry; after the jewelry is inspected, the* STREET HUSTLER *accepts the money, and* SKULL *moves on with* LEIONAH *in pursuit.* SKULL *now responds to a hissing sound from behind upstage plastic material: a suspicious looking character,* ALLEY

RAT, *pokes his head through, then the rest of his body.* ALLEY RAT *collects the lovely white hat and shoes from* SKULL, *accepts a few dollars, then alerts* SKULL *to a "shadow" in the alley. As the* ALLEY RAT *darts out of sight,* SKULL, *now reduced to a less awesome spectacle, spots* LEIONAH *who is now less impressed and, in an effort to conceal her fear, as well as get away, assumes a "hardened" disposition.*

SKULL (*as* LEIONAH *attempts to leave*) Hey, lil girl, that you?

LEIONAH (*stops, catches breath, turns*) You who?

SKULL You, baaaaabeeeeeee! You and me makes two of us!

LEIONAH Us? What us? I don't know nothin' bout us! You here alone, and I'm on my way home!

SKULL (*reaches out to grab her*) Hold on, lil momma!

LEIONAH (*withdrawing forcefully*) Don't put yo' hands on me, nigga! You don't know me! Don't you e-e-ever put yo' funky hands on me.

SKULL Come down, momma, I told yuh you couldn't stand the pace.

LEIONAH (*trying to out-maneuver* SKULL) I ain't even in the race, nigga. So you can't tell me nothin'!

SKULL Be cool, fool, and don't break no rules. 'Cause I see I'm gonna have to send you back to school.

LEIONAH School who? Don't talk crazy, baby. How a broke-down, low-life, no-count fool like you gonna teach me some rules? If you asked me, you need to do some bookin' on how to survive, as bad as you look, out here on the corner beggin' and stuff!

SKULL (*forcing her upstage right*) I ain't beggin', momma!

LEIONAH Sure, you beggin'! Yeah, you beggin', honey. Ain't no need in me lyin' . . . and you neither, for that matter.

SKULL What matter's, lil momma, is that you are here. And there ain't nowhere for you to go.

LEIONAH (*somewhat nervous now*) Like I been trying to tell you, I'm on my way home.

Upstage-right wagon/platform moves on with bed and clothes rack, indicating shabby effects of SKULL*'s room.*

SKULL (*urging* LEIONAH *onto bed*) Rest yo' mind at ease, Honey Chile, 'cause you gonna stay here for a little while.

LEIONAH (*fretful; almost tearful*) But I can't stay. I . . . I . . . I got thangs to do!

SKULL Ain't no way, lil momma. You had yo' chance to go. Now you gots-to-get-down!

Transitional Beat. LEIONAH *reclines tearfully, somewhat nervously on bed, as* SKULL *reduces himself further by taking off his "conked" wig, exposing a stocking cap underneath, and removing his shabby clothes until he is down to underwear.*

You'll see, lil momma, once you get hip to me, I ain't bad. I'm jes baaaad, that's all. But everybody knows I'm a ball. Ain't never in a mood to be crude, which is why any chick who is slick, and does what she's told, can get my gold. Shit, I don't need no boost, but I do be the King of the Robber's Roost. When the world gets uptight in some bad action, I give everybody satisfaction. Even Uncle Sam wanted me 'cause of what I am. I'm a cool fool, to say the least. I've climbed Rocky Mountains, fought grizzly bears, even tracked wild panthers to their hidden lair. Lissen! I've crossed the Sahara Desert, momma, and swam the Rio Grande, fought with Pancho Villa and every Wasp in the land. I've knocked down doors, and broken gorilla's jaws. Used tiger teeth for toothpicks, drunk lion's blood for soup. I'm a player and parlayer when I come across a chicken coop. Yesterday, a rattlesnake bit me, crawled away, and died, and you know, pretty momma, I ain't got no reason to lie. And when you see a hurricane or cyclone breezing through a city, you can bet everything you got that Skull, me, is drivin' it. So that's what you got to deal with here, momma. So get down, and get-up somethin' quick!

As SKULL *leans over the frightened* LEIONAH, *he reaches into his underwear: lights out, leaving only* SKULL*'s head to glow in the dark; he is now reduced to a greater state of unnatural imperfection, a skull.* LEIONAH *screams;* SKULL *curses. Lights up; she had bolted away, but is now restrained at the edge of the bed by two figures appearing skull-masked who block her retreat.*

Bring her sweet buns right back up here!

The TWO SKULETONS *force her down onto the bed.*

Okay! we might as well break her in right, right?
SKULETONS (*together*) Rhhaaaight!

Wagon/platform wheeled off as lights dim. Transitional Beat. Entering from downstage, MACDADDY *seeks out* SKULL, *thus approaches* FAST LIFE MEN *and* WOMEN *gathered around the craps-table upstage left.* MUSICIANS *playing fast-life blues theme. Without uttering a word,* MACDADDY'*s forceful appearance commands the dice. He rubs his juju-cane and makes three quick passes to the gathering's delight.* SKULL *enters the gaming-room. He usurps all the attention from* MACDADDY *who, also apparently awe-struck by* SKULL'*s completely-together potent appearance, humbly gives up the dice, then leaves the gaming-room to sing the blues.*

MACDADDY (*blues/ballad, i.e. "Stormy Monday"*)

Who could blame the woman
  who would follow
  when she can
the complete gentleman.

Who could blame the woman
  who would follow
  when she can
the complete gentleman

If I were that woman
  I too would wanna be the feather
  in the hat
  of the man
  who's got it all together.

Yeah,
  he's mean
  as the eye can see

if he were in battle
he wouldn't get touched by a war machine.

Yeah,
he's mean
as the eye can see
if he were in battle
he wouldn't get touched by a war machine.

If a bomb would dare to fall
it would not want to touch him at all
it would rather explode in Hell
than touch a thread on that man's lapel.

Yeah, he's mean!

Oh,
it hurts the eyes to see him
bringing tears to my eyes
wonderin' why
God had not blessed me with such beauty.

Yeah,
it hurts the eyes to see him
bringing tears to my eyes
wonderin' why
God had not blessed me with such beauty

But,
on the other hand,
since this beauty is only
a Skull,
I thank my God
I was created a man.

Yeah, yeah, yeah,
I thank my God,
to beat the band,
since this beauty

is only a Skull,
I thank my God
I was created a man!

Confidence recovered through singing the song, MACDADDY *approaches the craps-table once more, and, with the head of his juju-cane, stops the roll of* SKULL*'s dice abruptly: everyone gasps; music stops. He boldly stares at* SKULL *as the gathering quickly disperses, leaving the two men alone. Having made the confrontation,* MACDADDY *then leaves and positions himself downstage-right. With a cold, and calculated countenance,* SKULL *picks up his winnings and leaves the gaming-room which is rolled away.* SKULL *stops, spies* MACDADDY, *and approaches with deliberation. He taps* MACDADDY *on the shoulder, but as he turns around, he appears now to be a "gray cat," a cat-mask having emerged from the juju-cane and held up before* MACDADDY*'s face.* SKULL *ignores him. Now, as earlier, confident that he is alone,* SKULL *postures in the "car" and waits for* CAR DEALER, *the "gray cat" lurking behind him as the lights fade downstage. Transitional Beat. Upstage-right,* LEIONAH *lays indecorously spread across the bed with a large ring in her nose. She is mounted by a* SKULETON *who wears a chain around his waist, the end of it connected to the ring in* LEIONAH*'s nose; making carnal gestures, he grunts and groans while the other* SKULETON *squats in front of the bed posts.* SKULL *enters—reduced to a* SKULL *as earlier—with the unsuspecting "gray cat"—*MACDADDY*—at his heels. The* SKULETON *mounting* LEIONAH *stops and disconnects the chain from her nose, and wearily dismounts.* SKULL, *also with chain around his waist, squats next to the squatting* SKULETON *as the "gray cat" moves around bed inspecting* LEIONAH.

SKULL (*to* SKULETON *dismounting* LEIONAH) How you doin', boon coon?

FIRST SKULETON Just about wore this one down to the nitty gritty!

SECOND SKULETON And just about wore me out!

SKULL What's yo' story, Mornin' Glory?

SECOND SKULETON Tired!

SKULL Wha-choo-say?

SECOND SKULETON Whupped!

FIRST SKULETON Me too! So move over and let me squat awhile.

SKULL (*squatting with them*) Damn!

FIRST SKULETON Ain't much fun no more. All she do is lay up on her ass.

SKULL Wha-choo-say!

SECOND SKULETON She ain't movin'! We gotta do all the goddamned work.

SKULL All I wanna know is did you do yo' job?

SECOND SKULETON If you ask me, I think we overdid it!

SKULL Wha-choo-say?

FIRST SKULETON She got an overdose of the treatment. She done played out!

SECOND SKULETON We did everything you told us to do, Skull. Got her hooked with a ring in her nose that won't let go. She hooked up pretty good, but I don't know what she's good for.

SKULL Anything we want her to do!

FIRST SKULETON Well, she ain't actin' right, so I ain't gonna bust myself up on her dead ass no more today.

SKULL She ain't dead, just dead-alive. But when the Jones comes down on her funky butt, she'll make a livin' for all of us. (*Shouts at "gray cat" who is stroking* LEIONAH'*s forehead, trying to revive her.*) Get away from there, pussy!

SECOND SKULETON I think I'm gonna nod!

FIRST SKULETON Me too!

*The three of them, squatting at the foot of the bed-posts, nod into sleep: the "gray cat"—*MACDADDY*—furtively takes the ends of their chains and locks them to bed-posts. He then leads* LEIONAH *away from the bed/platform, past* SKULL *and* SKULETONS *who suddenly awake.*

SKULL *and* SKULETONS (*shouting*) Hey, pussy, come back here with our snatch!

As they shout furiously, the bed/platform wagon is withdrawn, and lights dim out. Transitional Beat. MACDADDY *observing* SOLDIER'*s efforts to fully revive daughter, vainly trying to remove ring in her nose as she leans forward on ground.*

SOLDIER Leionah! Leionah, chile, come on back. This is yo' daddy talkin'. Leionah! What in the world have they done to yuh, honey? Can you hear me, chile?

MACDADDY Ain't no use. Nothin' else to be done about it, Soldier.

SOLDIER (*anxiously; pacing*) You gotta do somethin', God-son. You promised to bring my baby back.

MACDADDY And I did! Now, I gotta go catch up with Wine . . .

SOLDIER Uh-uh, no good, God-son. My baby ain't even nearly back. If she can't come to herself she ain't got a hope in the world.

MACDADDY It ain't my fault! I did the best I could.

SOLDIER Well yo' best ain't worth a damn. All the trouble I got in the world keepin' my nose off the grindstone, and you talk 'bout yo' best. Hell, I can't even leave here on time.

MACDADDY Awright, goddammit, just don't cry on my shoulder. I'll try one more thing. Any natural weed around here?

SOLDIER Got some dippin' snuff here, will that do? (*He pours a bit into* MACDADDY'*s palm.*)

MACDADDY Got any wine left? Pour a little into my palm. (MACDADDY *works mixture into his palms, raises clenched fist and juju-cane in other hand upward, and chants.*) Like your son, God, you can do no wrong! (*He repeats phrase.*)

He leans over LEIONAH *and gestures as if feeding her some of the mixture; then, as she quickens, with great deliberation, he slowly begins to remove the ring in her nose.* LEIONAH *stretches her arms and yawns as if having had a deep sleep.*

LEIONAH Uhump! Don't you get tired!

SOLDIER (*elated*) Well, I'll be damned, God-son, you sho know how to do yo' stuff! How you feelin', daughter?

LEIONAH Fine, Daddy, jes fine! (*As* LEIONAH *stands up, it is now apparent that she is pregnant as she rubs her stomach.* MACDADDY, *ignoring the scene, prepares to leave.*)

SOLDIER (*inspecting her stomach*) What you got there, chile?

LEIONAH Got a little surprise for Daddy.

SOLDIER (*elated; patting* MACDADDY *on shoulder*) Well, I'll be God-damned, MacDaddy. You sho 'nuff for real know how to do yo' stuff.

MACDADDY (*as* LEIONAH *smiles affectionately*) Look, I don't know nothin' 'bout all that . . .

SOLDIER Oh, I understand, MacDaddy. You ain't got to boast when you got the most!

MACDADDY (*to* LEIONAH) Look here, girl, you'd better tell your Daddy somethin'!

LEIONAH (*smiling affectionately*) He sho is fine, ain't he, Daddy?

MACDADDY Wha . . . ?

SOLDIER (*to* LEIONAH) Ain't you the sweetest thang! Hate to lose you, chile, but I don't mind steppin' down for the Great MacDaddy, the greatest Daddy of 'em all!

MACDADDY You ain't lost nothin', Jack, 'cause Mac ain't goin' for that!

SOLDIER (*offering canteen*) Maybe you can go for some of this wine, son?

MACDADDY That's exactly what I had in mind. Which way did he go?

SOLDIER Take yo' time, MacDaddy. Consider' Leionah's condition and all, she might not be ready for travellin'.

MACDADDY Look, that's up to Leionah, but I'm damn sho gonna!

SOLDIER How you feelin', chile?

LEIONAH (*beaming at* MACDADDY) Feelin' fine as wine, Daddy.

As MACDADDY *and* SOLDIER *discuss the issue to one side,* LEIONAH *sings a lively blues—Ma Rainey style.*

I'm feeling fine
with the man
I call mine.
He's the host
of my life,
and I'm glad
to be his wife.

He's the man
with the most
that is why
I call him boss.

I don't care
what people say
cause they gon'
say it anyway.
I'm gonna walk
hand in hand
with my man.

I'm gonna walk,
walk, walk,
no matter how they
talk, talk, talk.
Can't give a damn
long as my man
has got my hand.

He's the host
with the most
and in my belly
is his jelly;

So if anybody ask you
when I'm gone
how I 'spects
to get along,
tell everybody
to rest their minds
cause I am
feelin' fine.

SOLDIER *embraces* LEIONAH *as* MACDADDY *looks on perplexed by the unresolved solutions.*

SOLDIER (*handing* LEIONAH *his suitcase with all his worldly possessions*) Take care of yourself, chile. I'm on my way.

MACDADDY Where you think you goin'?

SOLDIER Outta this world! Where I should've been long time ago. You see, I was jes passin' through. Bye yawl!

MACDADDY What about Wine?

SOLDIER (*as he exits*) Just lay with Leionah. She'll show the way through!

LEIONAH (*holding suitcase*) Guess we can leave now, Mac.

MACDADDY What you mean, *we? We* ain't goin' nowhere. But MacDaddy is leavin' here, dig it?

LEIONAH What about *our* baby?

Members of the OUTRAGED COMMUNITY/CHORUS *drift onto stage within earshot of the dispute and take notice: they whisper and signify about confrontation.*

MACDADDY *Our* baby, is *your* baby . . . which ain't got nothin' to do with me.

LEIONAH Well, I sho didn't make this baby by myself.

MACDADDY (*trying to exit quietly*) It's been done. Just ask Jesus!

LEIONAH (*grabbing* MACDADDY'*s arm*) You ain't goin' nowhere, nigga! You ain't leavin' me with this baby!

MACDADDY (*conscious of* OUTRAGED COMMUNITY) Let me go, woman! Find yourself another sponsor! Let go!

LEIONAH (*directly to* OUTRAGED COMMUNITY) Who's gonna take care of my baby? Who's gonna take care of my baby?

MACDADDY Shut up, woman, you're drawin' a crowd!

LEIONAH All you niggas wanna lay with Leionah, but when the shit goes down, yeah, when her belly gets round, all she ever gets from yawl is frown. Well frown done drowned in my tears, 'cause, let's face it, Mac, you ain't as slick as all that! You gonna take care of my baby and all 'ems that come back-to-back!

MACDADDY (*angered, he violently strikes her in stomach with juju-cane*) Goddamn your baby!

The OUTRAGED COMMUNITY *gasps: out pops the* SIGNIFYIN' BABY *through the plastic environment upstage center, adult sized and wearing a diaper.*

SIGNIFYIN' BABY (*dancing about frenetically*) Hoo-popsie-doo, how do you do! What you see is what you got! Oooooo!

LEIONAH (*rubbing flat stomach as she rises*) Ahhhh, Mac, ain't he cute? Go on, Mac, say somethin' nice to him.

SIGNIFYIN' BABY If you ain't got nothin' nice to say, don't say nothin' at all. Ooooo!

MACDADDY Yawl ain't puttin' me in no trick. I ain't got no claim on that boy!

SIGNIFYIN' BABY You got that right, so come down, MacBrown, you know I'm outta sight.

MACDADDY MacDaddy! The Great MacDaddy!

SIGNIFYIN' BABY You gotta prove it to me, MacGee! Weeeeeeee!

LEIONAH (*admiringly*) Shall we name him after you, Mac?

The OUTRAGED COMMUNITY/CHORUS *responds to the frenetic child with astonishment and titillation, shaking their heads admonishingly.*

SIGNIFYIN' BABY

Hold on, momma, put yourself at ease;
I got a name and pedigree.

MACDADDY How somethin' like you get a name?

SIGNIFYIN' BABY

What's it to yuh, momma screwer,
  you ain't 'ceptin' no blame.
But if anybody asks you
  what's my name,
you go on tell 'em,
  Puddin'nin Tain!

MACDADDY What's yo' name?

SIGNIFYIN' BABY

Puddin'nin Tain!
Ask me again, I'll tell you the same!

OUTRAGED COMMUNITY (*together*)

Better do somethin' 'bout that child,
  he don't be natural;
better do somethin' 'bout that child,
  he be a foundless foundling;

better do somethin' 'bout that child,
  he gonna turn havoc loose on the block!

SIGNIFYIN' BABY (*breaks his frenetic motion to assail member of the* OUTRAGED COMMUNITY)

Don't none of yawl be bad moufin' me,
'cause I'll raise my leg and on yawl I'll pee!

SCAG *enters scene laughing. Now being led around by* SCAG *whom* MACDADDY *watches closely, directing* SIGNIFYIN' BABY'*s attack on members of the* OUTRAGED COMMUNITY.

Ugly? Who you callin' ugly? You got some nerve to call me ugly! You so ugly that yo' momma got to put a sheet over your face so sleep can creep up on you. And yo' wife ain't no cuter. Man, is yo' wife ugly! Me and yo' wife went out to get a lil drink, before I got my bit, and she was so ugly she had to put on sneakers to sneak up on the drinks. (*To* SCAG *who laughs raucously.*) Now you know that don't make no sense. She look like somethin' I used to feed peanuts to in the zoo.

LEIONAH *is unable to restrain* SIGNIFYIN' BABY *and is quite concerned about the growing hostilities ignited in* OUTRAGED COMMUNITY *who begin to chorally utter, "Uhm-umm-uhmp!"*

LEIONAH Good Lord, MacDaddy, can't you do somethin'? You gotta do somethin' quick for the baaa-bah!

LEIONAH *tries desperately to break up a fight instigated by* SCAG *whom* MACDADDY *studies more intently as he ruminates over the options of what must be done:* SIGNIFYIN' BABY *assails a man who is being contained by his wife.*

SIGNIFYIN' BABY

Don't you be givin' me no evil eye!
I saw the last fight you were in
  and you were truly jive.
You 'member when I had to stop you the other day
  to tell you what this dude had to say down the way.

The way he talked 'bout yo' was a goddamned shame;
even heard him curse 'bout yo' grandmammy's name.
So you go runnin' off with an uproar, beatin' yo' chest like an ape;
and the dude just beat yo' ass all outta shape.
You made this chickenshit pass,
the dude stepped back and kicked your natural ass.
He put knots on yo' head, and kicked your ribs outta place,
the way he messed over yo' eye was truly a disgrace.
Now, you get back here more dead than alive
and got the nerve to be signifyin'.
Shit, if you had called me, I would have fought the dude myself,
cause anybody could see you needed a helluva lot of help.

MACDADDY *points his cane at* DRUM *among the* MUSICIANS, *who plays a rhythmic pulse that grips the* SIGNIFYIN' BABY.

Ooooooooowweee! Ooooweeeeee!

As the SIGNIFYIN' BABY *moves around frenetically,* MACDADDY *points juju-cane at* DANCE, *a member of* OUTRAGED COMMUNITY, *who dances with* SIGNIFYIN' BABY, *occupying his energies.* MACDADDY *then points to* SONG, *another member of the community who sings a song to civilize the force of* SIGNIFYIN' BABY *while the rest of the* OUTRAGED COMMUNITY, *at a different rhythm, utter "Uhm-umm-uhmm": a poly-rhythmic mode.*

SONG/WOMAN (*gospel*)

Oh, lead me on, I pray, Savior divine,
Let me commune with Thee, and let me find.
When storms of life appear

That Thou wilt linger near
to quell each rising fear
and lead me on.

Oh, lead me on, I pray, Lord, God of Light,
When deep'nin' shades I see, when coming night;
Engulfs the path I go,

I feareth naught I know
  Thou still doth go
before to lead me on.

SIGNIFYIN' BABY *becomes occupied and absorbed by all three modes,* SONG, DANCE, *and* DRUM, *until his energies dissipate: at this point, the* MICKEY MOUSE ORDERLY, *wearing white hospital attendant's jacket, enters and begins to wrap* SIGNIFYIN' BABY *in a strait-jacket;* LEIONAH *protests, but* MACDADDY *restrains her as the child is led off.*

LEIONAH Mac, they're takin' away my baby. No! No! Not my baby. Mac, do somethin'! I love my baby. Oh, Mac, please don't let them take my baby!

CHORUS, SONG, DANCE, *and* DRUM *continue their activity until the baby is taken off stage.* SCAG *blocks* MICKEY MOUSE ORDERLY'*s exit momentarily, but moves aside when stared down, and retreats.* MACDADDY *still holding the sobbing* LEIONAH *as the* OUTRAGED COMMUNITY *slowly disperses; stage empty,* MACDADDY *releases* LEIONAH *and prepares to leave once more.*

MACDADDY Stop cryin', woman! You'll get over it!

LEIONAH My baby . . . the only thing I had in the world.

MACDADDY Look! He's better off where he is. You would've lost him anyhow. That baby didn't have a chance out here. So, forget about him!

LEIONAH (*plaintively*) How you 'spect me to forget about my child?

MACDADDY (*tightens up appearance/attitude*) Yeah! Okay! But there'll be others. (*Prepares to leave.*) Well, anyway, I'm gone.

LEIONAH What am I supposed to do?

MACDADDY (*stops*) I don't know. Do what you been doin'!

LEIONAH Alone?

MACDADDY (*tightens-up his jaws: disgruntled, and without turning around, he shouts*) Shit! C'mon, woman!!!

She picks up suitcase and follows.

BEAT THREE

Arizona: Dog Races. ANNOUNCER'S VOICE *at a greyhound dog race track announcing last call for placing bets. Downstage,* FOUR JACKALS, *local Arizona types in white masks, sit on their haunches passing money between them. Upstage,* MACDADDY *stands wearily next to* LEIONAH *on wagon/platform watching the scene; she now wears a simple, full length sheath and a matching shawl around her head as she sits on suitcase.*

ANNOUNCER'S VOICE (*off-stage*) Hurry . . . hurry . . . hurry . . . place your bets. Put your money on the line for the bitch of your kind. Hurry . . . hurry!

MACDADDY We gotta make some dough quick, baby, before we go another fu'ther!

LEIONAH Dog racin' jes ain't yo' game, Mac!

MACDADDY Don't worry 'bout it, Momma, I still got a few games to play.

ANNOUNCER'S VOICE (*off-stage*) The doges are eeeeaaadee . . . theeeiirrr goes the rabbit . . . and they're off!

Sound of a bell. General crowd noises as ANNOUNCER'S VOICE *calls the race. The* FOUR JACKALS *rise up off their haunches and enthusiastically follow the course of the dogs in a circle. As the race ends, a final cheer, the* JACKALS *sit once more on their haunches, facing downstage, and pass money between themselves.* MACDADDY *hits upon an idea; he urges* LEIONAH *to stand, place one leg upon her suitcase, and raise the hem of her dress above the knee, and assume a seductive attitude. He now moves downstage in front of the* JACKALS *who, upon seeing him, scramble to pick up their money, yet remain on haunches.*

MACDADDY (*salesman pitch*) 'Afternoon, gentlemen, how-do-you-do? On a bright sunny Sunday like today, I can tell by your winnings you're having your way. But would you believe it if I told you I've got somethin' new for you.

The JACKALS *begin to slowly rise off their haunches, but are checked in place by* MACDADDY, *despite their suspicions.*

Now, don't crowd me! There's enough to go 'round for everybody. It may be sweet or sour, but there's sure enough for anybody whose dough is big enough for a taste. The biggest dough, of course, goes first. But make up your minds, I ain't got no time to waste. What's it gonna be, gentlemen? Money talks, nobody walks! And just to put yo' minds at ease, so yawl don't think I'm a tease, turn around and look for yo' self!

The JACKALS *swivel around on their haunches and lasciviously gaze at* LEIONAH, *making comments about her with local attitudes.*

There she bees, gentlemen, some of the best black bottom in these parts. Her name is Leionah. Now, when have yawl seen such sweet meat in Arizona? Who got the thirst to lay with Leionah first? Money talks, nobody walks! The firmest black bottom in Sodom, right down to the bone. But hold it! Just hold onto your seats! Yawl ain't heard 'bout the special treat. A sleeve-job! Leionah gives the best sleeve job in Gomorrah!

The JACKALS *look at each other perplexed.*

Now, I know yawl heard about the sleeve job. (*No response.*) Ain't yawl heard 'bout the sleeve job?

JACKALS *shake their heads.*

Now, now, now, think of that . . . we got some gentlemen here who ain't never had a sleeve job. Well, yawl got a friend in MacDaddy indeed. 'Cause once you've had a sleeve job you won't settle for no more chickenfeed. So roll up yo' sleeves and step right up. Don't miss yo' ebony opportunity!

FIRST JACKAL I'll buy one of 'em!
SECOND JACKAL Me too!
THIRD JACKAL Me three!
FOURTH JACKAL Make that four!
MACDADDY (*collecting money*) Like I said, gentlemen, money talks, nobody walks! But being asmuch as yawl never had no sleeve job, I'm gonna help yawl get over the embarrassment of the first time. So as not to spoil the fun, I'm gonna introduce yawl one-by-one. Roll up those sleeves. Higher. Higher! And to make sure everybody gets the most outta Leionah without any alibis, we gonna tie a cloth around everybody's eyes.

MACDADDY *uses the kerchiefs around the* JACKALS' *necks to blindfold them.*

It just ain't righteous to peek on a fellow when the sleeve job starts to get mellow.

MACDADDY *moves the* FIRST JACKAL *upstage right with his bare arms outstretched, stations him, and constantly exhorts the anticipating* JACKALS *to "roll sleeves higher," "spread yo' legs," "stretch out those arms," "easy does it," etc. Moving the* SECOND JACKAL *to the same location, he places his hands on the arm of the first, and commands "hold on tight"; the* THIRD JACKAL'*s outstretched hands are placed on the arm of the second; the fourth on the arm of the third so that they appear to be locked into a square formation.*

Hold on tight, yawl, and don't let go. By the time yawl count to ten, the fun will just begin.

JACKALS *begin to count in unison, and with much agitated anticipation, as* MACDADDY *steals away with* LEIONAH: *sound of a train passing faintly heard.*

JACKALS One . . . two . . . three . . . four . . . five . . . six . . .

Lights fade on JACKALS. *Transitional Beat. Sound of a train passing over a track with loud whistle. It is dark.* MACDADDY *and* LEIONAH *stand by a railroad track, eyes following a passing train, as if contemplating "hopping" a freight. A figure upstage of them approaches with a searchlight which breaks the darkness:* WHITE TRACK MAN, *wearing white mask, white shirt, and trousers, white straw hat, and carrying shotgun.*

WHITE TRACK MAN (*pointing shotgun*) Who's that?

MACDADDY (*spins around startled*) Who's that?

WHITE TRACK MAN Who's that, say who's that, when I say who's that?

MACDADDY Ain't nobody here but us chickens, Jack.

WHITE TRACK MAN And you sho 'nuff in for a roastin', Bub, 'less you got some explanation for bein' out here on this track.

MACDADDY Hey, lissen, we just passin' through . . . when we stumbled up on this track.

WHITE TRACK MAN Uh-huh, you just stumbled up on this track, just like that, huh? Well it's my business to see that you stumble right on back where you came from, 'cause we don't allow no messin' 'round with our track.

MACDADDY Ain't nobody messin' 'round. As a matter of fact, we only out searchin' for wood.

WHITE TRACK MAN What kinda wood?

MACDADDY Firewood!

WHITE TRACK MAN Now, you folks wouldn't be figurin' on usin' no track for your fire, would yuh? Let me have a look here! (*He checks track.*)

MACDADDY Nawwwww, we wasn't figurin' on nothin' like that! But you got to admit, Mistah Track Man, it do get cold out here at night.

WHITE TRACK MAN (*drops guard momentarily*) You sure as Hell got that right. Can't stand the night. Only part of my job I don't like. But yuh gotta keep your eye on the railroad day and night. Even if the wind do bite. It's all about progress. An eye on the future. Can't look away from the track even if it is a cold damn night. But that's the kinda sacrifice we Americans gotta make, or the Injuns will steal the track right out from under our feet. They ain't like us, you know. When it comes to progress, they ain't got an ounce of sympathy.

LEIONAH That sho is cold!

WHITE TRACK MAN Yeah! and me without a coat. Misplaced my coat somewhere along the track. And you know, that's a whole lotta track. Been searchin' out here all night. Yawl didn't happen to stumble up on my coat, did yuh?

MACDADDY (*shaking head*) Uhm-uhmmmm! But if we could get this fire thang goin', we could make it big enough for three.

WHITE TRACK MAN Guess we could, Bub, but we ain't got no wood.

MACDADDY There's plenty wood in 'em tracks.

WHITE TRACK MAN (*greatly agitated*) Take that back! Take that right back! That ain't no way for no American to be talkin'!

MACDADDY (*backing off from shotgun*) Raise, Track Man, I just thought you said you were cold.

WHITE TRACK MAN Colder than a witch's tit! Blood done chilled up in my veins so bad I'm afraid to turn my head too fast without breakin' my neck!

LEIONAH That sho is cold!

MACDADDY Well, no wood, no fire. Guess we'll be movin' on down the line.

WHITE TRACK MAN Hold up there, Bub! What's the big hurry?

MACDADDY Ain't no use in all of us standin' 'round out here. Somebody's got to find some wood.

WHITE TRACK MAN Now, you wouldn't be holdin' out on a fellow American, would yuh?

MACDADDY You gotta believe me, Track Man, I ain't holdin' nothin'!

WHITE TRACK MAN (*gesturing at juju-cane*) What's that you got in your hand?

MACDADDY *My daddy's juju!*

WHITE TRACK MAN Looks like right good kindlin' to me.

MACDADDY *unresponsive.*

LEIONAH That sho is cold!

WHITE TRACK MAN (*agitated*) I said, it looks like mighty fine kindlin'!

MACDADDY Yeah. Yeah, I guess it could be. Too bad I ain't got no match.

WHITE TRACK MAN (*pumping shotgun*) I got yuh match, Bub . . . right down in this barrel. Now you folks beginnin' to act as cold as night. Yuh didn't have it in your mind to be actin' like no Injun, did yuh? Maybe sneak up on us Americans and burn up our track?

MACDADDY Hey, why would I do a thing like that? Us Americans got to stick together, right?

WHITE TRACK MAN Well *us* is just about to have a bust!

LEIONAH That sho is cold!

WHITE TRACK MAN Never figured no nigga to be actin' like no Injun since yawl do speak our tongue, even though you do lie and cheat . . .

MACDADDY We speak in many tongues!

WHITE TRACK MAN There you go lyin' again! Well you won't trick me. (*Levels shotgun.*) So for the sake of progress, let me see how fast you can work up on that fire. And I hear tell you niggas got plenty of it!

Responding to the urgency of the threat, LEIONAH *sits on the end of her suitcase, spreads her legs, snaps her finger and invites* MACDADDY *to place his juju-cane between her thighs: when he removes the cane, the tip is "glowing" red.*

MACDADDY (*raising his juju-cane*) How's that for fire, my man?

He takes LEIONAH *around the shoulder and starts up the track with* WHITE TRACK MAN *in pursuit.*

WHITE TRACK MAN Hold up, Bub, let me next to that fire!

MACDADDY Make your own!

WHITE TRACK MAN Don't talk loco! I already own that fire.

MACDADDY You mean, you used to own it!

WHITE TRACK MAN Yuh outta line 'er, Bub. I own everything on this side of the track!

MACDADDY And what about the other side?

WHITE TRACK MAN That's the other fella's business. I ain't got no business over there.

MACDADDY *and* LEIONAH *gingerly cross over to the other side of the track.*

Hey, what yuh doin'? That's trespassin'! Come back here with that fire!

MACDADDY C'mon over and get some!

WHITE TRACK MAN That's trespassin'! Ain't supposed to trespass on your neighbor's property. Come back, it's cold over here. Don't be like no Injun! Yuh wouldn't desert a fellow American, would yuh?

MACDADDY Wouldn't I?

LEIONAH That sho is cold!

As lights dim, sound of passing "freight" along track drowns out WHITE TRACK MAN'*s voice, while* MACDADDY *and* LEIONAH *gesture as if "hopping" the train, their leaping attitude frozen as lights dim out.*

BEAT FOUR

Texas. MUSICIANS *playing country-western rhythm. Upstage-right, the swinging door of a saloon; downstage left, a bar on which sits a white-masked* COWBOY *who sings a country-western tune while a black* WAITER *does a "jig" dance for the amusement of the white-masked* BARTENDER *and* SHERIFF—SCAG *in another manifestation/personification.*

COWBOY (*singing*)

I got a boy and his name is Blue,
bet ten dollars he's a good boy too.
Never talks back like some coons do,
works like a horse and well trained too.

Hey Blue, you good boy, you!

Ain't nothin' shiftless 'bout my boy Blue,
'cept when he's out playin' with his girlfriend Sue.
Heavy as molasses is sweet Sue's rump,
bet'cha Blue can cut it with his ole tree trunk.

Hey Blue, you good boy, you!

Happy as a Blue Jay sittin' on a fence,
dancin' for his supper like he's got some sense.
Ain't nothin' in this world that Blue won't do,
to keep me off his buttocks with my hob-nob shoes.

Hey Blue, you good boy, you!

COWBOY *starts to repeat the first verse, but trails off as* MACDADDY *intrudes forcefully through the swinging doors and stands boldly: his attitude/appearance tightened up, though showing signs of wear, he surveys the scene. Everyone's attention, except that of* NIGGERTOE, *the waiter, is at the door.*

BARTENDER Check out that dude!

SHERIFF That ain't no dude. That's a niggah!

COWBOY Hah, you must be gettin' color blind!

MACDADDY (*signals outside*) C'mon in, baby!

LEIONAH (*enters and stands with trepidation by the door*) I better wait, Mighty Mac, 'til you make the path straight!

MACDADDY *checks out* NIGGERTOE *as he makes his way toward the bar.* LEIONAH *also observes him with apparent disgust.*

BARTENDER Niggertoe! Who tole you to stop dancin'?

NIGGERTOE If yuh please, suh, the music stopped.

BARTENDER So what? Keep on dancin'!

NIGGERTOE If yuh please, suh, yes suh! (*He continues "jig."*)

MACDADDY (*everyone pretends to ignore his presence as he stands at the bar; shouts*) Bartender! ! !

BARTENDER (*begrudgingly moves toward him*) You want somethin', boy?

MACDADDY What you got to drink?

BARTENDER Sheriff, this boy here wants to know what we got to drink.

SHERIFF Then tell 'im!

BARTENDER Sass-parilla!

MACDADDY Ain't you got no wine?

BARTENDER (*to* SHERIFF) You reckon somethin' wrong with this boy's hearin'? Y'all hear-d me say sass-parilla, didn't yuh?

COWBOY (*as* MACDADDY *observes* NIGGERTOE) Maybe the boy is deaf!

SHERIFF And dumb! Everybody knows we don't 'llow no cuffy put their lips on alcohol 'round o'here.

MACDADDY (*to* BARTENDER) Sassparilla!

BARTENDER Did you say somethin'?

MACDADDY I said sassparilla. And two glasses.

BARTENDER (*to* SHERIFF) Did you hear this boy say two glasses of sass-parilla?

SHERIFF And that's all I heard!

BARTENDER Maybe you'd better try that one more time, boy. Don't wanna make no mistake 'bout what I'm hearin'.

MACDADDY (*emphatically*) Sass-parilla! Two . . . glasses!

BARTENDER If you . . . ?

MACDADDY What?

BARTENDER If you . . . ?

MACDADDY If you *got 'em,* Peckerwood!

BARTENDER, SHERIFF, *and* COWBOY *recoil;* LEIONAH *sighs, suspecting trouble, and* NIGGERTOE *mumbles toward the ceiling as if in silent prayer, but continues dancing.*

SHERIFF (*subdued confidence*) Now, boy, you ought 't know better than to sass the man like that over a lil sassparillee. The man asked you a civilized question and all he wants is a civilized answer. Cause, you see, you ain't that tall in the rump that you can't get thumped, follow me?

MACDADDY Sassparilla! Two glasses! Do I get 'em, or don't I?

SHERIFF Boy, let me tell you a little story. I 'member when the Dodge Boys came through. Had plenty horse power too. They started kickin' up their heels the way a lotta niggas do. But they didn't count on my fire power! No, boy, they didn't count on that! Had to run 'em outta town before sundown. And without their sassparillee. Now, if you act right, and cause me no strife, you might even get outta here with your life.

MACDADDY Well, might had damn sho better be right!

BARTENDER That settled it right there! The cuffy ain't gettin' served. Can't get nothin' here but a barrel of trouble.

SHERIFF Now, see there, boy, huh? See what yuh done gone did? You done gone made the man mad, 'er, see? Boys like you make it tough on other niggas to come in here and drink, you know.

COWBOY Jes can't treat 'em right! Never could!

MACDADDY Ain't no big thang, Sheriff. Yawl ain't got no wine, and I don't know too many niggas who wanna drink that funky sassparilla yawl drink no how. I thought I was doin' yawl a favor comin' in here, but since yawl ain't got nothin' better to do than fuck with me, I'll jes leave!

SHERIFF (*blocking* MACDADDY'*s passage and looking him over*) Now, now, now, hold on, boy!

COWBOY That there's one cuffy I wouldn't bet a Buffalo nickle on. He ain't nearly true as Blue!

SHERIFF Have I ever seen you in these parts before?

MACDADDY Maybe! Maybe not! But in case you didn't, have a good look so you can recognize me when I come back through.

SHERIFF Hold your horses, boy. (*To* BARTENDER.) Give the boy a drink on me.

BARTENDER Yuh gotta be kiddin', Sheriff.

SHERIFF Yuh heard me, Prairie Dog, give the boy a drink! (*Beckons to* LEIONAH.) C'mon gurlie, you too.

LEIONAH *approaches with trepidation.*

MACDADDY (*as* BARTENDER *pours*) Don't do me no favors.

SHERIFF (*handing* LEIONAH *and* MACDADDY *drinks*) Don'tcha bet on it, boy. That ain't no favor. That's a drink for the road . . . with the signpost warnin' *get outta town*! When you get on that road, jes keep gettin' up, you understand, 'cause I done seen the bad of the bad without ever blinkin'. You name 'em, I've seen 'em. When the West was at its best, Jesse James and his brother Frank put everybody to a test, 'cept me who they tried to make a pal, hearin' 'bout my reputation at the O.K. Corral. You 'member the Dalton Brothers, don'tcha? They were four of a kind. Shot a poor sombitch for a raggedy dime. And there's one mean renegade I'm sure you must know . . . thinks they calls him Geronimo! Even came across a few bad coons before, and you don't nearly measure up to what I saw.

MACDADDY You must not know who I am!

LEIONAH *arches eyebrows.*

SHERIFF Don't have to! If you've seen one cuffy, you've seen 'em all.

MACDADDY (*turns on* NIGGERTOE) Stop dancin', nigga, you makin' me tired!

NIGGERTOE *stops.*

BARTENDER Who . . . ? Boy, who told you to stop dancin'?

NIGGERTOE *points meekly, confusedly, at* MACDADDY.

Wha . . . Boy, you'd better get back up on your toes!

NIGGERTOE *dances.*

MACDADDY (*as* SHERIFF *stands by benignly knotting a rope*) Stop! (*Stares angrily.*) And I'm not gonna tell you again.

COWBOY Somebody corral that cuffy before Texas gets a bad name.

BARTENDER Ain't no cuffy gonna stand on my grandpappy's grave and run my show. The Niggertoe will do what I want it to do. Get movin', boy!

NIGGERTOE *moves once more and is clearly confused, as* LEIONAH *anxiously tries to get* MACDADDY *to leave the saloon.*

MACDADDY (*his back to* NIGGERTOE) When I turn around, you'd better still be standin', nigga. And tall! Straight up on your feet!

BARTENDER (*shaking finger*) Now you gonna get it! You really gonna get it!

LEIONAH (*urging* MACDADDY *to leave*) Well, time done passed outta my cup, Mac. Time do fly!

MACDADDY Have another drink!

COWBOY Boy, I'm gonna sing a song about yuh when we drag yuh carcass up Boot Hill.

MACDADDY All I wanna know is who would dare to put it there?

BARTENDER Who do you think you are, huh? Just who do you think you are, cuffy?

MACDADDY 'Bout time you asked, Shoefly, 'cause if you knew you wouldn't be fuckin' with me. I am the Great MacDaddy, son of the Big MacDaddy who is dead, making me the greatest Daddy of all the MacDaddies who can do anything in this world!

SHERIFF (*holds up end of knotted rope*) You know what kind of knot this is?

MACDADDY Ain't interested!

SHERIFF You should. It's a nig-knot! Think you great enough to slip it?

They stare at each other momentarily.

MACDADDY Shiiidddd! If you can't show me nothin' better we might as well split. C'mon baby. And you too, Niggertoe!

SHERIFF (*ruffled; draws gun*) Don't you walk away from me, boy, when I'm talkin' to yuh. Hear me, boy? You ain't jes talkin' to no redneck trash. I ain't no trash, boy, hear me . . . ?

MACDADDY (LEIONAH *and* NIGGERTOE *stand by nervously*) I smell every word you say, Sheriff. And I can see from the ring around your collar that yo' neck is as red as sour grapes. Furthermore, I got a graveyard disposition and a tombstone mind . . . I'm a bad muthafuka that's why I don't mind dyin'! So go on, shoot!

BARTENDER (*as trio heads for doors*) Stop 'em, Sheriff! They stealin' my niggah!

SHERIFF (*flustered; waving gun, he shouts incantatively*) In the name of Jehovah . . . In the name of Jehovah . . . In the name of Jehovah . . .

Before MACDADDY, LEIONAH, *and* NIGGERTOE *can reach the swinging doors of the saloon, the* BEASTS OF PREY *emerge from upstage: three enormous, demonic figures—raised on platformed shoes—covered like Ku Klux Klanners with a single eye/light which blinks on and off as room darkens. They direct their beam of light towards the retreating trio as if trying to brand them, causing them to scurry about the stage desperately in an effort to stay out of range of the flashes of light.* NIGGERTOE, *though afraid, begins to dance in an effort to distract the beams of light away from* MACDADDY *and* LEIONAH *so that they might escape: he dances furiously as the* BEASTS OF PREY *close in on him with their flashing, branding eyes.* NIGGERTOE *absorbs all the light, sustains the abuse courageously, dancing until he is broken down by the beams of light, sacrificing his life while* MACDADDY *and* LEIONAH, *who had hesitated a moment before leaving, make good their escape, and the* SHERIFF, BARTENDER, *and* COWBOY *stand by in a frozen, hostile, attitude.* MUSICIANS *play calamitously.*

BEAT FIVE

A suburb in Arkansas. Upstage-right, on wagon/platform, a white-masked woman, MRS. MIDDLESEX, *sits in a wicker rocker knitting, while her husband,* MR. MIDDLESEX, *also in white-mask, sits in a wicker chair and reads the* Wall Street Journal. *They are sitting on a porch. At center stage is the* SCARECROW, *another manifestation/personification of* SCAG. MR. MIDDLESEX *bemoans the decline of the stock market;* MRS. MIDDLESEX *bemoans the black intrusion in Heavensville.* MACDADDY *and* LEIONAH *enter downstage right, their backs to the* SCARECROW, *anxiously surveying the audience, as if looking for traces of the* BEASTS OF PREY. *Their vigil is interrupted by the voice of the* SCARECROW.

SCARECROW Stop!

MACDADDY *and* LEIONAH *turn around quickly; observe* SCARECROW, *then turn away.*

MR. MIDDLESEX (*eyes riveted to his newspaper*) Prices are smokin', and money is frozen!

SCARECROW Stop!

MACDADDY *and* LEIONAH *spin around again to seek out voice; observe* SCARECROW, *then turn away.*

MR. MIDDLESEX Things look bad for this country, Mrs. Middlesex.

SCARECROW Stop! Go! Blow! Ain't gonna tell yuh no moe!

MACDADDY *and* LEIONAH *stare incredulously at* SCARECROW.

MR. MIDDLESEX This land was built on blood, sweat, and tears, Mrs. Middlesex. It jes don't seem fair!

MACDADDY (*pointing toward* SCARECROW) That voice came from over there.

LEIONAH Ain't nothin' there to know but an old scarecrow!

SCARECROW And I ain't no door-mat, so go!

MACDADDY *and* LEIONAH *size up the* SCARECROW. MRS. MIDDLESEX *stops knitting, slowly stands, and stares out as if inspecting her property for intruders.*

MACDADDY (*jocularly*) You know, for a minute, I thought I heard this scarecrow say go!

SCARECROW And I did!

LEIONAH (*sensing trouble, attempts to lead* MACDADDY *away*) Ain't nothin' here to know but an old scarecrow!

SCARECROW (*as* MACDADDY *searches for gimmick*) That jes goes to show how much you know 'bout ole Jim Crow. Better flap your wings away from this door!

MACDADDY (*incredulously*) A talkin' scarecrow! ! ? ?

SCARECROW

Eenee, meenee, minee, moe,
beat a nigger with old Jim Crow;
if he hollers, snap his collar,
eenee, meenee, minee, moe!

LEIONAH (*attempting to draw* MACDADDY *away from his inspection of* SCARECROW) Ain't nothin' here to know but an old scarecrow!

MACDADDY (*pulling away; annoyed*) Wait a minute!

MRS. MIDDLESEX You know somethin', Middlesex . . . ? I could swear I see nigras in our yard.

MR. MIDDLESEX (*eyes on* Wall Street Journal) Who'd ever believe it could happen here in Heavensville!

MACDADDY (*absurdly defiant to* SCARECROW)

Hickery dickery dock,
the mouse ran up the clock;
the clock struck ten,
the mouse broke wind,

and if you open yo' mouth once again,
I'll flatten you with my cane!

Raises juju-cane threateningly over SCARECROW *who is now silent.*

MRS. MIDDLESEX (*alarmed*) They is nigras in our yard. And they meddlin' with our scarecrow!

MR. MIDDLESEX Heavensville can't stand this pressure much longer.

SCARECROW (*after* MACDADDY *seems satisfied, lowers cane, and starts to walk away*)

Fly, Blackbird, fly away home!
 Fly, fly, fly!
Fly, Blackbird, fly away home!
 Fly, fly, fly!

MACDADDY *turns on* SCARECROW *furiously with raised cane but is restrained by* LEIONAH *who grabs his arm.*

LEIONAH Don't waste your energy down to the wick. Ain't nothin' here but spittle and sticks!

MRS. MIDDLESEX (*greatly alarmed*) Middlesex, 'ems some evil nigras out there. And it looks to me like they stayin'.

MR. MIDDLESEX (*absorbed in* Wall Street Journal) This is a dark day for Heavensville!

MACDADDY (*lowering cane once more*) Hell, I ain't studin' the bag of hay. But I ain't gonna let no scarecrow make a fool outta me.

SCARECROW You a fool if you stay! Better flap your wings while you got a chance to get away.

MACDADDY You still got something to say?

SCARECROW Yeah, I got plenty to say! We don't allow no carousin' out here, pissin' in doorways, squattin' on the grass, or playin' stink-finger with the moon. This ain't Coontown. Ain't no way a spade can stay, spade for spade!

MACDADDY Look, if you don't shut up, I'll dig you today, and spade you all the way up into next week!

SCARECROW Two little blackbirds sittin' in the thicket, tryin' to get to Heaven on a jive wolf-ticket!

MACDADDY (*searching pockets*) Where're my matches? (*To* LEIONAH.) Look in your bag for some matches! (*To* SCARECROW.) When I find my matches, I'm burnin' yo' ass down to the ground.

MRS. MIDDLESEX (*alarmed*) Middlesex! They squattin' on our property! That lil heffer down there with that buck, done opened up her suitcase. Next thing you know they'll have a string of dirty drawers strung across the yard.

MR. MIDDLESEX Looks bad. That's what an Open Door policy will get'cha!

LEIONAH *closes suitcase and shakes head, having not found any matches.* SCARECROW, *who only a moment ago watched them anxiously, now smiles.*

MACDADDY I don't know what you're smilin' at! I'm jes two minutes off yo' stack without a match!

SCARECROW (*singing*)

'Tis better that you steal on home,
than get your feathers tarred-to-the-bone,
  bye, bye, Blackbird!

MACDADDY *absurdly irritated;* LEIONAH *tries to pull him away.*

LEIONAH Let's split, Mac. Ain't nothin' here a good drought can't fix!

MACDADDY (*pulling away from her*) Uh-uh, naw, I ain't goin' nowhere!

SCARECROW Shoo-shoo, fool, before I call my man the eagle down on you!

MACDADDY (*incensed*) What goddamn eagle?

SCARECROW The Great American Eagle!

MACDADDY Well, I'm the Great MacDaddy, you understand?

LEIONAH *sighs.*

Son of the Big MacDaddy who is dead, making me the greatest Daddy of all the MacDaddies who can do anything in this world. So call yo' sad assed eagle, Jim, I'll ride his back until he grins! Go on, call him!

SCARECROW *murmurs toward the sky as* MACDADDY *directs* LEIONAH *to keep an eye out for* EAGLE. *They circle* SCARECROW *vigilantly.*

MRS. MIDDLESEX It jes ain't American what these nigras do. They understand nothin' 'bout private property.

MR. MIDDLESEX Done placed a lotta stock in Heavensville too.

SCARECROW (*shouting*) C'mon Eagle, come on through. Gotta show these blackbirds what Eagle can do!

EAGLE *appears from upstage flapping his wings: a grotesquely featured creature covered with soiled money, dancing menacingly around* MACDADDY *and* LEIONAH.

Sic 'em, Eagle. Sic 'em!

Retreating from EAGLE, MACDADDY *and* LEIONAH *back into* SCARECROW. *For the first time,* SCARECROW *moves from his stationary position, causing* MACDADDY *and* LEIONAH *to fall to the ground.*

MRS. MIDDLESEX What those nigras need is a good thrashing. The heffer's layin' down on the ground with that buck. Bet they ain't even married or nothin'.

MR. MIDDLESEX It's a sin and a shame for a God-lovin' country to sink so low!

MACDADDY *and* LEIONAH *lay stretched out on the ground.* SCARECROW *places straw-clips on their wrists and ankles as if anchoring them to the ground, while* EAGLE *dances about menacingly. A large, oversized, hypodermic needle and a plastic bag of white powder "fly in" from above and is suspended over the couples' heads.* EAGLE *becomes excited.*

SCARECROW (*reaching toward "works"*) Now, we keeps something up our tree that always makes the Eagle happy! (*Detaching hypodermic needle from wire.*) Get back, Eagle! Just so you birds don't think we're without humanity, I'm gonna show you a little Christian pity, just to ease your pain.

As MACDADDY *and* LEIONAH *struggle vainly,* SCARECROW *injects them with the hypo-needle, then replaces it on wire to be sus-*

pended over their heads like bait to urge EAGLE *to dance ferociously at their feet.*

Go on, Eagle, work yo' show! Yeah, do it to 'em!

MACDADDY, *in an effort to overcome the influences of the drug, and the imminent attack by* EAGLE, *begins to shout incantatively as if trying to awaken a stronger source of power to free them.*

MACDADDY God is so great! God is so great! (*He repeats this phrase which is interpolated with a response from* LEIONAH *of "Thank yuh, Jesus!"*)

MRS. MIDDLESEX Did you know that nigras use the Lord's name in vain?

MR. MIDDLESEX Can't happen here in Heavensville!

As MACDADDY *and* LEIONAH *repeat their phrases with varying rhythmic tonalities, improvisationally, a work-gang, the* SPIRIT OF WOE, *suddenly appears from upstage-left, chained together, pounding their sledge hammers rhythmically, punctuating their song, "My Country 'Tis of Thee," which is sung with a gospel inflection. Leading the* SPIRIT OF WOE *is the manifestation/personification of* WINE.

MRS. MIDDLESEX Oh no, good God! It's happening, Middlesex. Exactly what folks always say 'bout nigras. The moment you let one in they start bringing their friends around.

MR. MIDDLESEX Heavensville will never be the same after this!

SPIRIT OF WOE (MACDADDY *and* LEIONAH *shouting in between the phrases which reinforces the dynamics of the musical mode with call 'n response*)

My
  coun-try 'tis
  of thee
sweet
  land of
  lib-erty
for
  this I
sing.

Land
where my
fa-thers died!
land
of the
Pil-grims pride;
from
ev-ery
moun-tainside,
O Lord,
let free-dom
let free-dom
let-it-ring!

MRS. MIDDLESEX Before you know it, they'll be havin' all-night parties out there.

MR. MIDDLESEX Heavensville, my Heavensville!

The SPIRIT OF WOE *repeats the same verses one more time, along with the interlocking invocations of* MACDADDY *and* LEIONAH, *thus intensifying the musical mode which distracts* EAGLE *from his "bait," actually wears him out, his "killing dance" becoming subdued by the spiritual force of the work-song.* SCARECROW *scolds* EAGLE *to keep dancing. He is now astonished and chagrined to see* EAGLE *"peck," pull up the clips that had fastened* MACDADDY *and* LEIONAH *to the ground. As the* SPIRIT OF WOE *exits, dragging its chains and singing vigorously,* EAGLE *trails docilely behind them.*

SCARECROW What's wrong with you, Eagle? You supposed to be my partner. Come back! You makin' a fool outta the whole goddamned nation! Come on back here! This ain't no time to go soft-on-the-job. Lotta people dependin' on you and me, Eagle, come-on-back!

MACDADDY *stands while* LEIONAH *remains in a state of grace for having been freed by the spirits, and tips up behind* SCARECROW *who faces the exit.*

MACDADDY (*as* SCARECROW *turns around*) Booo!

Horrified, SCARECROW *runs off-stage.*

MRS. MIDDLESEX (*despairingly*) Ain't there somethin' we can do, Middlesex?

MR. MIDDLESEX (*looking away from the* Journal *for the first time to stroke his chin reflectively*) They tell me cyanide is colorless, odorless, and painless.

MRS. MIDDLESEX *collapses in her chair with a horrified expression on her face, gazing at her husband as wagon/platform is wheeled offstage.* MACDADDY *detaches hypo-needle and bag of powder from wire.*

MACDADDY Wonder what this is?

LEIONAH Ain't nothin' more fearful than idle curiosity!

MACDADDY Nothin' wrong with bein' curious. That shit he shot into us was powerful. For a minute, I thought I was in the valley of the shadow of Death. Always was afraid of needles, though I fear no evil. Here, put this in your bag. The only way to beat fear is to get used to having it around.

LEIONAH (*forewarning as she takes hypo and powder*) The cheapest way to help a man through the world is to pile up flowers on his tombstone!

Lights fade out as MACDADDY *seems puzzled by her response.*

BEAT SIX

St. Louis. Lights up on MACDADDY *and* LEIONAH *looking at a sign upstage-left which reads* THE FAITHFUL REST, *hanging over a boarding-house "stoop" upon which sits* MOTHER FAITH, *wearing a housedress, bedroom slippers, and fanning herself with a church fan as she casually leans forward to observe the street scene. Downstage-right is* STAGOLEE *standing around with a "street corner" attitude.* MACDADDY *and* LEIONAH, *both appearing quite tired, approach the "stoop."*

MOTHER FAITH (*responding congenially*) 'Afternoon, children!

MACDADDY How you doin'? You know who runs this place?

MOTHER FAITH Why, sho . . . Mother Faith!

MACDADDY Where she bees right about now?

MOTHER FAITH You lookin' at her, chile. Anything I can do for you?

MACDADDY (*hesitantly*) Well . . . er . . . that depends. Got any beds free?

MOTHER FAITH (*business attitude*) Why sho! Got plenty beds . . . but they ain't *free!*

MACDADDY (*somewhat embarrassed*) Well . . . er . . . how much are they?

MOTHER FAITH (*surreptitious tone*) For . . . two?

MACDADDY (*uncomfortably*) Hmm? . . . er . . . yeah!

MOTHER FAITH Ah dollar and ah half ah day! Clean linen and two meals!

MACDADDY (*apparently broke*) I see . . . well . . . er . . . we'll be back a bit later, okay?

MOTHER FAITH Why, sho, anytime yawl ready. Mother Faith ain't goin' nowhere.

She begins to fan once more and follow MACDADDY *and* LEIONAH *with her eyes as they hesitantly approach* STAGOLEE.

MACDADDY (*tentatively*) How you doin', cousin?

STAGOLEE (*spins around; suspiciously*) Don't *cousin* me! My name is Stagolee!

MACDADDY That's awright with me. I jes thought I'd see if you could spare a dime.

STAGOLEE

A dime! Man, you must be outta yo' mind.
Do I look like some kinda money-tree?
Ain't nothin' out in these bushes free!

MACDADDY Look here, brutha . . .

STAGOLEE Uh-uh, I ain't got no brutha! My momma only made one like me!

MACDADDY Well anyway, dig on what I got to say. Me and my ole lady ain't had no sleep nor somethin' to eat for nearly ah week!

STAGOLEE

So what you want from me, pity?
My middle name ain't Charity!
Out here it's every man for hisself.
If you wanna keep yo' game in check,
  you gotta get yo'self a rep,
  by any means necessary.
Hell, I done fucked over every nigguh alive
  so that I might survive.
So don't be askin' me for no sympathy,
  you'd better get out here
  and beat these bushes like me.
Or pick up yo' stick
  and split.
Cause you'll get nothin' here
  but yo' head shook,
  yo' pennies took,
  and yo' name put
  in the St. Louis General
  Hospital book!

MOTHER FAITH *observes the scene downstage with great consternation.*

MACDADDY So yo jes gonna over us, huh? What kind of city you nigguhs livin' in without no pity? Can't you see this sista is hungry?

STAGOLEE

I ain't got no sista, either. And before you try to make a
sissy outta me, I'm gonna tell you somethin' 'bout bein' hungry.
Back in '22 when times was hard,
  had a sawed-off shotgun with a crooked deck of cards;
  had a pin-striped suit, and a broke-down hat;
  had a T-model Ford without a payment on that.

Had a cute lil 'hoe who throwed me out in the cold.
  When I asked why, she said, "Our love is growin' old."
So I walked on down to Market Street,
  down where the baddest nigguhs in town used to meet.
Walked through water and waded through mud,
  'til I came to a place called "The Bucket of Blood."

I walked in, asked the man for somethin' to eat.
He brought me a stale glass of water
  and a fucked-up piece of meat.
I said, "Raise, chicken-shit, do you know who I am?"
He said, "Frankly, sad ass, I don't give a damn!"
I said, "This is me, bad Stagolee!"
He said, "Yeah, been hearin' 'bout you 'cross the way,
  but I feed hungrier and badder nigguhs each and every day."
I knowed right then that this bird was dead;
  throwed a thirty-eight shell right through the sucker's head.

And if I'm lyin', I'm flyin'!

LEIONAH (*insinuating disbelief*) Countin' the stars don't help the meal-box!

MACDADDY (*responding pragmatically*) Look here, Stagolee, we ain't got much . . . (*Opens* LEIONAH*'s suitcase.*) but maybe we can sell you somethin' . . . like a pretty dress for your woman or somethin'.

STAGOLEE (*checking out suitcase*) Lissen, chump, my name is Stagolee, not Sugar Daddy. Any buyin' to be done, will be buyin' for me! What's that in the corner, somethin' to eat?

MACDADDY *holds up plastic bag of white powder.*

MACDADDY This? Uh-uh, don't think you can handle it, Stagolee. Much too mean. Even meaner than you.

STAGOLEE (*takes bag; dips finger in for a taste*) Ain't nothin' that mean! And if it is, I oughta get to know it. (*Tastes.*) Ooooweeee! it sho do have a bite. But I damn sho ain't gonna let a little white-stuff give me no fright. What's the price?

MACDADDY I'm tellin' yuh, Stag, that stuff will grab you like death-dipped-in-misery!

STAGOLEE How you sound, Clown? I know all about misery. Just give up the price!

LEIONAH A blind mule ain't hardly 'fraid of darkness!

MACDADDY Ah dollar and ah half!

STAGOLEE (*as he counts out money*) You got it! Now, how do you get next to this white-stuff without using yo' fingers?

MACDADDY (*holding up hypo-needle*) Here's the shot, but I'm afraid I can't sell it to you 'cause it's such a fearful thing and I'm still gettin' used to havin' it around. But . . . er . . . I guess I could rent it to you for another dollar.

STAGOLEE (*taking hypo-needle*) Fifty cents! and that's all you get.

MACDADDY (*accepts money;* STAGOLEE *walks off*) Hope that white-stuff don't knock you down, Stagolee.

STAGOLEE (*exiting*) If it's that bad, we'll jes have to lock assess 'til one of us falls dead, and you know, I ain't been beat lately!

MACDADDY *and* LEIONAH *look away from* STAGOLEE *and discover* MOTHER FAITH *vigorously beckoning them; they approach.*

MOTHER FAITH (*admonishingly*) C'mon over here, chile, and let me talk to yuh! Whay you children doin' talkin' to that bad Stagolee. He ain't gonna do you no good.

MACDADDY Ain't nothin' to it, really. We jes had to hit on Stag for some bread so we could ease up on that meal and bed you be advertisin'.

MOTHER FAITH (*directing them inside*) Stagolee is the last person in the world yawl should have to go see. I got eyes, ain't ah?

I can see yawl need a rest. If you didn't have no money, why didn't you say so.

LEIONAH *sulks as she leads them onto stoop in preparation to go inside.*

Now, yawl just come on in here. Mother Faith ain't never turned nobody 'way from her door. C'mon in, chile!

Wagon/platform rolled offstage. Transitional Beat. Lights up on stage-right while MUSICIANS *play honky-tonk. Several black people,* THE COMMUNITY AT REST/CHORUS, *seated at a long table. At one end,* WOMEN *eating from soup bowls and dipping bread; at the other end,* MEN *are playing cards noisily while the* WOMEN *chat with abandon.* MOTHER FAITH *enters with* MACDADDY *and* LEIONAH. *She directs them to a table.*

MOTHER FAITH That's right, yawl jes come right in here and rest yo' souls. We ain't got much, like everybody else out here, but yawl jes make yo'selves at home. Stay as long as you like, we'll find a way. (*To others.*) Yawl make room for these children. (*To* MACDADDY *and* LEIONAH.) And after supper, yawl be sure to get some sleep, even though the bed do take two! Keep the faith, children.

FIRST CARDPLAYER (*to* MACDADDY) Hey man, you wanna take my hand? I'm 'bout to give it up!

POPPA (*another manifestation/personification of* WINE; *grouchily*) You oughta! Can't play no way!

MACDADDY (*starts to accept the offer, but looks over at* LEIONAH *and is reminded through a glance the limitations of his monies, thus merely sits next to* POPPA) Naw! That's awright! Kinda hungry right through here.

LEIONAH *enters into lively conversation with the other women.* MACDADDY *suddenly becomes aware of the grouchy* POPPA.

POPPA (*signifyin'*) Can't none of yawl play. Uhmmp! looka there!

FIRST CARDPLAYER Stay out the game!

POPPA What game? Yawl ain't got no game. (*Poking* MACDADDY'*s elbow.*) They never could play The Man's game down front!

MACDADDY *merely nods placatingly.*

Trump card! Uhump! that sho was po'!

SECOND CARDPLAYER Didn't the man say stay outta the game?

POPPA (*poking* MACDADDY'*s elbow*) Can't tell these young squirrels nothin'! They think they know it all. (*Re-intrudes the game.*) Trump 'im! Ain't that somethin'!

THIRD CARDPLAYER (*having just played the wrong card*) Now, we ain't gonna tell yuh no moe' . . . keep yo' cottonpickin' nose outta my cards!

MOTHER FAITH (*admonishingly*) Uh-uh, wait one minute here. Yawl know yawl ought'n do Poppa like that. He's only tryin' to tell you somethin'!

FOURTH CARDPLAYER How he gonna know what I know when he ain't even in the game?

POPPA I know you got a handful of trumps, Short Change, and you don't even know it. (*To* MACDADDY.) And if he did know it, he wouldn't know what to do with 'em.

FIRST CARDPLAYER (*waves* POPPA *off*) Awwww, man, you ain't said nothin'! Let's play cards!

POPPA (*to* MACDADDY) 'Em fellas ain't learned nothin' 'bout The Man's game.

MACDADDY *merely nods placatingly.*

I know, 'cause I done seen 'em all. Ain't no new game. Only the card deck is new and the stakes higher. Same old shuffle, though. (*Becomes more agitated.*) Common sense will tell you that the man with the biggest trump will thump everytime. Trump card is powerful, you know. Every niggah's got one! If we put 'em all together and use 'em right, we'd all be powerful. (*He stands up, moves down the end of table, looks away as he takes a swig from his half pint of Old Grandad. Suddenly he spins, slams his fist down on the table, and ejaculates a statement that stuns the whole table into silence. His speech and attitude is redolent of Marcus Garvey.*) Saw seven bust eleven in the pants . . . (*Everyone is startled.*) . . . and make snake-eyes give him some respect! A trump can bust anybody in the rump. That's the true test of Time. I know about Time!

They stare at him as one does a man who speaks with a drunkard's tongue, but possesses wisdom. MACDADDY *is particularly curious as the women reinforce his speech with responses.*

There was a time when black people had all the trumps, and white folks got bumps on their behinds sittin' in caves. And that's a fact! And the time when black women were to men what daylight is to darkness, a change for the better, shedding light on the mysteries of life. Couldn't do without her then, and no real man can do without her now. But you gotta have your trump card! It ain't no virtue to be poor all yo' life. It's a crime! When you poor, you be hungry without hope of food, sick without a drop of medicine, tired without a bed to lay your sleepy head, naked without clothes to hide your sores. Without that trump card you be despised! Hell, ain't nothin' left but crime! Yeah, the trump card is power! If you don't believe me, ask The Man . . . you always askin' him for somethin'! I know what I say, 'cause I been hungrier longer than anybody here today. The Man got the trump card, and his family too! That's why he got more power than you. They done played full house and got a nation. A nation! hear me, a nation! Is that trump enough for you? If you want yo'self a nation, you'd better figure out how he stacked that deck and get you some trump cards too. Cause the man who can't play the game is cheatin' on God's image. Hear me? God wanted you . . . to be the complete master of yo'self, so he could go on bein' the Almighty trump card!

MOTHER FAITH (*she repeats the last few words, then launches into song "Amazing Grace" as* POPPA *words improvisationally—call 'n response—throughout phrases of the song*)

T'was grace that taught my heart to fear
and grace my fears relieved;
Oh, how precious did that grace appear
the hour I first believed.

Amazing grace
how sweet the sound
that saved
a wretch like me;

oh, I once was lost
but now I'm found
was blind
but now I see.

MOTHER FAITH *repeats the verses once more. Her song has restored spiritual harmony at the table as* POPPA *braces himself with another swig of Old Grandad.* MACDADDY, *confidence restored, moves in closer to card game.*

MACDADDY Deal me in . . . brutha!

Lights fade out. Transitional Beat. MACDADDY *and* LEIONAH *encounter the nerve-wracked figure of* STAGOLEE, *now* SCAGOLEE, *on the "street corner." He scratches and talks to himself as they approach him.*

Wuz happenin', Stagolee?

SCAGOLEE (*spins around nervously; suspiciously*) Who you talkin' to? You don't know me. My name is Scagolee!

MACDADDY Hey, man, this is me, MacDaddy.

SCAGOLEE (*vacantly*) Yeaaaaah! (*Almost nodding.*)

MACDADDY Look, I got some bucks. I thought I'd buy that stuff back.

SCAGOLEE (*snapping upright*) Ain't no moe'! I done whupped Death's ass. I put fist all in white-stuff's face. Dude tried to do Scagolee dirty. I put a hurtin' on him, Jim.

LEIONAH (*signifyin'*) Hard for me to see who hurts the worse!

MACDADDY You sho 'nuff been in a fight, Scagolee. How the dude get yo' jaws so tight?

SCAGOLEE The dude did this funny thing, Braaaahhh! You know me, Scagolee, I always keep some bread for my shit, you understand. Ain't nobody ever caught me beggin' for nothin'! So I'm sittin' out there by my ride when ole white-stuff slid up on me with this ghostly lookin' dude. Yeah, right down here in the Jetto!

SCAG *appears upstage and mimics the literal, as well as the visceral, levels of the story.* LEIONAH *responds with utterances and gestures to indicate her contempt for what is implied by the carnal level of the story; she insinuates, while punctuating the story, that she rejects such experiences which are merely "typical" and the consequences of such events she almost welcomes.*

First, I thought he was The Man, so I was cool, but he kept on rappin', you know, leanin' on my ear, fillin' my head up with white-stuff. Said she was his ole lady, you know. Said he was tryin' to get into somethin', right down here in the Jetto, Jim! And I say, that's cool, not wantin' to act-the-fool, you understand. So he say, "how 'bout some little-girl?" Now, I lean back on my ride and checks the dude out. I checks out some more of white-stuff too. Then I say, no, I ain't interested in no little girl. So he looks at me kinda funny and say, coke? And I say, I don't drink no coke. He say, "you mean you don't like white-stuff at all?" Then he reached down in his pocket and come out with the little girl, Jack! I start sniffin' a little bit of her right there on the corner, you understand, and it was good.

MUSICIANS, SCAG, *and* LEIONAH *all making impressions which heighten the story rhythmically.* SCAGOLEE, *quite frenetic in his pacing;* MACDADDY *subdued.*

Now we cuts down to the dude's hotel, outside the Jetto, cause we gonna party! No sooner do we get there, ole white-stuff start doin' strange, takin' off her clothes and shit! Before I know it, she done stretched out on the bed neckid! But I don't pay no 'tention, cause all I wants is some moe' of that little girl. Still, he asked me just the same 'bout his ole lady, asked me how I liked her. I say, she ain't bad, where's the little girl? And he say, with his hands strokin' white-stuff's thighs, "in the hay," you know, like you tell somebody on-the-cuff, "in the hay is your little girl, white as snow, sweet as cotton candy." So, now I sees what's comin' down, and I say, "No good, Jim, your ole lady can't do nothin' for me. Just give me my taste of coke and I'll split. I'll even pay for it!" He say, "That won't be necessary, Buddy" . . . he called me Buddy . . . cause if I could get down with johnson and give white-stuff a turn, I could have a whole bunch of little girl free.

LEIONAH *furious;* SCAG *dancing gloatingly.*

MACDADDY Now, I know a bad nigguh like you didn't go for that!

SCAGOLEE Didn't I? Sure I did! What else could I do? But that ain't the worse of it, that ain't really what burned Scagolee. You see, it wasn't easy talkin' johnson into that kind of action, the dude standin' over me and shit. But we gets it together, like Scagolee always do, and johnson is hard as Chinese 'rithmetic! And I start pile drivin' into ole white-stuff like I was breakin' ground for a projects. I was doin' it to death, Jim, but now she really puts me in a trick, you understand.

SCAG *becomes almost orgiastic in his movements;* LEIONAH *more embittered.*

She got both my legs pinned down to the bed. And when I raised my head to peek out the corner of my eye, my heart almost stopped. This dude is standin' over me with his own johnson choked around the neck. And he is pumpin', Jim, jes-a-pumpin'! (SCAG *mimics fiercely.*) Now I know it's time to get up from here, but this white-stuff is strong, she got me all strung out. She starts moanin' and stuff, and I struggle to break free, almost breakin' my back! But her grip is a monster. And jes when I was about to crack her upside her head, I felt it, Jack, all up and down my back. All up and down my spine, you understand!!! The dude had blown his whole load up and down my back!

MACDADDY *laughs.*

That shit ain't funny!!! The dude might as well had fucked me in the ass!

SCAG *indicates his pleasure;* LEIONAH, *great disappointment;* MACDADDY, *dismay.*

MACDADDY What did you do about it?

SCAGOLEE (*more subdued, as in music*) I went crazy on 'em. Took out my razor and went crazy on 'em muthafukas!

MACDADDY Before, or after the little girl?

SCAGOLEE (*vacantly*) Yeeaaaaaah!

Lights dim on a nodding SCAGOLEE.

BEAT SEVEN

Louisiana. Lights come up red. Percussion rhythms. MACDADDY *and* LEIONAH *standing in same area downstage as earlier, searching the empty redness that surrounds. They become startled by the sudden appearance of* RED WOMAN *who dances on and toward them with sensual, Afro-Caribbean movements as if trying to get* MACDADDY'*s attention.*

MACDADDY Who's that?

LEIONAH *checks out* RED WOMAN *with a 'tude.*

She callin' you?

LEIONAH *shakes her head.*

She callin' somebody, and I don't even know the lady. You sure you don't know her?

LEIONAH *looks up at* MACDADDY *with a 'tude.*

Then what she want with me?

LEIONAH (*as* RED WOMAN *comes in close, then backs away rhythmically, beckoning* MACDADDY *the while*) Maybe we oughta see jes what she's puttin' down!

MACDADDY Uh-uh, you never see me followin' no strange 'hoes around!

LEIONAH (*hand on hip; curious*) C'mon! fear is only dangerous for the heart when you let it get yo' mind. Let's go!

LEIONAH *struts arrogantly on top of* RED WOMAN *who tries to look around her as she backs away, so as to maintain* MACDADDY'*s attention, as he follows, peering over* LEIONAH'*s shoulder. They move upstage to a certain point where* RED WOMAN *stops, looks past them, reacts fearfully, and runs away.* MACDADDY *and* LEIONAH *spin around sharply. They encounter the grotesque features of* BENNY *and* RED, *two drug forces.* BENNY *is hyperactive and fast talking;* RED *is slow, dawdling, hesitant in speech.*

BENNY (*startled by* MACDADDY'*s swift spin*)

Look out, nigger, and hold your ground,
ain't nobody told you to turn around!

RED (*slowly*) No-body told you nuthin'!

No response from MACDADDY *who ushers* LEIONAH *to one side, then stands firm, his appearance/attitude tightened up, supporting himself on his juju-cane.*

BENNY

And don't be actin' cute,
'cause you all dressed up
in yo' Sunday suit.
Don't wanna hear no cryin'
this time!

RED Don't wanna hear it!

No response. LEIONAH *upstage vigilantly.*

BENNY

And don't be givin' me no glass eye;
ain't never met a nigguh
who wasn't 'fraid to die.
You might not be the usual pick
but that don't matter
one damn bit!

RED Don't be matterin' no way!

BENNY

Maybe you don't know who I am?
My name is Benny;
this here is my
girlfriend Minnie!

RED Awww, Benny man, drop dead! You know my name is Red!

MACDADDY (*with arched deliberation*) And I am the Great MacDaddy, son of the Big MacDaddy who is dead, makin' me the greatest Daddy of all the MacDaddies who can do anything in this world.

BENNY

Oh yeah?
Then you must be the goddamned meat
for my goddamned cat.
Not too
goddamned lean;
nor too
goddamned fat.
Ready to be packed in a neat sack!

MACDADDY

Yeah,
I'm your goddamned meat
for your goddamned cat.
Not too
goddamned lean,
nor too
goddamned fat.
And if you don't get
your goddamned ass
outta here quick,
I'm gonna break it
with this goddamned stick!

RED Ooooooooohhhh! Wwwweeeeeeee!

BENNY

Who you think you playin' with, Jack?
I couldn't give a damn if yo' momma calls you Mac!

RED (*slow reaction, but titillated*) Hah . . . Momma Mac!

BENNY (*excitedly*)

> You don't know what you doin' messin' with me.
> Messin' with me will make your nerves twitch,
> your backside itch,
> and your bowels switch
> so badly they
> empty out yo' mouth
> so you only talk shit!

RED Phewwwweeeeee!

BENNY That's right, Mac, you'd rather be locked up in a phone-booth sandpaperin' a lion's ass than to be messin' with me. Dig it? You'd be better off suckin' milk outta a gorilla's left breast than to be thinkin' 'bout jumpin' in my chest.

RED Beat 'im to death, Benny!

BENNY Let me tell you one more goddamned thing. Don't you know I ain't worried 'bout you . . . 'cause I'll run up yo' god-damned throat, jump down yo' goddamned lungs, tap dance on yo' kidneys, do-the-grind on yo' liver, stomp yo' balls into a nod, then kill yo' goddamned rod, even die in yo' funky but 'til yo' heart stops beatin'!

RED And you gets double-trouble messin' with Red!

MACDADDY (*cold and deliberate*) I'm gonna turn around and count to three. And if yawl still here when I look back, thunder and lightnin' will close your traps!

BENNY (*stalks* MACDADDY *cautiously*) Ain't that some bitch!

MACDADDY (*searching* LEIONAH'*s eyes which register their positions*) One . . . !

BENNY Move in on 'im Red, he's as good as dead!

MACDADDY (*holding juju-cane firmly*) Two . . . !

RED Not so fast, Benny!

MACDADDY Three!

BENNY Grab that stick!

MACDADDY *spins around with the juju-cane extended with both hands: a single, loud blast from the juju-cane and* BENNY *and* RED *fall dead. Lights change to normal as* MACDADDY *and* LEIONAH *stand over the bodies. The* BLOOD FOLK *community rush on to review the outcome of the confrontation. They are horrified by what has transpired, and fear reprisals.*

BLOOD LEADER (*manifestation/personification of* WINE) What did you do? Is that Benny and Red that you've slammed dead? Don't you know you can't get away with a thing like that in Louisiana?

MACDADDY Look, Blood, it's over and done with. Ain't no moe' problem.

BLOOD LEADER When 'em cracker-flies see this, they gonna give us a fit for real. Let's get outta here. Everybody out quick!

Fear causes everyone to panic. Strobe light indicates calamity as everyone runs in different directions, and in the confusion, even LEIONAH *is swept off, leaving* MACDADDY *alone. Transitional Beat. Lights back to normal,* MACDADDY *frantically searches audience for* LEIONAH. *He is worried.*

MACDADDY Leionah! Leionah! Leionah!

HUMDRUM, *another manifestation/personification of* SCAG, *enters upstage-right carting a large, stuffed, burlap bag load on a rolling dolly.*

HUMDRUM (*street-crier rhythm*)

Got Black Cat
Got Black Cat
Got Black Cat today-oh
  catch me now
  while I'm givin'
  'im away-oh!
Dry lo-ad!
Dry lo-ad!
  Dry load for pine
  Dry load passin' time.
Make up yo' mind
  take up my cry-oww!
Make up yo' mind,

'foe I pass by-oww!
I'll sell it to the rich
I'll sell it to the poor
I'll sell it to the baby girl
standin' in the door-oww!

MACDADDY (*approaches* HUMDRUM *anxiously*) Hey, man, you see some people pass this way?

HUMDRUM (*settling load*) Humdrum sees people each and every day.

MACDADDY I'm lookin' for some particular people. Some Bloods! See some Blood go by?

HUMDRUM Humdrum do all he can not to miss them. Best customers I got out here in the street.

MACDADDY (*impatient*) Yeah . . . yeah, that's cool. But which way did they go? My woman is with them! Gotta find them now, you understand?

Two TREES *appear.* BLOOD LEADER *and* RED WOMAN *each with large umbrellas with strips of plastic material draped over the side obscuring their faces. The* TREES *enter from stage left and right, come together briefly upstage of* HUMDRUM *and* MACDADDY, *then exit upstage right and left. They seem to be humming.*

HUMDRUM Sure, I understand. You lookin' for your woman, and you in a hurry. Well, I'm in a hurry too. So if you help me with this load we can get to them even faster.

MACDADDY (*agreeing*) Ain't no big thang! Which way do we go?

HUMDRUM Jes follow those trees!

As they move upstage, the BLOOD FOLK, *including* BLOOD LEADER *and* RED WOMAN *appear.* LEIONAH *is with them.* MACDADDY *leaves* HUMDRUM *to deliver the load at the feet of the* BLOOD LEADER *as he embraces* LEIONAH. *As they query about the contents of the load, and prepare to inspect it upon the invitation from* HUMDRUM, MACDADDY *sings one brisk chorus of a blues/ballad.*

MACDADDY

Leionah!
Leionah, bab-ee!
  you sure
  are a sight
  for sore eyes.

Leionah!
Leionah, momma!
  you sure
  did open
  my eyes.

A man ain't worth a quarter
  without some other man's
  daughter,
  I'm glad
  you're at
  my side!

Throughout the brief song, HUMDRUM *prods the* BLOOD FOLK *community to open the sack. Upon doing so, they discover the body of the* BLOOD SON.

BLOOD LEADER (*stridently*) Blood Son! It's my Blood Son! Who would do a thing like this to my Blood Son? (*Searching faces in the audience.*) Somebody tell me, who would do such a thing to my Blood Son? Huh? Do you know? (*Shouting toward audience.*) Somebody tell me, why should my Blood Son be the victim of this scaggy life?

HUMDRUM That's a goddamned shame, ain't it? If I had known that load was such a burden, I never would've helped that fellow!

BLOOD LEADER Who?

HUMDRUM (*pointing finger at* MACDADDY) Him! How could I know? I was jes helpin'!

The BLOOD FOLK *angrily seize* MACDADDY, *while* HUMDRUM *feigns innocence, but are stopped by* BLOOD LEADER.

BLOOD LEADER Wait! We have no time to chastise that man. We must celebrate the Blood Son's spirit before it becomes cold. Let's dance and sing 'til seven bells ring, so that his spirit will be assured of rest. And this man will join us!

BLOOD LEADER *moves toward* MACDADDY *to relieve him of his juju-cane.* MACDADDY *withdraws, but under the pressure of the community, he gives up the juju-cane.* BLOOD LEADER *now places the cane on the chest of the* BLOOD SON.

Get up, Blood Son, and show us the way!

MUSICIANS *play New Orleans funeral procession music.* BLOOD SON *rises, takes the juju-cane, and solemnly leads a double line, men on one side, women on the other, across stage in the first line.* HUMDRUM, *anxious to join them, takes the dolly and sack offstage, cries out for them to wait for him, and joins the back of the line to pick up the rhythmic handclap. From upstage-center,* BLOOD SON *leads group downstage forming a "strip" as men and women now face each other.* BLOOD SON *now gestures toward the* MUSICIANS *with the juju-cane, and the tempo of the rhythm is accelerated for the beginning of the second line.* BLOOD SON *dances vigorously up the "strip": on his way down, he hands the juju-cane to the man at the top of the line who now enters the "strip" with the woman facing him, initiates a dance step which she follows, gives juju-cane to next man, then moves on down the "strip" with the woman, ending up at the end of the line. Each man and woman follow the same procedure twice around. However, each time* HUMDRUM *is in line to receive the juju-cane, he is passed up, thus, he goes to the end of the line in order to try again. Having been passed up twice,* HUMDRUM *jumps into the middle of the "strip" and dances wildly by himself: the* COMMUNITY *stops to watch as the music trails off.*

HUMDRUM (*awkwardly dancing alone*) C'mon, yawl. Wha'cha stoppin' for? Where's the music? Ain't yawl dancin' no more?

They stare suspiciously at HUMDRUM.

All I wanna do is join the crowd. (*No response.*) Well, why shouldn't I? (*Points at* MACDADDY.) Why should he have all the fun, huh, tell me, why should he? (*No response.*) What yawl got against me? I like stylin', flim flam, Cake Walk too! (*No response.*) He don't deserve to be here anyway . . . cause I did it! I killed your son. Hear that! Me, Humdrum, killed your Blood Son!

BLOOD LEADER (*the last to get the juju-cane; ceremoniously*) Then we gotta dance for you for real!

BLOOD LEADER *gestures toward* DRUM *with the juju-cane, who initiates a fast rhythm with* MUSICIANS. *As the women back away into a tight group, clapping their hands, the men form a dancing circle with* HUMDRUM *in the center.* BLOOD LEADER *gestures with juju-cane toward the* RED WOMAN *who becomes* DANCE; *she enters the circle with* HUMDRUM. *He now points toward one of the women in the chorus,* SONG, *who leads them into a jubilant rendering of "By-and-By." The gospel sound is infused with African percussive attitudes which informs the dancing rhythm of* DANCE *and* HUMDRUM, *while the men in the circle dance at a slower tempo, thereby insinuating a polyrhythmic quality in the total mode.*

SONG

Temptations hidden snares,
    often take us unaware.
And our hearts are made to bleed
    for each thoughtless word or deed.
And we wonder why the test
    when we try to do our best.
But we'll understand it better
    by-and-by.

BLOOD FOLK WOMEN (*rhythmic hand clapping*)

By and by
    oh when the mornin' comes
All the saints

of God are gatherin' home
(And we will) tell the story
how we've overcome
And we'll understand it better
by-and-by.

The chorus is repeated several times as SONG, DANCE, *and* DRUM *wear down* HUMDRUM. DANCE *drives* HUMDRUM *out of the circle and offstage, the singing women in pursuit, the men following, leaving the* BLOOD SON *to dance jubilantly at center stage where he receives a handshake from* BLOOD LEADER *before exiting in the opposite direction.* MACDADDY *grabs* LEIONAH, *who is infused with the spirit, before she leaves with the other women and prepares to leave downstage while* BLOOD LEADER *solemnly listens upstage for the seven bells which signal the* BLOOD SON'*s spirit at rest. The voices of the women can still be heard.*

BLOOD LEADER (*returning the juju-cane to* MACDADDY *following the sound of seven bells*) MacDaddy! If you want to find Wine, listen back . . . listen back, and you'll hear what's happenin' up . . . listen *up,* and you'll be able to take what's goin' down. Jes keep an eye on the Blood Son!

BLOOD SON *exits quickly to catch up with the singing voices, leaving* MACDADDY *confused, at first, about which direction to exit. He follows* BLOOD SON.

TERMINAL RHYTHM

South Carolina sea island. Lights up on MACDADDY *and* LEIONAH *standing on bare platform/wagons upstage gazing at the awesome spectacle of the ashen-gray environment that surrounds them—the plastic material now suspended throughout the house—appearing as vines or old trees of a dense swamp. It is quiet, with the exception of the percussive pulses of the* MUSICIANS. *As* LEIONAH *sits on her suitcase to gaze with disbelief,* MACDADDY *steps down from platform to inspect environment more closely.* LEIONAH *alerts* MACDADDY *to the sudden appearance of an ashen-gray figure that backs its way into the environment. It is* WINE.

MACDADDY (*curiously*) Wine! Is that you?

WINE (*wiping brown; backing toward platform*) Well, well, well, ain't that swell. Young MacDaddy!

MACDADDY Great MacDaddy, Wine, and don't you ever forget that! Where in hell you been? I been lookin' all over creation for you.

WINE You been here that long? Thought I knew everybody in Creation. Don't see how I could have missed yuh here in Carolina.

MACDADDY Jes got here!

WINE Oh, I see. It must have been kinda sudden.

MACDADDY Are you kiddin'? That was one helluva trip!

WINE You mean to tell me, yawl come this far and ain't dead yet?

LEIONAH A feather-bed ain't much service to the young corn!

WINE (*easing down onto edge of platform*) Well, if yawl that snappy, don't see how yawl gonna be able to stay 'round here. Got too much life in yuh!

MACDADDY Ain't plannin' on stayin', really.

WINE (*lounging attitude*) Don't yawl get me wrong, now. Love to see you young people 'round. But yawl come back when yuh ready to settle down. When you really ready for a rest. Ain't much else to do here but rest, you know, stretch out the ole limbs, that's best. Ain't nothin' in the world like it!

MACDADDY It do look pretty dead around here. Well, anyway, since you done got your rest, I'm ready to take you back to L.A.

WINE Uh-uh, nothin' doin'!

MACDADDY I don't wanna hear it, Wine. I come too far to find you. Now you goin' home!

WINE Already home! And I'm home to stay.

MACDADDY Don't be talkin' crazy, Wine! You know, when you left me strung-out in L.A. I was madder than a broke-dick dog! If I had caught up with you one minute sooner, I would've stomped your ass in the ground!

WINE Yeah, I guess there ain't much you can do to me now.

LEIONAH You know, Mac, you should never sweep dirt out of a door at night, or you'll sweep yourself out of a home.

WINE Well, great-green-corn, this 'ere is a wise lil woman you got. Pretty as a grape, too. You sho know how to pick 'em!

MACDADDY I know it! ! !

WINE Uhm-umm-mmm! How you stumble up on somethin' like that?

MACDADDY Lookin' for you! I never figured you to do me in, Wine. Embarrassin' me in front of all my friends. Why would you do that to me, the son of Big Mac, why?

WINE Got tired of The Man!

MACDADDY What man?

WINE All The Mans in the world! They kinda rough Wine up a taste. What in the world was I gonna do, the law always chompin' on my head, the lawless takin' my bread. If it wasn't one, it was the other Man.

MACDADDY Listen, all you had to do was pull-my-coat!

WINE And it would have come off yo' back too! Look, not a week went by without my gettin' tested or arrested. One time, ole Wine was on the wagon, my own wagon, too. But the police wouldn't even give me time to change my mind, said they were takin' me in for questionin', wanna know how I got on this wagon! Now, they jes happen to have two white boys down there accused of stealin' a horse and a cow. So I figures, since they look like The Man, they must know how to read his hand, so I would follow through on whatever they do. The first case come up b'foe the judge was the white boy accused of stealin' a horse. Judge say, "Guilty or not guilty," and the boy say "not guilty," cause he owned that horse ever since it was a colt. Case dismissed! Judge then asked the boy accused of stealin that cow, "Guilty or not guilty," and he owned that cow ever since it was a calf. Case dismissed too! Then he come on out and accuse me of stealin' that wagon and I said "not guilty," cause I owned that wagon ever since it was a wheelbarrow. Sombitch gave me thirty days!

LEIONAH (*sympathetically*) The worst road to the courthouse is through the pig pen!

WINE You ain't jes passin' water, daughter!

MACDADDY Okay, okay, when we get back, I'll get it all cleaned up. I'll even forget you left if you come back for a little breath.

WINE Ain't that much breath left in L.A. Naw, MacDaddy, ain't nothin' finer than to be in Carolina.

MACDADDY Awright then, have it your way! Just give me the formula and we'll split.

WINE What formula?

MACDADDY For the palm wine you do!

WINE Aw, shucks, that won't do you no good. Ain't nobody enjoyin' what comes natural no more. You couldn't sell a pint! The Man got somethin' new goin' 'round, the worse thing in the world you ever did see, causin' havoc, makin' people raggedy and hungry for days. I tried to tell you 'bout it 'foe I left, but I didn't have time. The Man had put somethin' on my mind!

MACDADDY What you talkin' 'bout, Wine?

WINE This other Man, he gimme a taste of this new thing goin' 'round. It turned my stomach so bad that the Green Runner came to me in my sleep.

MACDADDY (*irritated*) What Green Runner?

WINE You know 'bout the Green Runner, don'cha? He always comes to yuh when things get rough. He's outta this world! He's the strongest brutha that ever pulled a river straight. I've seen him sit down and eat a barrel of flour, a side of meat, and a water-bucket full of greens and syrup, all in one meal. Then he would swell up and tell the heebie-jeebies to turn four bruthas loose from their labors cause he would do their jobs. And that's how I got a lotta of my wine done. And it was him that come and pulled that monkey off my back when The Man had fouled up my stomach track!

LEIONAH Don't cross your eyes at a blinkin' owl, Mac, or you'll miss the point!

MACDADDY So, Wine is through!

WINE *nods.*

And you're stayin . . . !

WINE *nods.*

Well, I guess comin' after you sure wasn't worth the trip.

WINE (*as they prepare to leave*) Oh, I don't know, it might a been. Had a talk with the Green Runner the other day. He gimme his personal formula for gettin' anybody back on their feet. Shoot, I reckoned it would win you more friends than any lost without Wine.

MACDADDY Well, I sure hate to go back empty-handed. So, if you've got the word, let me have it.

WINE Uhmmm! Are you sure you can handle it?

MACDADDY I can do anything in this world!

WINE Oh yeah? . . . Then tell me somethin' one half scientific!

MACDADDY Scientific? What kinda scientific?

WINE You know, somethin' that you break-down and put-together . . . like yo' momma mighta taught you. Somethin' simple, so I can see if you can handle my recipe.

MACDADDY (LEIONAH *whispers in his ear; confidently, he replies*) Py-R-Squared!

WINE Wrong! But you almost got it!

MACDADDY *stares at* LEIONAH *disgustedly as* WINE *gets up.*

Pie . . . are round, and cornbread . . . ar squared! (*Facing them as he begins to leave backward.*) Now, yawl make the best of your long haul to L.A.!

MACDADDY (*confounded*) Wine, wait . . . say it again . . . about the cornbread . . . !

WINE (*backing off*) You got the word, now take it on back out there where yawl from and use it! Bye yawl! (*Exits.*)

MACDADDY (*perplexed*) Pie are round . . . cornbread are squared . . . is that all we got to take home?

LEIONAH If the ash is out before the oak, it will be a summer of fire and smoke!

Lights fade as they exit through the ashened environment. Transitional Beat. Lights come up on CHORUS/COMMUNITY *posed, as they were in primal rhythm, in a still-freeze party/dance attitude with* SCAG PHOTOGRAPHER *downstage with his head under black cloth of camera, arm raised with flash preparing to take a picture.* MUSICIANS *are playing up-tempoed Charleston. A flash from* SCAG PHOTOGRAPHER *sends up a billow of smoke, and rather than an energetic Charleston dance, the* COMMUNITY/CHORUS *droops over listlessly and begins the "Junkie Crawl" with saddened expressions on their faces, and the music changing to the attitude.* MACDADDY *and* LEIONAH *enter through the door upstage right as* SCAG *comes out from under black cloth and observes them curiously. He is holding up a pan of cornbread, while she holds up a pan of pie.*

MACDADDY Hey now everybody, MacDaddy's back in town . . . and he's brought you somethin' square 'n round!

SCAG PHOTOGRAPHER How did I miss yawl in this picture?

MACDADDY (*approaching* SCAG PHOTOGRAPHER *furiously and pointing juju-cane*) Get outta my life! Get outta my life and stay out!

SCAG PHOTOGRAPHER *moves away, but seeks out better vantage points on stage to focus in on audience, even arranging segments of the audience for the proper angle, going under and out of the black cloth repeatedly as he adjusts his lens.* MACDADDY *and*

LEIONAH *make vain efforts to get the* CHORUS/COMMUNITY *to accept the pie and cornbread, but are unresponsive, the weight of the Jones being too heavy.*)

Cornbread . . . c'mon, get yo' cornbread . . . it's good to yuh! . . . c'mon yawl, I'm talkin' 'bout cornbread . . . !

LEIONAH (*repeatedly*) Get yo' piece-of-the-pie!

MACDADDY, *as* LEIONAH *continues moving among the* CHORUS/COMMUNITY, *disappointed and angered, moves downstage and holds the cornbread aloft in one hand, the juju-cane aloft in the other, and begins an incantation toward the audience as if beseeching the appearance of a super-force, a great spirit.*

MACDADDY

Great Guggah Muggah!
This is MacDaddy talkin'!
Son of the Big MacDaddy
who is dead,
makin' me the greatest Daddy
of all the MacDaddies
who can do anything in this world
'cept feed my bruthas!

Great Guggah Muggah,
if you be out there
and care,
give me yo' ear!

We got trouble in this city,
Great Guggah Muggah,
can't you show us a little pity?
The bruthas are wastin' away.
Whatever happen to those good ole
grits and gravvy days?

C'mon, Guggah Muggah,
show me a rainbow sign,
not just yo' tired behind!

Don't get me wrong,
Guggah Muggah,
I ain't mad with you.
All I wanna see is
what you gon' do!

Beat on yo' chest
and make the wind blow!
Beat on yo' chest
shake ground like a fandango!
Beat on yo' chest
send thunderbolts through the clouds
like our man Shango!

The music becomes more intense, and the "Junkie Crawl" more desperate as the CHORUS/COMMUNITY *seems to disintegrate, the Jones coming down hard as they experience agonized pains of withdrawal induced by* MACDADDY'*s incantation. The* SCAG PHOTOGRAPHER *goes about his business gingerly, setting the audience up for a portrait.*

Great Guggah Muggah!
if you all that they say
you be,
you must be
at least
as bad as me!
So do somethin'
pleeezzzzze!
Can't you see these Bloods
be sufferin' from
a cripplin' disease?

They in a rut!
I know what I'd do,
if I were you,
I'd kick some butt!
If I were you
and they refused to eat

I'd make 'em eat doo-doo!
If I were you
    and they stopped producin' yo' image,
    I'd castrate them too!
If I were you,
    and they stopped celebratin' yo' spirit,
    I'd take away they dancin' shoes!

It is a calamitous moment: the CHORUS/COMMUNITY *writhing on ground.*

No I wouldn't,
    I take it all back,
    Guggah Muggah,
    I wouldn't do nothin' like that.

These are my bruthas and sistas
    and I love everyone of 'em.
I'm just tryin' to help us get back
    where we been.
'Memberin' when nigguhs were happy,
    quick as a whip
    and twice as snappy.
I got the cornbread,
    square out the ground;
my woman's got the pie,
    round as a world
    kissed by the sky.
And we thinkin' 'bout good times now,
    'em bad pots hummin' loud
Come 'n get it!
    candied-yams and dumplin!
    'em black-eyed peas is somethin'!
Collard greens, chicken and rice,
    c'mon get yo' cornbread, children,
    the staff of life!

The calamity having subsided, the CHORUS/COMMUNITY *having shaken the Jones, they slowly rise and join* LEIONAH, *who has already begun to sing/talk, in song.* MUSICIANS *make a slow transition in the tempo and attitude of music.* SCAG PHOTOGRAPHER, *his camera positioned upstage center, now, facing audience, takes note of the* CHORUS/COMMUNITY's *revitalization. He tries desperately to re-group them, but to no avail.* MACDADDY's *staunch presence forces him to back off and exit.*

LEIONAH

We gonna rise up
 this mornin'
We gonna stay up
 all day.

Ain't
 no more sleepin'
 our lives away.

We gonna rise up
 this mornin'
We gonna stay up
 all day.

We ain't payin' out
 no more dues
 to-day.

We gonna rise up
 this mornin'
We gonna stay up
 all day.

Ain't
 gonna let
 nobody stand
 in our way.

We gonna rise up
 this mornin'
We gonna stay up
 all day.

Brutha/sista
  gonna find
  their way home
  someday.

Every effort is made by the CHORUS/COMMUNITY *to get the audience/community to join them in the celebration. At the high point in the singing, the* CHORUS/COMMUNITY, LEIONAH *pulling a satisfied* MACDADDY *off last, exit out the door upstage-right, with* MACDADDY *closing the door. Everything dims out with the exception of the* SCAG PHOTOGRAPHER'*s camera which is focused on the audience: if the audience is still singing, the light/special on the camera gradually fades out; if not, the* MUSICIANS *stop playing and camera light/special remains focused on the audience until they decide to exit the house.*